Worked Up Selves

Also by Elaine Swan

GENDER AND DIVERSITY IN MANAGEMENT: A Concise Introduction (*with Caroline Gatrell*)

Worked Up Selves

Personal Development Workers, Self-Work and Therapeutic Cultures

Elaine Swan
Senior Teaching Fellow, Lancaster University Management School

palgrave
macmillan

First published 2010 by
PALGRAVE MACMILLAN

Palgrave Macmillan in the UK is an imprint of Macmillan Publishers Limited, registered in England, company number 785998, of Houndmills, Basingstoke, Hampshire RG21 6XS.

Palgrave Macmillan in the US is a division of St Martin's Press LLC, 175 Fifth Avenue, New York, NY 10010.

Palgrave Macmillan is the global academic imprint of the above companies and has companies and representatives throughout the world.

Palgrave® and Macmillan® are registered trademarks in the United States, the United Kingdom, Europe and other countries

ISBN-13: 978-0-230-20136-1 hardback

This book is printed on paper suitable for recycling and made from fully managed and sustained forest sources. Logging, pulping and manufacturing processes are expected to conform to the environmental regulations of the country of origin.

A catalogue record for this book is available from the British Library.

A catalogue record for this book is available from the Library of Congress.

10 9 8 7 6 5 4 3 2 1
19 18 17 16 15 14 13 12 11 10

Printed and bound in Great Britain by
CPI Antony Rowe, Chippenham and Eastbourne

To Steve

Contents

Acknowledgements

Thanks to Paul Milner, Virgina Thorp and Ursula Gavin at Palgrave, particularly to Paul for all his patience.

I would like to thank the Women's PhD Pressure Group for their emotional support, and love of Happy Hour cocktails: Sue Eccles, Carole Elliott, Caroline Gatrell, Ellie Hamilton, Valerie Stead, Sharon Turnbull and Helen Woodruffe. A special thanks to Caroline Gatrell, Ellie Hamilton and Valerie Stead for reading and commenting on chapters and for being such inspiring academics and friends. Thank you too, Andy Bailey, my colleague in MDD for providing much needed good humour and practical support over the years.

A big thanks to Jackie Stacey for supervising my PhD, providing unstinting encouragement and warm support over a very long time.

A special mention goes to David Cripps and Sarah Vogel for their interest in the book and debates on therapeutic cultures. Furthermore, I'd like to thank all of the practitioners interviewed for this research, who gave up their time to share their insights and experiences so generously with me.

Thanks to Sparky and the late departed Gretchen for being so furry.

Finally, I am indebted to Steve Fox for his untiring support and vigorous confidence in me.

1
Changing Selves

Introduction

> One must recognise that the desire to invent a life is no longer evidence of narcissistic self-involvement or an emancipator countercultural impulse, but rather is increasingly required as a new form of 'immaterial labour' – mental, social and emotional tasks – required for participation in the labour market.
>
> (McGee, 2005: 24)

This quote encapsulates the topic of this book: the emergence of new modes of work and workers. Thus *Worked Up Selves* is an exploration of the growth of personal development, a form of immaterial labour or more precisely, 'self-work' (Tipton, 1983; Heelas, 2002; Chappell et al., 2003). In personal development this self-work involves self-exploration, self-expression, self-reflection, self-improvement and experimentation with appearance, capacities, behaviours, emotions and thinking. *Worked Up Selves* focuses, in particular, on the personal development workers who help people to undertake this type of labour outlined above. These types of workers include management trainers; life- performance- business- and executive-coaches; learning consultants; personal development consultants; facilitators, and management developers. Up to now, this group have been somewhat neglected as an occupational group in organisational theory and wider social theory.

A useful way to understand this proliferating type of worker and the work they do is to draw on Pierre Bourdieu's concept of 'cultural intermediaries' (Bourdieu, 1984). This is a term introduced by Bourdieu to describe a new category of middle-class worker emerging in the past thirty years – post-industrial service occupations. These roles involve the provision of symbolic and material goods and services in areas such as presentation of the self, and care of the mind and body (Gray, 2003a, 2003b). Several writers have extended the application of cultural intermediary to newer occupations such as management consultants, image consultants, nutritionist, alternative medicine, therapies and communication skills trainers. Cultural intermediaries are fascinated by selves, identities, self-presentation, appearance and lifestyle at home and at work (Featherstone, 1991: 60).

Personal development workers fit in this description very nicely. Representing an off-shoot of the traditional helping professions, they offer the service of providing advice, techniques, expertise and experience focused on mental, social, psychological and emotional tasks, which they see as helping people to develop their selves so that they become more effective at work, at leisure and at home. I discuss how personal development workers claim to do this kind of work throughout *Worked Up Selves*, drawing on interviews with a range of different personal development workers from coaches, facilitators to management trainers. As a cultural intermediary occupation, personal development workers represent a growing form of therapeutic work and operate at the interface between therapeutic cultures and various workplaces, drawing upon therapeutic, emotional, experiential and psychological sensibilities and habituses to help them. I will discuss in Chapter 8 what this interface might mean for expanding our understanding of the cultural intermediary.

Worked Up Selves

Having described the focus for the book, I now turn to outline its rationale. I chose the title of *Worked Up Selves* for this book for a number of reasons. Outlining these reasons below will help situate the introduction and the book within the wider set of debates about therapeutic cultures and the turn to the self in social theory and organisation studies. It will structure the first part of this introductory chapter. My first reason is that this book discusses the shaping and cultivating of – the working up of – selves seen to be a predominant project in contemporary society. This project is the main topic for what we might call the emergent 'sociology of therapeutic cultures'. I use the phrase 'sociology of therapeutic cultures', to refer to a limited, but growing set of literature by social theorists which argues that therapeutic ways of being have become more dominant in contemporary society and culture. Personal development in the workplace can be understood as a form of therapeutic culture.

There is a consistent argument in this sociology of therapeutic cultures that our contemporary era is characterised by an intensification and proliferation of therapeutic ways of thinking. Critics within this field characterise this expansion of therapeutic mores in concepts such as 'the age of therapism' (Weldon, 1999), the rise of the therapeutic state (Nolan, 1998), the proliferation of the therapeutic ethos (Nolan, 1998), and the emergence of the 'therapeutocracy' (Chriss, 1999). In this vein, it is claimed that therapy is now one of the three core discourses of our times alongside of advertising and bureaucracy (Fairclough, 1989).

Proliferation of the therapeutic

Most critics agree that this spread can be seen in the way that therapeutic practices have moved away from the counselling room into our homes, our doctors' surgeries, our schools and our workplaces. For example, studies have shown that therapeutic ideas can be found in schools (Cloud, 1998; Nolan, 1998; Rose, 1989, 1996a; Ecclestone and Dennis Hayes, 2009); on television (Shattuc, 1997; Rapping, 1996; White, 1992), and in Hollywood films (Walker, 1993); in self-help books (Simonds, 1992, 1996; Lichterman, 1992); the twelve-step movement (Reinarman, 1995; Warhol and Michie, 1996), and the workplace (Brewis, 1996; Cameron, 1995, 2000a; Newton, Handy and Fineman, 1995; Rose, 1989, 1996a, 1996b; Swan, 2006, 2008; Swan and Fox, 2009; Fineman, 1993, 2000a, 2000b, 2000c, 2003; Heelas, 1996, 2002, 2008; Costea et al., 2007 and 2008; Hollway, 1991; Hatcher, 2003; Webb, 2004, 2006).

Therapy for the well

As a result, the ambit of the therapeutic is no longer just 'sick' selves but 'healthy' selves. Having extended into new spaces and new subjects, therapeutic interventions are seen to have targeted new aspects of our selves and our habits: gambling; shopping; eating; the use of the internet; sex (Miller and McHoul, 1998a, 1998b; Sedgwick, 1994; Rapping, 1996); our sleep (Williams, 2001); our debts (Rose, 1989); our pets and even our use of self-help books. This is what sociologist Nikolas Rose (1996a) refers to as the 'psychologisation of the mundane'.

These new therapeutic practices have generated their own services, workers, work practices and products. With this expansion, critics argue, come new understandings, configurations and moralities of the self. Thus for, Stanley Cohen the rise of the therapeutic can be defined as the 'colonisation of the subjective'. In his view, there has been this colonisation which has extended so much that there is what he calls 'a general coalescence of the therapeutic with mass culture itself' (1985: 232).

In sum, this literature suggests that these new ways of thinking about and shaping the self bring complex social and political consequences for both individuals and society (see for example Cameron, 1995, 2000a, 2000b; Cloud, 1998; Coward, 1989; Lasch, 1980, 1985; Nolan, 1998, 1999; Rose, 1989, 1996a, 1996b; Sennett, 1986; Simonds, 1992, 1996). One of the main concerns in this literature is the politics of the growing influence of therapeutic ideas. By focusing on the self, the personal and the subjective, therapeutic cultures are criticised for what is seen as their disregard for the political, social, historical and economic. In this view, more political, less individualised and privatised ways of understanding and relating to our selves are marginalised as we are turning towards therapeutic expertise, and therapeutic expertise is turned on us.

Professional therapeoisie

The starting point for this book is the way that 'therapeutic' workers are largely neglected in this discussion of the proliferation of therapeutic cultures. The effect of this is that a monolithic therapeutic culture is constructed in which different kinds of therapeutic practices and politics are lost. As an organisational sociologist I found this to be most noticeable in relation to workers such as 'management developers', 'coaches' and 'personal development trainers', who can be encountered in various workplaces in the private and not-for-profit sectors. These workers have a range of different titles and change their titles as different practices come to the fore. For example, many management trainers have now become executive coaches. Others refer to themselves as management consultants and yet in practice are quite narrow in the kinds of work they undertake, largely doing interpersonal skills training or coaching. Given this variety of changing terms, I will refer to them in this book as 'personal development workers'. In essence, these are people who use therapeutically based practices with the aim of helping someone work better, become a 'better' person or get a 'better life'. In line with the book's title, personal development workers then encourage people to 'work up', to shape, improve and transform their selves along particular psychological and behavioural contours.

Personal development workers

The use of this term personal development worker enables me to distinguish them and their work from more traditional therapists and counsellors working in mental health contexts. It also separates them out from the broader category of management consultant, a growing occupational group and the topic of recent organisational studies (Clarke, 1995; Clarke and Fincham, 2002; Sturdy et al., 2009). This is important as many management consultants work in organisations on other issues such as strategy, finance, marketing etc, utilising quite different knowledge bases and techniques than personal development workers.

Although there are increasing studies on management consultants (Clarke, 1995; Clarke and Fincham, 2002; Sturdy et al., 2009) and management gurus (Jackson, 2001), there is very little written about workplace trainers and personal development workers. This is even the case when management training, workplace spirituality and therapy are the focus of study (Costea et al., 2007 and 2008) or ethnographic research (Bell and Taylor, 2003, 2004) (see Cameron, 2000a; Sturdy, 2002 and Swan, 2004, 2008 for exceptions).

Cultural intermediaries

As mentioned above, personal development workers can be seen as 'cultural intermediaries'. Bourdieu defines these as occupations:

> Involving presentation and representation (sales, marketing, advertising, public relations, fashion, decoration and so forth) and in all the institutions providing symbolic goods and services. These include the various jobs in medical and social assistance (marriage guidance, sex therapy, diectics, vocational guidance, paediatric advice etc.) and in cultural production and organization. (1984: 359)

They are seen as active, self-conscious and reflexive (Negus, 2002). A key characteristic is that cultural intermediaries transmit, disseminate and promote cultural and symbolic goods, services and lifestyles to a wider audience (ibid). As such they constitute a type of cultural authority, shaping taste and inculcating certain dispositions (Nixon and du Gay, 2002). According to cultural theorist Mike Featherstone, they are more disposed to emotional exploration as part of their work and their wider life (1991: 126) as they draw on a mix of Romantic emotional and aesthetic sensitivities. They are also seen to blur a number of traditional distinctions: life and leisure/work; high art/popular culture and personal taste and professional judgment (Negus, 2002).

An important characteristic of cultural intermediaries is that they exemplify their own wares. Thus Bourdieu writes that they are:

> sellers of symbolic goods and services who always sell themselves as models and as guarantors of the value of their products, and who sell so well because they believe in what they sell...[and are] sincerely sold on the value of what [they sell]. (1984: 365)

In sum, they are their body of knowledge! They also represent the 'very ideal or image of the employable and competent individual' (ibid: 233). In this vein, personal development workers present themselves as 'more developed' than their clients or in some cases, as fully 'developed'.

Importantly, for Bourdieu, cultural intermediaries do not have the cultural and economic capital of the dominant class. As a result, they take on a learning and self-improvement approach to work, home, leisure and life – what Bourdieu refers to as learning mode to life (see also Featherstone, 1991: 44). As such, they are, he argues, 'perfect consumers' because they consume their own practices (1984: 371). Thus, personal development workers participate in various therapeutic cultures on an ongoing basis. This can be seen in the later chapters and my own autobiographic narrative in this chapter. In so doing, personal development workers are labouring at their own project of working up their selves and their techniques of working up others.

Therapeutic power and influence

Therapeutic workers as cultural intermediaries then are central to the development, dissemination and reconfiguration of therapeutic cultures. And up till now their experience has been largely overlooked in much of the sociology of therapeutic cultures. This is rather surprising given many critics' anxieties about the power and influence of experts, and expertise, and the increasing dependence on therapeutic experts and expertise in particular. There are some conversational analyses of counsellors in healthcare contexts but these concentrate on in situ practices in medical contexts (Silverman, 1997). Overall, we know very little about what practitioners think they are doing in their practices, and how they understand the self, its transformation and self-work (Tipton, 1983; Heelas, 2002; Chappell et al., 2003).

One of the effects of this omission is that different types of self-work and therapeutic practices get blurred. Personal development workers are different from other therapeutic practitioners in a number of ways: their practices are informed by a broader range of ideas; many are freelance and thus relations with their clients are inflected by this self-employed status; finally, their clients do not see them because they have mental health problems but because they want to, or have to, transform themselves. A number of questions are raised as a result of this relative absence in the literature: how do personal development workers understand what they do? What models of the self do they draw upon? How do they imagine the self can be changed? How do those who work in workplaces describe what they do? The purpose of this book is to start to address these questions and examine how personal development workers' conceptualisations of their practices fit with current understandings in the sociology of therapeutic cultures.

Worked up critics

This brings me neatly onto my second reason for entitling the book *Worked Up Selves:* that many commentators of therapeutic cultures are quite agitated, nettled or 'worked up' about the rise of therapeutic approaches. Hence, there are a number of influential critical accounts, for example Christopher Lasch (1980, 1985); Philip Rieff (1966); Richard Sennett (1986); Robert Bellah et al. (1985) which are highly critical of the rise of therapeutic cultures during the counter-cultural movement in the 1960s and 1970s for what they see as their anti-communal, depoliticising, narcissistic effects. Described as 'patrician' by more recent commentators (Ross, 1992), these authors are in no doubt that therapeutic ways of thinking and being are to be roundly condemned. This denunciative school of thought has permeated more recent accounts such as James Nolan (1998) Dana Cloud (1998), Frank Furedi (2004) and Katherine Ecclestone and Dennis Hayes (2009), Bogdan Costea, Norman Crump and Kostas Amiridis (2007, 2008) which are quite hostile to what they see as the more recent colonisation of therapeutic idioms into the state, the political arena, the workplace, education and the media.

Pseudo-therapy

In this highly critical take on therapeutic cultures, personal development is the worst kind of therapeutic practice on a number of counts.

First, it is seen as the most self-indulgent of all therapeutic cultures because its participants are seen as less desperate, more middle class and more instrumental than people undertaking traditional counselling in mental health contexts. Secondly, its reliance on popular psychology is believed to make its practices more superficial, trivialising and morally bankrupt. For example, in her discussion of diversity training, Elisabeth Lasch-Quinn writes quite hyperbolically that 'a whole army of diversity experts has penetrated mainstream America equipped with half-baked, contradictory, quasi-scientific pseudo-truths' (2002: xv).

In these accounts a hierarchy of knowledges is set up, in which psychoanalysis is seen as high culture, associated with being intellectual and highbrow, whereas popular psychology, chat show therapy and personal development are seen as low culture, with their eclecticism viewed as evidence of unreliability and confusion. Thirdly, personal development and management training in the workplace are understood as techniques of capital, a means of controlling employees and securing their consent, commitment, and deeper selves.

Monolithic therapy culture

One of the problems with these accounts is that they construct therapeutic cultures as monolithic. In so doing, therapeutic cultures are seen as sinister, totalising and hegemonic forms of social control. Consideration is not given to how practitioners conceptualise their practices. Nor is there much discussion of how a number of factors such as the eclecticism of their influences, the contradictory nature of their ideas, the contexts in which they work, and the scepticism of their clients, might mediate the effects of therapeutic cultures.

Another worry in the literature is the way that it is imagined that therapists have power over us. So it is believed that therapists can 'brainwash' us or seduce us to replace our own self-narratives, aspirations and ways of thinking with therapeutic narratives, ideals and philosophy, meaning that our selves are not really our own (see Hacking (1995); Plummer (1995); Anzte (1996) for discussion of these ideas). In popular views of false memory syndrome, for example, the therapist is seen to be responsible for making people believe things that are supposed not to have happened (see Hacking, 1995 and Lury, 1998). Celia Lury gives an extended discussion on the fears associated with therapists' power to influence clients in relation to psychoanalysis, hypnosis and false memory syndrome. She argues that the anxieties therapists' imagined power to 'brainwash' influence provokes are to do with the way this imagined power problematises masculine self-possession and self-creation. For Charles Taylor, this kind of anxiety is the result of the combination of 'soft relativism' (1991: 17) with a particular from of contemporary individualism, in which the belief is that no-one should dictate the contents of our selves (1991: 14). The contents and contours of our selves are imagined to be the result of our decisions and influence.

An extension of this argument is that the state itself uses therapeutic interventions to colonise the private through a variety of techniques and agencies (see Rose, 1989; Nolan, 1998). Finally, critics are concerned with the way that therapists use techniques that are imagined to bring our insides out into the open, getting the private into the public, leading to a lack of decorum and blurring of public and private. For much of this literature then, therapeutic cultures are a major problem.

A different view

My own experience as a client and practitioner in personal development has made me question these types of dismissive, monolithic accounts. My first encounter with personal development was in 1982 when I had just finished university, had started work and decided to go to an evening class on assertiveness run by Anne Dickson, the author of a book entitled *A Woman in Your Own Right* (1982). Assertiveness training has dominated my own participation in personal development as I attended several courses at work after this first evening class, and in 1995 trained for whole year on how to be an assertiveness trainer with Redwood, a charity organisation established by Anne Dickson, to train women in assertiveness training. From 1986 until 1992, I worked in the area of training and development in private sector organisations, was employed full-time, and attended over ten courses lasting two to three days on skills areas seen to be essential for managers and trainers, including influencing, negotiating, coaching, training and facilitation, and on top of this, several personal development conferences. In 1992, I became a freelance management trainer and continued to attend skills courses, undertaking a two-year part-time Diploma in Career Counselling and Consulting run by Birkbeck College, part of which involved me having counselling supervision. My attendance on courses was both mandatory when I had been employed as a manager and trainer, and more voluntary when I was freelance, although prompted by the precariousness of my labour market position and the feeling that I needed to 'up-date' my knowledge, skills and techniques and credentialise what I was doing. My own response to my participation in personal development practice was highly variable, with some of the programmes I attended being immensely helpful in my personal and professional life and others seeming formulaic and trite.

Soft capitalism

It was in the mid-1980s that most medium to large organisations in the private and public sector employed dedicated training staff to run what are called 'soft skills' training courses. These included training in interpersonal skills, assertiveness, negotiating skills, personal effectiveness and influencing skills, and were seen as distinct from technical skills training courses such as finance or IT training by both employers and attendees. Although employers saw these courses as different from counselling or therapy, some participants came with concerns about their therapeutic underpinnings, often phrased in their references to 'navel gazing', 'American psychobabble' and 'touchy-feely stuff'. There was also a shift in terminology during the 1980s as the use of 'training' changed to that of 'development', with my title changing from training officer to management development officer. These changes denoted the move in the way learning was seen to require the involvement of the learner, and to show that training was too narrow and instrumental in its aims, with development being seen as less technical and more holistic, involving the 'whole person'.

My own encounters with personal development as both a client and a practitioner suggest a different kind of experience that has been left out of a large percentage of the critical literature. As a client myself, I did not feel self-indulgent, anti-communal or de-politicised by these practices as some of this literature suggests, nor would I characterise the people who attended these events in those terms. Some of this literature proposes that as a client I would have been manipulated into believing that I have been helped, when in fact I would have been simply comforted in such a way that any political criticality I may have had was effectively neutralised (Cloud, 1998). It is also argued that as a practitioner I may genuinely have wanted to help people but did not realise the de-politicising effects of my actions (Nolan, 1998; Cloud, 1998).

As an antidote to these claims, I do not want simply to suggest that personal development is a radical form of politics but I do want to argue that there are three important aspects underplayed in the literature. First, reactions to personal development were highly varied. Many participants I came across claimed to find personal development courses to be what they called 'life-changing', whether the events ran for two days or much longer. Other participants, or different programmes, invoked more muted or resistant responses.

A mixed bag

My own view was that personal development was a highly contradictory set of ideas and practices, which led to mixed responses from clients. As a client I found some experiences interesting, intense and helpful and others mundane, boring and tiresome. Secondly, many people, myself included, found personal development inspiring and comforting. It spoke to a dimension of social change not addressed by traditional politics and allowed us a space not available in other contexts in which we could contemplate and discuss our subjective life, explore our feelings and our relationships. Offering a place of care, hope and fantasy, it enabled us to try on different ways of being. Thirdly, my fellow practitioners and I and our participants were sensitive to popular critiques of therapeutic ideas. As a practitioner, I would have a range of tactics for anticipating and trying to overcome criticism, mockery and cynicism (Sturdy, 2002).

My experience raised a number of questions for me in response to critics' views: why were there so relatively few representations of practitioners' understandings of therapeutic cultures in the critical literature? Had I been party to something that had such pernicious effects? How else could we think about personal development to enable us to account for the positive effects people claimed without claiming it as a form of radical politics? As Lora Romero (1997) argues with respect to popular culture, perhaps we need to take the view that personal development and therapeutic cultures can be radical in some ways and reactionary in others: oppositional but not liberating, conservative but not outright colonising or rationalising. This was the motivation for my study based on an ethnographically informed approach focused on personal development workers.

Working the self

A third reason I called the book *Worked Up Selves* is to address what I see as a major absence in much of the literature around the territory of personal development and its interface with the workplace. The title *Worked Up Selves* points to the importance of the workplace as a site for self-work (Heelas, 2002; Chappell et al., 2003; Rose, 1989, 1996a, 1996b; Hollway, 1991). As indicated in this introduction, personal development has its own historical trajectory and influences compared with other therapeutic cultures. It also has particular contexts of reception, including the workplace, which will inflect how it is understood. These aspects are worth giving more detailed attention as they affect the kinds of transformations and selves believed to be achievable through personal development practices. They are of relevance to the sociology of therapeutic cultures because many of the criticisms that are levelled on therapeutic cultures are based on assumptions about the conceptualisation of self and the consequent political implications of such conceptualisations.

There are several reasons for this choice of personal development: there are few studies of personal development within larger studies on therapeutic cultures, which has meant that its specificities are largely ignored. In particular, the intersection between therapeutic cultures, the workplace and management training has been under-researched and under-analysed, both within the sociology of therapeutic cultures and organisational studies (see Swan, 2006, 2008; Swan and Fox, 2009; Costea et al., 2007, 2008; Cameron, 2000a for exceptions). This is an oversight given the wide spread of personal development ideas and practices, and the way that they are affecting our understandings of the workplace, and what it is to do 'work'. It raises questions about how this interface affects ideas about the self and its transformation in personal development.

Personal development

As I suggested above therapeutic cultures cover a wide range of practices and can be encountered in a range of domains. This means that there are different and even contradictory ideas about the self and how to transform it across different therapeutic practices. Personal development represents a particular set of techniques and ideas which distinguish it from more traditional therapy or counselling. Sometimes called 'therapy for the well', personal development is, however, difficult to define. Writing nearly thirty years ago, Roy Wallis suggests it is characterised by 'vagueness and elasticity of [its]... boundaries'. It has shifting features (Wallis, 1989: 152), and operates on 'a plane neither "public" nor "private", neither "statutory" nor "voluntary"' (Rose,

1989: 214). Personal Development overlaps with some New Age ideas and practices but does not centre on the spirituality aspect as much as these. Thus Paul Heelas defines the New Age as 'a spirituality "of" and "for" what it is to live out of life...a spirituality "of" and "for" being truly human' (2008: 17). It is not the significance of the workplace which distinguishes personal development from New Age as New Age and workplace spiritual practices can be found in the work place (Heelas, 1996, 2002; Casey, 2002a, 2002b; Bell and Taylor, 2003, 2004). In fact, Heelas goes on to write that spiritualities fall on a spectrum from anti-capitalist to ethical guidance within capitalism to capitalist spiritualities (Heelas, 1996, 2002).

Self-improvement pedagogics

Personal development is different from workplace spirituality. Thus, it does not present itself as religious or in touch with the divine as some spiritual management development practices (Bell and Taylor, 2004). It is not about 'a mystical, unrestricted question for meaning in life...involving recognition of the soul or god within' (ibid: 461). Personal development rarely draws upon explicitly religious practices such as prayer and meditation (Bell and Taylor, 2003). Personal development, in the main, is concerned with techniques and pedagogics which help people become more effective at work, or at home or in personal relations through focusing on emotional, psychological and behavioural knowledge and techniques. Whilst drawing upon some holistic and mystical ideas, its overarching aim is to be pragmatic, resourceful and problem-solving focused. Personal development is about self-improvement and 'practical change' albeit through emotional and psychological exploration and experimentation. Its horizons are often quite narrow – problems with people at work, lack of confidence at work, work-life balance issues and this often framed within a psychological frame. Personal development has much in common with counselling and therapy but is more hybrid in the ideas it draws on and broader in the places it can be encountered.

Magpie expertise

Personal development is particularly difficult to pin down because of the eclecticism of its sources. For example, *The Dictionary of Personal Development* (2002) has 500 entries for what the authors, Paul Tosey and Josie Gregory, both academics at Surrey University, see as the most prominent terms, all taken from what they define as the main fields of personal development: Adult and Experiential Learning; BodyMind Development; Counselling; Gestalt Therapy; Group work; Humanistic Psychology; Jungian Psychology; Interpersonal Skills Training; Management Development; New Age; Neuro-Linguistic Programming; Psychology; Psychosynthesis; Spirituality; Systems Thinking; Transactional Analysis; and Transpersonal Psychology (2002: vii–viii).

Although therapeutic practices in general are quite diverse in their sources of knowledge and practices, personal development is more profligate. Personal practitioners often pride themselves on what they call their 'magpie' skills of working and taking from different sources, and what critics dismissively call 'pick and mix'. Thus it draws upon a wide range of different and sometimes opposing, psychological schools simultaneously, including popular psychology, psychoanalysis, humanistic psychology, behaviourism and cognitive behaviourism. Culling more widely, personal development is also influenced by historical traditions of the self such as romanticism (Taylor, 1989; Campbell, 1989) and liberal individualism (Rose, 1989, 1996a), Western religions such as Puritanism (Cushman, 1990, 1995; Starker, 1989; Plummer, 1995), Eastern religions and philosophies (Drury, 1989; Heelas, 1996), and Modernist beliefs about progress and growth, including social Darwinism (Nisbet, 1969; Woolfolk and Richardson, 1984). In her discussion on communication skills training in the workplace, Deborah Cameron refers to this eclecticism somewhat disparagingly a 'ragbag quality' (2000a: 72). For Cameron (2000a) these training materials combine respectable academic sources of knowledge with what she calls 'unreputable sources'. She writes of these training materials:

> they do not adopt a unified approach but draw on various bodies of knowledge or expertise. These range from the clinical/therapeutic precepts of assertiveness training to the anecdotalism of popular how-to-succeed-in-business books... Consequently, there is some incoherence in the materials; for instance, two somewhat different accounts may be given of the same phenomenon, or principles may be adduced which conflict with each other. It is seldom explained where the accounts or principles come from – in most cases they are presented as obvious and indisputable pieces of common wisdom. Appeals to experience are more prominent than appeals to scientific authority...This kind of training is meant to be practical rather than 'academic'. (2000a: 67)

Unlike other eclectic movements such as complementary medicine (Sharma, 1995) or expressive alternative lifestyles (Hetherington, 1998), personal development does not gain coherence by defining itself as oppositional to other social or cultural practices. Its eclecticism is further extended by another important factor: practitioners have usually worked in other fields such as marketing, sales or teaching before becoming personal development workers and so draw upon these fields in tandem with ideas from personal development in their practices (see for example Deborah Cameron's discussion on communication trainers, who had worked in advertising, journalism, counselling, management and teaching, 2000a: 26).

Contextual hybridity

Importantly, the particular contexts in which personal development workers operate inflect the ideas and practices used. For example, it makes a difference to the ideas and techniques used by personal development workers whether personal development practices are being delivered within the workplace or more recreationally, perhaps in an evening class. Even within the workplace, there is much variation in the types of techniques and ideas that are used depending on the sector of the workplace and the roles and institutional power of the audience. In the final chapter, I will examine how this kind of eclecticism and bricolage might fit with the idea of postmodern pedagogies which Mike Featherstone sees as a central role of cultural intermediaries in seeking to educate different publics (1991: 5).

Overall, personal development is less institutionalised than traditional therapeutic practices. Its practitioners work across a range of sites such as management training departments, in private and non-for-profit sectors; others work in health care, community work, and teaching and many are freelance, working across all of these domains.

Increasingly, local authorities put on evening classes in assertiveness, and personal effectiveness, universities run similar courses for students and staff. Physiotherapists advertise personal development services in their waiting rooms. In sum, then personal development intersects with, but is not synonymous with: the new age movement (Heelas, 1996; Ross, 1991), alternative medicines (Coward, 1989; Stacey, 1997), workplace training (Brewis, 1996; Hollway, 1991; Cameron, 1995 2000a), new management practices (du Gay, 1996; Rose, 1989, 1996a), expressive alternative lifestyles (Hetherington, 1998), and counselling (Bondi and Fewell, 2003; Feltham, 1995). The diversity of these contexts, purposes and practitioners mean that personal development has become amorphous, heterogeneous, and mobile.

All of this means that personal development needs to be defined in different terms. Given the lack of coherence in relation to the content or practices of personal development, it is better to understand it in terms of its aims and aspirations. In this vein, I am using the term personal development to point to a range of approaches for thinking about, and intervening in the self, its experiences and its relations with others. In essence, personal development approaches are characterised by the idea that the self can be changed psychologically and behaviourally in order to improve its experiences. Unlike traditional mental health or counselling practices, personal development does not claim to help people with mental health problems but instead to support people to get more out of life. In this thinking, as Lisa Blackman argues, life's failures are now seen as things which can be 'overcome and transformed en route to self-development' (1999: 114). Personal development represents a shift from the use of therapeutic methods for dealing with what are seen as difficult psychological problems, to enabling people to improve 'their lot'. Charles Lindholm (2001) identifies one aspect of this shift as the turn away from repression and neurosis in psychoanalysis to a concern with constructing new selves. In short, personal development is about 'making well people better' (Ehrenreich and English, 1978: 270). This can be extended when thinking about the workplace as 'making well people work better.'

DIY self society

Whether on a voluntary basis or not, social theorists suggest that we need sources like personal development to help us create our selves. This is because it is argued that the self is no longer prescribed by traditions, but is something that we have to make ourselves (See for example Anthony Giddens, 1991, 1992). The key messages of self-help literature according to Barbara Ehrenreich and Deidre English is 'you can be what you want to be, you choose your life, your environment, even your appearance and your emotions... you can choose to feel what you want to feel' (1978: 273). This means that we have to work at producing our selves. In doing so, we need new knowledges, training and skills in self-formation, and access to technologies of the self and practices of self-transformation (Blackman, 2000). Alongside consumer culture, personal development is increasingly one significant fund for these self-formation resources and practices. In this view, cultivation of the self becomes an imperative as indicated in the opening quotation at the start of this chapter and developed in *Worked Up Selves*, rather than as a narcissistic indulgence as some critics argue (Lasch, 1980; Craib, 1998).

Creating our selves also involves on-going transformation. See for example Lisa Blackman (1999); Lisa Blackman and Valerie Walkerdine (2001); Nikolas Rose (1989). Rather than once-only productions, the self is seen as something to be continuously improved. As critics note, there is a long history of techniques and initiatives to incite people to change the way that they behave. This is particularly so for women, as Nancy Armstrong (1987) has suggested. As I argue (Swan and Fox, 2009) elsewhere, the difference today is that all aspects of ourselves and our lives are now seen as malleable and improvable, particularly in the workplace. According to Lisa Blackman and Valerie Walkerdine (2001) among others, self-improvement is seen as a moral and social obligation that we need to meet in order to keep the economy and democracy going.

Workplace therapeutic approaches

As mentioned earlier, personal development will be inflected by the context in which it is encountered. One of the main sites is the workplace and here our encounters with personal development may be through choice, but they may have also been imposed on us. For example, we might elect to go on a personal development training course at work because we want to find out more, or it may have been 'suggested' that we need to attend by our manager in a 'performance appraisal', or we may have been 'sent' on a programme by our manager to address what has been seen as a remedial need, or our attendance may be mandatory as part of an organisation-wide initiative. The use of this verb 'sent' is very common shorthand amongst personal development workers to denote someone who is likely to be troublesome because they have not chosen to attend a course but it has been imposed on them (See Ackers and Preston (1997); Chappell et al. (2003); du Gay (1996); Gee, Hull and Lankshear (1996); Hopfl and Linstead (1993); and Turnbull (1999) for ethnographic accounts of such programmes). Our encounters with personal development then can be private, public, voluntary, compulsory, temporary or more enduring.

Organisational work

There are a number of different ways in which personal development practices may be encountered in the workplace. The main two are organisationally imposed and individually chosen. I discuss each of these in turn. Under the rubric of culture change, values alignment, Human Resource Development and teambuilding organisations now undertake practices to transform individual employees, and groups of employees. In essence it is imagined that re-making employees in particular ways will help the organisation's 'survival' in some way, shape, or form. These practices can include training, team building, corporate workshops, coaching, performance appraisal, outdoor training, experiential training, action learning sets and 360 degree feedback tools (See for example Ackers and Preston, 1997; Chappell et al., 2003; du Gay, 1996; Fineman, 2000a, 2000b, 2000c; Martin, 1994; Rose, 1989, 1996a, 1996b; Swan, 2006, 2008; Swan and Fox, 2009). For many critics, these aim to change inner parts of its employees, 'what people think and feel, not just how they behave', their 'hearts and minds', with emotions seen as the means and the target of many of these interventions (Wilmott, 1993: 516). For many organisational theorists, these practices represent an extension of management control into a new, and deeper, domain, the emotional and existential, which had previously been left alone (Townley, 1994, 1995; Costea et al., 2008).

Overall, it is believed that managers and employees needed to be changed at this deeper level in order for them to identify with and commit to the organisation. This can be seen as an attempt to collapse the divisions between personal life, personal values and beliefs, inside and outside work, work and non-work (See for example du Gay and Salaman, 1992; Legge 1995; Wilmott, 1992). As Axel Honneth writes:

> The creation of biographical originality has become something required of individuals themselves: more and more the presentation of an 'authentic' self is one of the demands placed upon individuals, above all in the sphere of labour. (2004: 467)

However, not all organisational theorists agree on this. For example, Paul Thompson and Patricia Findlay (1999) argue that this academic view that workplaces can go deeper into employees ironically reproduces the beliefs of personal development workers that this internal access is possible. They disagree with this view, saying that employees have their own strategies of resistance and self-protection and that responses to therapeutic interventions are uneven and varied (See also Fineman (2003) on this point).

There has also been widespread cynicism in the press on these transforming practices. For example, in his critique of change programmes in organisations, David Wilson cites the *Economist* on management training programmes. The *Economist* wrote that management training programmes transformed 'well-proportioned young men and women ... into critters with lopsided brains, icy hearts and shrunken souls' (1992: 13).

Transformations of individuals are imagined to provide a radical reconfiguring of the organisation's culture. As part of this, just as employees are seen as having interiorities, organisations too are imagined as having deeper levels, in the form of 'cultures'. There is an extensive debate on the problems of defining organisational cultures and on transforming them (See for example Anthony (1994); Hancock and Tyler (2001); Martin (2002); Parker (2000); Axtell Ray (1986); Wilmott (1993). As Stephen Fineman (2003) points out, the attempt to intervene in shaping organisational culture and employees' emotions was not as new as some commentators made out, but the scale and intensity of these programmes is. The history of organisational personal development interventions will be discussed in more detail in Chapter 2.

Choosing to develop

As mentioned above, personal development practices may be chosen by individuals rather than being imposed on them, particular at more senior levels within organisations. Thus, individuals undertake different training courses and personal development practices as part of their ongoing workplace development and learning. One core reason is in order to render themselves more employable (Garsten and Jacobsson, 2004). Changes in the labour market mean that 'new demands [are] placed on the individual' (ibid: 1). Personal development can provide resources for coping with these new demands such as being more flexible and for demonstrating on-going learning (Swan and Fox, 2009).

These ideas and practices involve us in not only transforming our selves, but being responsible for these transformations, and becoming proselytisers of transformation in a world seen to be full of change (See for example Donzelot, 1991 and Salaman, 2002). To cope with change and uncertainty, we are incited by increasing government initiatives to take up education and training, 'lifelong learning' and even 'family' learning, in order to improve our own individual capital and that of society's too.

There are also new ideas within neoliberalism about possibilities of the individual and their selves. Thus, Emily Martin (1997) suggests that in neoliberal work policy and practices, individuals are imagined as being made through their interactions with the environment (cited in Thedvall, 2004). As Renita Thedvall writes:

> Martin (1997) argues that there has been a shift in the view of the individual and how change is perceived in individuals. The 'truth' of the individual resides '...neither in the subject, made up of inner memory, childhood, a single history, nor will it be made up of Marxism's forces that bear down on subjects from outside' (Martin, 1997: 245). The individual is viewed as being 'constructed' in her or his meeting with the environment. Martin (1997) proposes the idea of an interface zone. The interface zone is a space where the possibilities and capacities of individuals are endless, since the surrounding environment changes in different contexts. 'Individuals come to consist of potentials to be realized and capacities to be fulfilled' (Martin, 1997: 247). This perspective influences the way individuals view themselves. It makes it possible for individuals to see themselves as a project to be constructed by themselves. It is connected to the neo-liberal idea of the independent individual taking responsibility over her or his future. Individuals become their own agents. Individuals become their own creators. (Thedvall, 2004: 135)

The possibilities for individuals shift as the environment changes from context to context. As a result, individuals are imagined as constantly malleable and changing to cope with the rise of 'manufactured uncertainty' (Giddens, 1994, cited Garsten and Jacobbson, 2004: 162). This has led to the rise of what I call pedagogies of self-flexibility, personal development practices aimed at encouraging workers to develop more malleable, flexible selves (Swan and Fox, 2009).

Another reason people undertake personal development is that work is being presented as a 'good in itself' (Donzelot, 1991), a means for self-fulfilment rather than an obligation. With this comes a reinvention of what it means to be an employee (See du Gay, 1996; Heelas, 1996, 2002, 2008; Rose, 1989, 1996a, 1996b; Salaman, 2002). In undertaking personal development, people may be able to get more fulfilling work or improve how they do their work so that they get more of the good, self-fulfilling work.

There is also an argument that people take up personal development because it helps them with the false promises or psycho-pathologies of capitalism, individualism and neoliberalism (Blackman and Walkerdine, 2001; Honneth, 2004; Swan, 2008; Sennett, 1986). In this view, personal development can provide resources, techniques, practices, self-reflexivity with which to understand or mediate the difficulties of work, life, new gender relations. It offers a structure of support (McRobbie, 2002) for coping with failure, disappointment, anxiety, confusion and frustration. For example, the unprecedented rise in executive coaching can be seen as providing spaces for discussing the difficulties of being a leader, being entrepreneurial and living with audit cultures and the pressures from living with the simulacra of reality produced through a focus on performativities (Swan, 2008).

Gendering the therapeutic self

Much of the literature makes the point that transformation of the self is not endorsed on any terms. According to this view, these therapeutic practices are designed to shape a particular configuration of the self, characterised by many as the 'enterprising' self (See for example Blackman (1999); Blackman and Walkerdine (2001); du Gay (1996); Gee et al. (1996); Rose (1989, 1996a); Salaman (2002); Swan (2006, 2008); see Fournier and Grey (1999) for a critique of this argument). Seen to be the spawn of the enterprise culture, with its tenets of self-reliance, autonomy, responsibility and initiative, the enterprising self involves us in trying to 'take control of our careers, transform ourselves into high fliers, achieve excellence and fulfil ourselves, not in spite of work, but by means of work' (Rose, 1989: 14). In a discussion on the individual qualities of enterprise, Russell Keat argues that there is a great deal of congruence between these and those valued in practices informed by 1960s humanistic psychology such as non-directive counselling, student-centred learning and certain forms of management training: 'an active, self-motivated individual, accepting responsibility for its own fate, keen to identify clearly its aims and desires, to remove barriers to its fulfilment, to monitor its success in realizing them' (1991: 11) (See Heelas (1996) for a similar argument. Cummins and Hoggett (1995) note the congruence between counselling language and personnel management language).

Thus the self of personal development may be understood in terms of gender. Several theorists have argued that these characteristics of autonomy, independence derring-do, and get up and go, are associated with certain forms of masculinity (Swan, 2006).

Feminine selves

In contrast, there is a view that rather than the masculine enterprising self, a more feminine version of the self is now being valorised at work.

In a move to what some critics call 'soft capitalism' (Kellner and Heuberger, 1994; Heelas, 2002; Thrift, 1999), organisations are encouraging their employees to develop skills culturally coded as feminine. Seen as an extension of the 'feminisation' of society and culture, a new 'culture of intimacy' in which emotionality, irrationality, fragility and passivity have become 'part of a project of self-development where the ability to feel, to nurture, to empathise and confess were valorised and celebrated' (Blackman, 1999: 112).

This is seen to have extended to the workplace in a number of guises. For Stephen Fineman, it is part of the 'customerisation' of services (2000b: 107), in which organisations across different sectors require a particular performance of emotions, intimacy and embodiment. Several theorists have written about the emotionalisation and aestheticisation of labour. Thus, the presentation of our self in terms of how we look, how we sound, how we use our emotions and bodies has become part of how business is done (Fineman, 2000a, 2000b; McDowell, 1997; Adkins, 2002a, 2002b; Cameron, 2000a; Kerfoot, 1999; Misztal, 2002). In some forms of work it involves the 'emotional proletariat' (Macdonald and Sirianni cited by Fineman, 2000a: 4) but has extended to managers, as they are being encouraged to develop 'warmer' relations with their employees, as well as their customers, with expectations that managers will be more open, and trusting, and act like a friend, teacher, family member, leader, mentor, or coach (Ackers and Preston, 1997; Casey, 2002a/b). Personal development workers claim to help workers improve in these types of emotional skills and social relationships. These workers are part of, as Deborah Cameron (2000a) puts it, the styling of employees.

As many feminists theorist note, the emphasis on feminine skills or capital has not addressed women's power in the workplace (Adkins and Lury, 1999; Hatcher, 2003). In fact, for Lisa Adkins (2002a, 2002b) it is men's ability to move between femininity and masculinity which is reaffirming their power in the workplace. Thus personal development can be seen to teach certain versions of femininity and masculinity, and how to move between them as I discuss elsewhere (Swan, 2006). They can also be seen as space for coping with the struggles and strains of having to be both emotionally feminised and, at the same time, agentic, enterprising and independent.

Re-enchantment

For other critics, the valorisation of feminine skills is more the result of 'soul searching' by employees themselves, rebelling against modernist technocratic rationality (see for example Casey, 2002a, 2002b; Heelas, 2002). In this view, it is middle-class professionals who are demanding a revitalisation of work, in which they want work to be the route to a better self, and a better life (see for example Casey, 2002a, 2002b; Heelas, 2002). One of the consequences of these new intimate types of work is the question about the authenticity of the self.

The problem of authenticity is raised in relation to the sincerity of the service encounter when it is over-styled or engineered (Cameron, 2000a; Fineman, 2000a, 2003), but also concerns worries about the self of the employee, and her/his ability to be 'real' when her/his conduct is being 'McDonaldised' (Fineman, 2003). As Stephen Fineman writes of the increasing workplace emphasis on emotional labour, 'one corollary of this is to make normal and acceptable emotion work and emotion management; they are necessary features of self-discovery' (2000a: 7). This has ushered in a recent growth in renewed ideas and practices on how to know and work on your self so that you can find the 'authentic you' and your 'real feelings'.

Self-improvement industry

As a result of these organisationally imposed and individually chosen participations in personal development, there has been an increasing institutionalisation of transformational practices aimed at the workplace. Training, seminars and other therapeutically-informed services, aimed at transforming individuals and teams, are increasing so that people can take on these new ways of behaving and feeling. There were over five hundred training organisations and tens of thousands of practitioners in training at the end of the 1990s (Puttick, 2000). Training is one of the fastest growing service industries across all sectors, and is now aimed across the board, at managers, professionals and trade unionists (Puttick, 2000). The focus on employees' attitudes, feelings and values rather than technical skills means that these practices use therapeutic ideas and practices in diversity training, emotional intelligence and charisma training, communication skills training (Lasch-Quinn, 2002; Fineman, 2000a, 2000b, 2000c, 2003; Cameron, 2000a on communication skills training). Rather surprisingly given the extent of this increase, these practices have been given very little academic attention in organisation studies, as Andrew Sturdy (2002) notes (see Cameron, 2000a, 2000b; Swan, 2006, 2008; Swan and Fox, 2009; Bell and Taylor, 2003 and 2004 for exceptions).

Through these practices, our notions of the self at work are being transformed, whether encouraged by employers, or by employees.

There has also been a marked increase in the number of practitioners operating in the field. It is difficult to find out how many practitioners are there because of the lack of a central organisation for personal development, the diverse spheres in which they practise and the fact that practitioners of personal development are often defined in other professional terms such as adult education lecturer, human resource manager, nurse etc. Some figures are published by some relevant associations but it needs to be borne in mind that practitioners often draw upon many different practices, so for example they may be simultaneously a 'life coach', a Gestalt therapist and an NLP practitioner. The UK-based Coaching Academy claims to have 2000 registered coaches. The North American-based Coaching-U states that it has trained over 7000 coaches in North America, UK, Israel, Japan and Canada. Related to this, there has also been an increase in the number of associations, for example *The Dictionary of Personal Development* lists over fifty centres, associations, networks and institutes in the area of personal development based in Britain (Tosey and Gregory, 2002) and postgraduate qualifications, aimed at these practitioners. Overall, the self-improvement industry or what early on its rise, Barbara Ehrenreich and Deidre English refer to as a 'pysch market' (1978: 273) is expanding.

Worked up empirical research

The final reason I have called this book *Worked Up Selves* is to get at another meaning of the verb to work up: to sharpen or to refine. As I mentioned earlier, most studies on therapeutic cultures have been carried out 'at a distance', being based largely on abstract theorisation rather than empirical research. This means that certain aspects of therapeutic cultures, such as their relationship to social changes, are emphasised whilst other aspects such as their heterogeneity or the influence of their particular contexts of reception, are underplayed or ignored. I wanted this book to provide a more close at hand examination of personal development workers and work. In medicine, work up means to examine a patient more thoroughly by subjecting them to a thorough diagnostic examination and it is something of this I want to achieve in this book.

Macro accounts

Even though theorists are critical of therapeutic practices and practitioners, there is still very little empirical work done on the practitioners themselves. This is because most critics concentrate on the relays between large-scale, socio-cultural changes and the rise in therapeutic ways of thinking. For example, Christopher Lasch (1980, 1985) links what he sees as the widespread depreciation of traditional forms of authority to an over-reliance on therapeutic experts; Anthony Giddens (1991, 1992) charts similar themes of de-traditionalisation and the rise of expertise but from a more sanguine perspective, seeing therapeutic ideas as a helpful resource; for Nikolas Rose (1989, 1996a), therapeutic ideas mirror and reproduce contemporary ideals of neoliberal democracy. Whilst this emphasis on widespread macro changes helps us to consider the broad factors in the spread of therapeutic thinking, it means that the particularity of therapeutic practices and workers gets relatively little attention.

As Liz Bondi and Judith Fewell (2003) argue, therapeutic practices are shaped by their distinct histories, geographies and contexts. Not surprisingly, from the bird's eye view of the macro, much of the distinctiveness and contextual specificities of therapeutic practices get blurred, or rendered invisible. As a result of this glossing, certain practices get to stand in for all of them. For personal development workers, this substitution of one type of practice to stand in for all practices would be highly problematic. Even though practitioners are highly eclectic and draw upon contradictory practices simultaneously, one practice does not mean the same thing as another.

Textual analyses

The majority of the empirical research that has been done has focused on textual analyses of self-help books, or in fewer cases, the reading practices of readers of self-help books. These have made useful contributions to the study of therapeutic cultures in that they examine some of the complex views of the self and transformation to be found in therapeutic thinking. They also suggest that readers show more ambivalence and creativity in their responses to self-help literature than might be thought from some of the more macro studies on therapeutic cultures. By concentrating largely on texts and in particular self-help books, questions about how other types of therapeutic cultures see the self and its transformation remain mostly unaddressed. Although we have insights into the extent of the spread of therapeutic cultures through the macro studies, and insights into the assumptions of self-help literature and its readers through the textual analyses, there are still some gaps that have yet to be addressed.

Newer practices

Another problem is that this literature does not take into account of newer or more marginal practices. Neuro-Linguistic Programming (NLP) is an example of a widespread therapeutic practice which can be encountered on various courses in the workplace from sales training to appraisal skills training, and can be encountered in a more recreational way through evening classes. Neuro-Linguistic Programming, abbreviated to NLP, originated in North America and has become popular in Britain in the past fifteen years. It is now an accredited school of psychotherapy but is also used extensively in training courses on selling, communication skills, personal effectiveness and management in the workplace. Invented by Richard Bandler and John Grindler, it draws upon cognitive psychology, linguistics, cybernetics and Gestalt therapy, to offer a range of techniques which are said to enable its users to change their mental strategies. Sometimes called 'Design Human Engineering', it has been critiqued for an over-emphasis on techniques rather than core values (Tosey and Gregory, 2002). Less obviously, doctors and teachers are also using it. The training in NLP has many stages and its own accreditation system, with qualifications costing as much as £10,000. At the moment, there are very few sociological or organisational studies of, or even references, to NLP.

The same could be said of 'coaching', a practice participated in by middle-class professionals, which is proliferating across North America and Britain in the workplace, through private practice and columns in the Sunday newspapers (see Swan, 2004, 2006; Arnaud, 2003 for exceptions). Coaching is a primarily work-based combination of sports coaching and counselling. Taking the form of a one-to-one relationship, it involves a focus on skills, and behaviour inside work, although in its form of 'life-coaching', it extends into private and home life. Using behavioural techniques such as role-plays, alongside cognitive therapy's ideas on self-talk, with less conventional activities such as visioning and regression, it has gained extensive popularity in the past five years in Britain, with several associations being set up to standardise, professionalise and credentialise its activities.

The practice of coaching is a relatively recent phenomenon. But it has proliferated phenomenally in the last ten years in the US, Japan, Europe and Australia and New Zealand, and across public, private and voluntary sectors. Coaching is seen to have exploded in the field of consulting (Arnaud, 2003). The numbers bear this out. It is speculated that there were 70,000 coaches in US in 2007, with a similar proportion in UK. The membership of the International Coaching Federation has soared from 1500 in 1999 to 8200 in 2005, spanning thirty countries, with members coming from different backgrounds – athletics, therapy, management and consultancy (Joo, 2005) and charging anything from £1–£2k per day, with the average fee being £975 per day (Carter, 2003). In the US there are over 100 coaching training 'academies' (Palmer, 2003). Used in private sector organisations such as American Express, AT&T, Citibank, Colgate, Levi Strauss, Northern Telecom, NYNEX Corporation, and Procter & Gamble, it is now a rapidly growing industry both in the US and UK (Olivero et al., 1997) and is moving rapidly through parts of the UK public sector including healthcare, education and the civil service. It has been suggested that 70% of leading private sector organisation use coaching in some form (Palmer, 2003). A recent CIPD survey in 2004 of more than 500 respondents said they were moving away from classrooms, and towards other forms of learning, leading to a 51% net increase in coaching and e learning (Fielden, 2004).

At the moment, there is very little academic research outlining its history and assessing its effects (Joo, 2005; Arnaud, 2003; Swan, 2004). But there is a growing number of literature reviews being commissioned by various public sector bodies (Fielden, 2004; Carter, 2003; Hartley and Hinksman, 2003; Hobson, 2003; Offley et al., 2005; Williams and Offley, 2005).

Research Focus

Worked Up Selves examines the accounts of practitioners in personal development, all of whom practise in relation to the workplace in some way. In order to provide greater understanding of how practitioners in personal development think about what they do, this study has concentrated on ethnographically-informed, in-depth interviews with fifteen practitioners from the field of personal development. I chose to undertake in-depth interviews rather than do more strictly ethnographic research, as I wanted to know how practitioners conceptualised what they did and to compare this with ideas in the sociology of therapeutic cultures.

This book considers practitioners, not clients, for two main reasons. First, although the study of clients in personal development is an important and under-researched area, it would not have enabled me to understand the views of people considered to be experts in personal development who are involved in the dissemination of personal development ideas and practices. Their perspectives have rarely been explored, and yet their actions are seen to be central to new reconfigurations of the self and politics. In addition, their practices have not been taken seriously except as symptoms of social change, or manifestations of the decay of the political sphere. Secondly, there is the issue of my own history as a practitioner, which meant that I believed that there was more to how practitioners conceptualised their practices than simply being 'an engineer of the soul' (Rose, 1989). This work was motivated by a commitment to finding out how practitioners' ideas compared to the critics' views. The practitioners interviewed are drawn from a range of practices, including assertiveness training, Gestalt therapy, coaching and management training. They were chosen not to form a representative sample of different approaches in personal development, but to enable me to examine some of the heterogeneity in personal development ideas and practices as indicated in the brief history provided above. The resulting 'data' contain insights into expert relations, the diversity of self-transformation practices and models of the self, and the category of emotion in personal development.

Structure of the book: Themes and issues

In sum then, the main aims of this book are three-fold: first, to provide an empirically grounded exploration of personal development workers and their work. Secondly, it is to examine how empirical data may extend current thinking on therapeutic cultures more broadly. A final aim is to explore what personal development workers and self-work in the workplace can contribute to contemporary thinking on changes in the nature of work. The empirical focus is on the UK, although the book draws on a number of theories and studies from outside the UK, and the significance of the analysis and ideas can go beyond a UK context.

Chapter 2 provides an historical overview of therapeutic ideas and the different views of the self that these have promulgated in wider society and in the workplace. It emphasises that different types of selves and concepts of interiorities have emerged at different points in time, influenced by a range of religious, etiquette, psychological and spirituality ideas. Although the history is necessarily schematic and brief, it provides a snap-shot of interventions into the self and the rising connection between the workplace and therapeutic ideas, particularly in relation to management.

Chapter 3 examines the debates on therapeutic cultures in the emerging sociology of therapeutic cultures. In order to address one of the aims of this book, which is to compare the conceptualisations of personal development workers with accounts in the literature on therapeutic cultures, this chapter examines the differences in emphases and arguments between different macro sociological positions in this literature.

Chapter 4 offers a review of textual analyses of cultural representations of therapeutic cultures, and finishes with a review of more ethnographic studies of therapeutic cultures. It provides several feminist takes on different therapeutic practices, particularly in relation to feminine culture. This chapter also emphasises the importance of understanding how 'users' relate to therapeutic ideas. The final part of this chapter provides a brief overview of the research and introduces the fourteen personal development workers interviewed for this study.

Chapter 5 examines one of the main themes in the sociology of therapeutic cultures, the relations of expertise. It does this through a consideration of the ways in which the personal development workers interviewed for the research conceptualised the kinds of relations they have with their clients. The chapter looks in particular at the concept of equality as understood by the practitioners interviewed and shows that it was understood in highly differentiated ways. In contrast to critics such as Rose (1989, 1996a), practitioners conceptualised their dynamic with clients in terms of 'equality'. The questions that are further explored in relation to these themes are: what mechanisms did practitioners think were needed to achieve equality? What concerns about their power meant that they wanted to understand their relations in terms of 'equality'? What were the main ways in which they understood their relations with their clients and how did this relate to their conceptualisations of expertise?

Chapter 6 continues with a discussion of the ways in which practitioners interviewed imagined the self could be changed through what they did. In particular, it explores the diverse set of 'models' through which transformation of the self was believed to be achievable. Thus, for some practitioners transformation involves a narrative of suffering, which involves a 'dark night of the soul' in which the self has to come to terms with 'its dark side'. For others, the self can be transformed quite fundamentally through 'the quick fix' and the 'makeover', a view that is in stark contrast to critics such as Craib (1998), for whom quick fixes are superficial and trivialising. What comes through these findings is the importance of the 'structure' of the narratives of transformation:

the relationship between the 'before self' and the 'after self'; and the gap between them. One of the main conclusions I draw is that these models of self-transformation are reconfiguring our understandings of the self and its relations with the past and future.

In Chapter 7 I look specifically at the category of emotion within the accounts of the practitioners who took part in the study. It examines in particular how practitioners understood the expression of emotion, and argues that what is particularly striking are the ways in which the form of the expression was as significant in terms of meaning as the expression's 'content'. So for them, emotional expressions were understood in terms of duration, speed of 'take-off' and bodily performance. Furthermore, particular expressions meant particular things. I link this discussion to the sociology of emotions, to argue that the category of emotion in relation to therapeutic cultures needs breaking down so that its meanings for practitioners can be understood more fully. For many critics, such as Sennett (1986) and Nolan (1998), the worst aspect of therapeutic practices is their valorisation of emotion and emotional expressions. In their view, the expression of emotion is leading to the decay of the public sphere by blurring how to behave in private with how to behave in public. In many of these accounts, emotional practices within therapeutic encounters are 'glossed' as 'people going to learn how to express their feelings'. In contrast, for the practitioners interviewed, the category of emotion, and its expressions, is far more complex.

Chapter 8 concludes the book, reviewing the main 'findings' of my research, and reflecting back upon the theoretical themes discussed in the light of my data. I argue that the specificities of personal development and in particular its understandings of the self, the self's transformation and emotion are largely lost in current studies of therapeutic cultures. I suggest that much of the critical literature is inadequate in the way that it creates the effect that therapeutic cultures are monolithic and homogenising. I finish this chapter by suggesting some important questions arising from this research which can be considered in future research on therapeutic cultures and personal development.

The purpose of this book can be summed up as follows: to examine how practitioners in personal development conceptualise their practices, given the specificity of personal development, the diversity of its cultural influences and contemporary work practices. Seeking to address the relative lack of concrete empirical studies of personal development, it examines the accounts of personal development workers who took part in this study in relation to their own meanings rather than simply as manifestations of wider social changes. It considers the following questions. What kinds of ideas about the self, emotion and transformation operate in practitioner accounts and how might these confirm or challenge our understandings of the self in contemporary culture? What meanings do practitioners mobilise which are not currently represented in the sociology of therapeutic cultures? This investigation is situated within the sociology of therapeutic cultures, but also draws upon theories, ideas and themes from cultural studies, the sociology of religion, organisational studies, critical psychology and anthropology.

2
History of Working the Self

Introduction

The introductory chapter laid out the aims for the book. I identified that a key project for the book is exploring the heterogeneity of therapeutic cultures and in particular, personal development approaches as understood by a cultural intermediary occupation, personal development workers. In Chapter 1, I discussed that one of the problems with the current critiques of therapeutic cultures is that the origins and influences on personal development are often overlooked. Personal development has a specific history that informs the kinds of ideas and practices that are mobilised by practitioners and clients. This history also inter-relates with the history of the workplace, its main site of encounter. In this chapter I provide an historical account of personal development and other therapeutic practices in the workplace, drawing on other writers' historical work to contextualise the data chapters in the book. This will help to demonstrate the multiple strands and varied ideas that interweave in personal development practices today. This account is necessarily brief, schematic and selective. It focuses on the waxing and waning of different therapeutic ideas in recent history in Britain and North America, and in particular on the intersections of therapeutic practices with the workplace. It will not be a history of the concept of the self, but will allude to the implications of changing practices of therapy for the self.

Puritanical self-work

Whilst it may be considered a post-World War Two phenomenon, several commentators such as Philip Cushman (1990, 1995) and Steven

Starker (1989) argue that therapeutic cultures started in the seventeenth century (see also Plummer, 1995; Miller and McHoul, 1998a; Cameron, 1995). For these writers, self-help books originate in the religious based self-improvement manuals of the New England Puritans. These books laid out prescriptions on how to lead a devout life through self-sacrifice, discipline and hard work. Other writers suggest an even earlier set of origins, for example Nancy Armstrong (1987) and Jane Shattuc (1997) argue that the roots of self-help books are to be found in medieval conduct books. For Charles Lindholm (2001), self-development begins with the Renaissance, as self-knowledge becomes a secular value, rather than as a search for God. This emphasises that ideas on how to improve the self have a long history and varied origins.

Emotions

Emotional expressivism, seen by critics as the quintessential therapeutic objective as will be discussed in Chapter 3, also has a long history (see for example Nolan, 1998 and Sennett, 1986). Many writers point to the influence of eighteenth-century Romanticism on the valorisation of emotions and their public display (see for example Campbell, 1989 and Taylor, 1989). In contrast, psychologist Philip Cushman (1995) argues that this kind of emotionality was also encouraged by an influential eighteenth-century Puritanical sect, which encouraged public displays of intense feelings. This interest in emotions was related to the expansion of the inner life in Puritanism (Zaretsky, 1976). For the Puritans, with their emphasis on self-examination, their anxiety about salvation, and the importance of discerning the voice of the true self as opposed to the devil, self-knowledge was a difficult and complicated process (Baumeister, 1987, 1999; Lindholm, 2001). Leading to the notion of a unique self with a hidden interiority and latent potential, Puritanical and emergent Romantic thinking emphasised that the self wasn't always what it should be (Baumeister, 1987; Taylor, 1989). These contrasting influences are all part of the debate about the origins and form of the 'modern' self.

Inside the self

The concept of interiority is seen to be a key part in the development of the modern self. The concern about the hidden self intensified after Freud lectured in North America in 1909, and his ideas became more popular, and popularised (See Burnham, 1988). As part of this popularisation, dissemination of therapeutic thinking through the mass media intensified. By 1915 representations of psychoanalysis were regularly appearing in women's magazines such as *Good Housekeeping*, receiving 'three-fifths as much attention as birth control, [and] more attention than divorce' (Nathan Hale cited in Pfister, 1995: 63). We also see the beginnings of particular psychological versions of interiority gaining purchase. Joel Pfister (1997b) suggests that it became chic, glamorous, fashionably radical and 'deliciously naughty' among the middle classes in North America from 1910–1920, to present themselves in psychoanalytic terms, and what John C. Burnham describes as possessing a 'wicked unconscious' (1988: 81). For example, one character in a play from 1924 says of her analyst that he 'probed the very depths of my being and oh the things we brought up out of my subconscious' (cited in Pfister, 1997b: 172). According to Pfister, the presence of the hidden self enabled people to justify any behaviour but also meant that particular possibilities and interventions were attached to this version of the self.

Mind power

At the same time as the power of the unconscious was being recognised, a contrasting model of the mind was being promoted. In the religion of 'New Thought', it was believed the technique of 'mind power' based on 'individual power and self-determination' would enable people to achieve wealth, health and happiness (Starker, 1989: 20–22). This new way of achieving success was completely at odds with traditional Protestant self-help books with their emphasis on deferred gratification, personal effort, and struggle (Starker, 1989). In advocating the power of the self, rather than some higher power such as God or nature, it represents a very modern way of imagining the self and its capabilities. This message of mind over matter has 'reverberated through most of the twentieth century, influencing millions of lives' through its notion of 'willpower' (Starker, 1989: 20–22). It forms a significant theme in today's therapeutic cultures, and has been neglected in critical accounts that place much emphasis on the influence of psychoanalysis and the unconscious. Although some argue the will is having a crisis, the notion of willpower is key to contemporary ideas on healthcare and management (See for example Sedgwick, 1994; Coward, 1989; Stacey, 1997).

Personality

In addition to the influence of psychoanalysis, Romanticism and Puritanism on therapeutic thinking, some historians also point to the effects of the media and consumption. T.J. Jackson Lears (1983) and Warren Susman (1985) argue that at the start of the twentieth century there was a move away in advertising and self-help manuals on the workplace, from a Puritan representation of the self as 'character' with its self-contained interiority, to seeing the self as 'personality', with an interiority that shone through and attracted others. This transition involved, according to Lears, the replacement of the traditional therapeutic model, with its emphasis on prudence and the careful management of personal resources by an abundance model of therapy, in which the psyche was imagined to be replete with potential and other personal resources, which when released would lead to a better life. Susman (1985) in a study of early twentieth-century advice manuals, notes a shift from the model of the self based on 'character' i.e. discipline, duty and work, with self-development seen as self-sacrifice, to a model of the self as 'personality', defined as magnetic, masterful and forceful, with self-development characterised as self-realisation. Personality was seen as something you could develop, and in particular, the workplace was viewed as a key place for the presentation of self as a personality, especially so for managers. These shifts represent not only different views of the self but an emphasis on its malleability (Cushman, 1990).

Psychoanalysis in the 1920s

Many critics imagine the intensified spread of therapeutic practices to be characteristic of our time. And yet in many ways, this is not the case: psychological ways of thinking had become so widespread post-World War One that the 1920s have been dubbed 'the Psychoanalytic Age' and the 'Age of Popular Psychology' (Pfister, 1995). This rise in psychology, psychiatry, psychoanalysis and behaviourism had a profound effect on work practices, popular culture, in advertising magazines, and self-help books. Hence, articles on psychoanalysis appeared in the 1920s in *Forum, Vanity Fair* and other magazines aimed at the professional-managerial class (Pfister, 1995).

Hidden selves

Part of this rise was due to the normalising of therapy. The use of therapeutic techniques on soldiers with shellshock after World War One legitimatised the idea that therapy was a kind of repair which could be used on normal people, since it was seen that even 'heroic' individuals had needed it (Pfister, 1997b). The inner life and shape of the self was increasingly regarded as important. According to John C. Burnham (1988), during the 1920s these became seen as dominated by motives, variously defined as primitive, hidden, childish, animalistic and habitual depending on whether understandings of the self were psychoanalytic or from emergent behavioural models.

The idea of hidden self meant that appearances could be deceptive and that one's potential lay hidden rather than on the surface. This gave rise to a mass interest in finding oneself, and in personal confessions in new magazines such as *True Stories* (Pfister, 1997b). These themes re-emerged during the 1960s and again more recently with the recovery movement.

Social control

During the 1920s, the aims of therapeutic cultures shifted from progressive societal amelioration to the possibilities of psychology as a new form of social control (Burnham, 1988). Eli Zaretsky (2000) argues that the idea of social control was seen in more positive terms at that time than would be the case today. Adam Lipsky, an author, wrote in 1925, 'The belief that we are at last on the track of psychological laws for controlling the minds of our fellow men has brought about a revolution in the popular attitude toward the science that teaches us to do it....Out of this change has sprung the universal interest in psychoanalysis, psychotherapy, hypnotism, character-analysis, mob-psychology, salesmanship, – all connoting a technique with which one may control the minds of others' (cited in John C. Burnham, 1988: 70).

Management psychology

This view was particularly prevalent in the workplace. Therapeutic ways of thinking, mixed with scientific management, began to infiltrate management practices, as corporations imagined psychology and therapeutics could help increase profits, productivity, improve industrial relations, and influence consumers through sales and marketing (Cushman, 1990). For Joel Pfister, the rise of the psychological as a 'mass-cultural commodity' is linked to the growth of the university-educated professional-managerial class and it is this class who brought therapeutic understandings into the workplace (1995: 65). In addition, he argues that there was a growing belief that the managerial, university-educated, class was more complex and deep than the working classes and minority groups, and therefore entitled to the 'right' to manage these groups in the workplace. According to Pfister, for the professional-managerial classes, Freud was seen as the new 'prophet of efficiency', the successor to Taylor and Ford (1995: 65). Advertisements for Freudian-informed how-to-succeed books pointed to the damage of repressing desires and suggested that you could become healthier, happier and more successful by not suppressing your desires.

Eli Zaretsky (1976) and Jill Morawski (1997) also connect the rise of higher education with the growth of psychotherapy. This classed view of the self's interiority as depth also meant that there was part of the self which offered a retreat from the workplace, a space that could not be 'standardised, controlled or owned' (Pfister, 1997b: 174). It also brought a classed concept of self-control to the fore with middle classes seen to be better able to control their inner selves and emotions (Morawski, 1997). The notion of unalienated, unmediated inner space has been a constant theme in more recent therapeutic cultures. More recently, this inner space is being seen as both the target of workplace therapeutic interventions, and for this managerial class, the workplace is now imagined to be a place in which this inner space can be explored and expanded.

Sentimental workers

The self at work has been central to debates about the politics of therapeutic cultures. Aspects of these politics include who gets to have what kind of psychological interiority, and what interventions are made on this inner self. Increasingly, people's inner selves in the workplace became seen as legitimate targets for intervention. At the same time as managers were viewed as having complex interiorities in North America, in Britain, in response to increasing fatigue and accidents amongst workers, both workers and managers started to be seen as individuals, each having their own particular unique psychological make-up, consisting of different emotional tendencies (Rose, 1989). Employees were understood as more emotionalised and irrational. Wendy Hollway refers to the new model of the employee as the 'sentimental worker', someone imagined to have 'feelings or emotions which affected his or her relation to work' (1996: 26). This idea of the sentimental worker arose from a particular take on management, known as the 'human relations' school, developed in the 1930s from the famous Hawthorne experiments. Loren Baritz (1974) provides a detailed historical account of the Hawthorne experiments. He shows that the importance of emotions in the workplace was recognised in the 1920s with psychologists writing about importance of a 'we feeling' in the modern factory (See Brammel and Friend (1981), and Gillespie (1988) for class critiques of the Hawthorne experiments).

Human relations was seen as an antidote to scientific management in the way that it attended to the inner self, its desires and needs, and saw the worker as socially, rather than economically, motivated (Hollway, 1991). The main idea behind human relations was that people would be more productive if their social and emotional needs were taken care of, as people were believed to be influenced at work by needs that originated at work and in the private sphere (Hollway, 1991; Zaretsky, 2000). Given workers' emotionalised interiors, it was believed that relations between workers and managers needed to be changed. To help them personalise their supervision, supervisors were trained in new post-Taylorist skills such as non-directive counselling (Hollway, 1991; Zaretsky, 2000).The programme in what became termed 'personnel counselling' began as part of the Hawthorne experiments in 1936 and finished in 1956 (Baritz, 1974). The precursor of more recent practices of non-directive counselling, the counsellors were instructed not to give advice or argue, and to deal with attitudes to problems not problems themselves (Baritz, 1974: 105).

By using counselling, it was believed, as the findings of the Hawthorne experiments suggested, that when workers were allowed to get things off their chests to a sympathetic listener, they would co-operate better and be more productive. As a result human relations conceptualised management and employees in terms of motivation, behaviour and relationships (Child, 1969). It marked the emergence of a science of work behaviour and the development of programmes aimed at dealing with individual employees individually (Baritz, 1974; Hollway, 1991). Henry Ford called human relations training 'human engineering' (Baritz, 1974). This type of psychological thinking permeates much contemporary management practice. As Hollway writes, 'its assumptions are so widespread that it is difficult to distance ourselves from them' (1991: 69).

Group therapy

The individual was not the only target of therapeutic techniques in the workplace. The group also becomes a significant part of the rise of therapeutic cultures. In the era post-World War Two, after the rise of authoritarianism, the group emerged as a particular focus for experimentation. For Kurt Lewin of the National Training Laboratory at MIT in North America, the examination of relations of authority and leadership in groups had therapeutic and democratic potential (Miller and Rose, 1994; Back, 1987). The most famous type of group work that emerged in this period is the T group, also known as training groups. Increasingly, T groups were run in organisations as group relations were imagined to be related to productivity. T groups were run in various forms from the mid-1950s by the British Institute of Management and the Industrial Welfare Society and attended by the National Coal Board, Esso Petroleum and the Council of Church Training Colleges (Miller and Rose, 1994). In 1957 the influential 'Leicester Conferences', involving group relations training, started in the Adult Education Department at Leicester University, with participants from Glaxo, a sausage manufacturer, a building contractor, psychologists from the London County Council and the British Iron and Steel Federation, the Steel Company of Wales, a headteacher, a probation officer and several academics (Miller and Rose, 1994).

People who attended groups were then trained as trainers and this technique was central to the 'multiplier effect' of these and other later, therapeutic ways of thinking (Miller and Rose, 1994: 57). This movement from client to practitioner is one of the leitmotives of therapeutic cultures.

Narcissistic self-growth

The 1960s saw an unprecedented proliferation in therapeutic practices and ideas. Mark Seltzer characterises this rise as 'a growth industry: the industry of growing persons' (1998: 110). This was the era, extending into the 1970s, that has been associated with 'selfism, selfishness, self-worship, individualism, narcissism' and sharply contrasted with the 'slavish conformity, rampant conservatism, religiosity, approval seeking, materialism and status seeking' of the post-World War Two generation (Starker, 1989: 126). Influential academic writers include Phillip Rieff (1966) on the rise of therapeutic culture; Richard D. Rosen (1978) on the dominance of 'psychobabble'; Christopher Lasch (1980) on the culture of narcissism; Richard Sennett (1986) on the retreat to the personal; Edward Schur (1977) on self-absorption instead of social change; see Cyra McFadden (1978) for a novel about the rise of the California human potential movement; Daniel Bell (1979) on the rise of hedonism and Alasdair MacIntyre (1985) on the therapist as contemporary archetype.

For most critics the rise of therapeutic cultures signalled an unhealthy preoccupation with immediate gratification, superficiality, and emotional satisfaction. Combining with ideas from the counter-culture and civil rights movements, therapeutic cultures moved away from the notion of therapy as solving problems to it being about liberating and growing the self. The liberation of the self was seen as a necessary precursor to wider social liberation.

Central to the rise of therapeutic cultures was the merging of democratic ideals with therapeutic practices (Herman, 1995). As part of this merging, new therapeutic models of the self and its relations with practitioners become prominent. Psychoanalysis with its perceived asymmetrical power relations between therapist and client, and its notion of the unconscious was seen to be undemocratic and inconsistent with the aims of the counter-cultural movement. In this vein, one of the leading figures of the human potential movement, Abraham Maslow called psychoanalysis 'high IQ whimpering on a cosmic scale' (cited in Herman, 1995: 265).

Humanistic psychology with its beliefs in equality, democracy and empowerment came to the fore. Ellen Herman writes the 'core imperatives of humanistic theory – to grow, to become, and to realise full human potential – were nothing less than democratic blueprints grafted onto the map of human subjectivity' (1995: 265). Rather than the therapist being the expert, the client was believed to be in a privileged position in relation to understanding her/his self, and knowing what to do for the best. In his history of psychoanalysis, Barry Richards argues that humanistic therapeutic cultures in the 1960s were based on 'an attack upon the internalised other, experienced as controlling, dominating, poisonous. Happiness must consist in the expulsion of the other; particularly the internalised authority of others... The alternative to authority was to trust the organism' (1989: 118). In this way of thinking he argues the 'imprint of the other' is seen as a threat, scar, alien, invasive and constricting, leading to an intolerance of the other within (1989: 111). The result, in Richards' view, was the creation of a false choice between two polarised types of therapist-client relations: 'permissive facilitation' or 'dominant control' (ibid).

This sense of democratisation was reproduced in new types of self-help book in which self-expression and self-development were promoted. One of the most important of these was Eric Berne's (1965) *Games People Play*, which sold 3.4 million copies by 1977, and topped the best-seller lists in 1965, 1966 and 1967 in the US. Starker (1989) suggests that the rejection of the elitism and complexity of psychoanalysis and a focus on the quick fix and self-analysis became the main characteristics of popular psychology books at this time. Berne's transactional therapy was described as 'a people's psychology', 'the first therapy that has made the complete transition from the Europeanised, intellectualised Freudianism to the church-supper optimism of Middle Western Americana' (cited in Starker, 1989: 117). Its predecessor, *I'm Ok You're Ok* by Thomas Harris (1967), was described as doing 'for psychotherapy the same thing that Henry Ford did for the automobile: made it available to the average person' (cited in Moskowitz, 2001: 224).

Habits of the self

At this time, there was also a resurgence in behavioural techniques. Behaviourism with its view of the self as habit and skills had originally risen to prominence in the 1920s (Burnham, 1988). Shorn of its 1920s grand claims, and divested of its associations with white-coated experts experimenting on unsuspecting subjects, in the 1960s and 1970s, behaviourism's lack of belief in the unconscious and its focus on technologies of self-control and self-learning meant that it was consistent with the general democratising impetus of therapeutic cultures (Richards, 2002). It was believed that anyone could use behavioural techniques, on themselves, or on others, and observe their immediate effects, without using esoteric ideas or intervening in people's inner selves (Cohen, 1985; Rose, 1989).

For some critics, behavioural practices are not democratic in spite of these claims. For Stanley Cohen (1985), their practices were used mainly on the working classes and involved a de-humanising move because of its model of the self, in which the focus was on the body and acts not the mind or the actor. For John C. Burnham (1988), they moved control inside the self, as the unconscious or biology could no longer be used to justify actions (Burnham, 1988). In this period then, the promise of rapid cures, tips and techniques, instead of protracted analysis, was seen as democratising rather than trivialising.

Good selves

The democratisation of relations between practitioner and client was dependent on a particular model of the self. In humanistic psychology during the 1960s, the self was seen as naturally good, and self-regulating. In contrast to the self of psychoanalysis, motivated by dark unconscious drives, the self of humanistic psychology was imagined to be comprised of goodness and authenticity, in the sense of being unmediated by social constraint. John Rowan, one of the leading lights of humanistic psychology, defined it as 'the study of how to enable people to fight their alienation and become more authentic' (1988: 15).

Inauthenticity and false selves were believed to be the result of social repression, including oppressive parenting, which suppressed the self's natural creativity and potential. Roy Wallis cites Michael Barnett, a leader in the Growth Movement in Britain, who said that 'the Human Potential Movement sees that we have sacrificed ourselves unknowingly, as children, in the name of society or of our parents' (1989: 25). Eva Moskowitz cites a handout given at an 'Awareness Extravaganza; from this time which said:

> you just need to be who you really are and who you are is whoever you are when you stop doing all the things you do to be someone other than who you are because you're so afraid that who you really are may not be all right. (2001: 218)

She also describes one exercise which was designed to overcome oppressive socialisation. This took the form of the 'Crotch eye-balling exercise' in which 'trainees were told to look at each other's genitals, whilst the trainer pointed at his saying this is where I shit, fuck, piss, and masturbate' (2001: 243)!

In particular, authenticity was believed to be achieved through an emphasis on the expression of emotions, and particular performances of 'honesty' as antidote to the wider anti-expressive culture. Moskowitz (2001) describes a best-selling game of that time called the 'Feel Wheel' in which players talked about how they felt, and the development of Sensitivity Inc greetings cards which sold twenty-five million and expressed statements such as 'Thank you for giving when I couldn't ask' and 'I think you use being hurt as a weapon against me'. Their inventor characterised them as what conversations build up to but don't actually get there (Moskowitz, 2001: 223). The release of true feelings and real authenticity often involved practices aimed at the body because it was imagined that the mind played games, but the body didn't lie (Moskowitz, 2001). It also involved the confrontation of pain through force and combative activities.

Given the innate goodness and potential of the self, one of the core ideas in humanistic psychology was that the true self should be allowed to come to the fore through a process known as self-actualisation. Self-actualisation was perceived to be positive for psychological health, but also evidence that possibilities for the self were not limited by human nature or environmental constraints (Blackman, 2001).

Encounter groups

By the 1970s this search for self-actualisation lead to a proliferation of personal development practices. Humanistic psychology began to influence many therapeutic practices and its understandings of the self spread across hospitals, schools and universities, and the workplace. In particular, group work – known as sensitivity training or encounter groups – proliferated at this time (Back, 1987; Rowan, 1988).

The encounter group is a 'gathering for a few hours or a few days of twelve or eighteen personable, responsible, certifiably normal people. Their destination is intimacy, trust, and awareness of why they behave as they do in groups; their vehicle is candor... In many instances they have never even met before, but, like the proverbial strangers on a train, quickly talk of their deepest emotions. Sometimes they use gadgets and exercises and props; sometimes they don't. Some of them shout, seethe, sob, attack and eventually embrace each other' (practitioner cited in Moskowitz, 2001: 229).

In his history of this era, Kurt Back (1987) refers to the personal growth centres where encounter groups and other sessions were run as leisure pursuits, as 'psych-resorts' to capture the extent to which the middle classes at this time began to see the analysis of their selves as a serious pastime. Sessions run had a range of titles: 'personal growth', 'intimacy for couples', 'sensory awakening', 'the body of god' and 'the crack in the cosmic egg' (Back, 1987). There were awareness events, intimacy labs, stranger labs, non-verbal labs, risk taking labs, creative divorce labs, and creative aggression labs (Moskowitz, 2001).

Rowan (1988) writes that in 1968, the Association for Humanistic Psychology listed thirty-two growth centres, by 1978, this had grown to 121 and in 1983, there were 265 in nine different countries. Groups were being run across Europe, Israel, Russia, and in Japan, where Routledge (1988) suggests there were over 400 people leading encounter and psychodrama groups. Kurt Back (1987) suggests that the sensitivity group spread through many universities in North America in the 1960s. Several of the practitioners interviewed talked of its use in a

Diploma in Psychology at the Polytechnic of North London in the 1960s which they undertook. There were two main trends in these groups: first, groups that were run with political aims, seeing groups as micro-societies enabling individuals to experience social and political structures in a controlled setting (Hollway, 1991); secondly, groups that were seen as having more therapeutic aims and psychological and individualistic underpinnings.

There was also a growth in corporate therapeutic practices such as scientology, Silva Mind Control, Transcendental Meditation, and overall an increasing commercialisation, institutionalisation and professionalisation of these practices (Wallis, 1989). As therapeutic cultures spread, the clients and practitioners moved from practice to practice, sampling a wide variety of different schools and approaches in search of their selves (Wallis, 1989).This pattern was evident in several of the interviews I did with practitioners who had participated in what they defined as the human potential or growth movement in the 1960s and 1970s.

The whole person

The shift in conceptions of the self and expertise influenced different workplace practices. The interiority of the self at work becomes significant again. Hollway (1991) argues that human relations training in the workplace took on a new hue, moving away from behaviourist training towards something which was seen to target something 'deeper' such as emotions, values and attitudes, to aim at changing the 'whole person'. This change in emphasis was seen to be necessary, Hollway suggests, because of the problem of 'authenticity' and the way that workers were believed to see through '"inauthentic" posturing by their superiors', and that 'managers had to be transformed so that they could live out the democratic and humanistic relations with subordinates with sufficient conviction' (1991: 93).

The target for therapeutic practices in the workplace moved from the employee to the manager but traditional training methods were seen as inadequate to the job of transforming managers' inner selves and values. The encounter or sensitivity group was seen as the best method for achieving this. The widespread and rapid use of these groups meant that managers were trained in multinationals at the same time as socialist local governments organised anti-racist training, the disarmament movement participated in 'despair workshops' whilst the police underwent sensitivity group training (Richards, 1989). As one influential author wrote, 'they cannot be "taught", "issued", "sold" or "plugged into" people' (Argyris, cited in Hollway, 1991: 94). A key question for these practices according to Hollway is 'how do you successfully influence resistant people and yet model democratic values?' (1991: 94).

The answer, exemplified by the idea of growth for Hollway, is that you convince the person who needs to change that they are choosing to change, and that change is 'neutral and desirable' and because the inner self is good and loving (1991: 95). Hollway writes, 'attempts to change individuals in organisations at this time were thus automatically justified. This was reinforced by, and helped to reproduce, a widespread belief in the value of change in the personal sphere' (1991: 95).

Feminism

The merging of political aims, behavioural techniques and therapeutic cultures comes to the fore with the second wave of feminism. Assertiveness in the form of courses and self-help books became a prominent means of personal development for women, although not found unproblematic by some feminists (Rakos, 1991). Assertiveness training had been used as a clinical therapeutic method in the 1950s to help both women and men with deal with anxiety, depression, schizophrenia and even substance abuse (Cameron, 1995). It became a feminist practice in the mid-1970s when feminists believed that assertiveness techniques of self-expression and the idea of individual rights could help women, who it was imagined, were socialised to be indirect and self-effacing. Although many feminists at this time had critiqued therapy quite trenchantly for its racist and sexist ideologies, Eva Moskowitz (2001), in her history of therapeutic practices, describes a time in May 1970 when radical feminists took over a meeting of the American Psychiatric Association, carrying slogans such as 'the psychiatry profession is built on the slavery of women'. Some of the more humanistic practices were seen to connect with the feminist belief that 'the personal is political' (Herman, 1995). (See Greenspan, 1993; McLellan, 1995; Kitzinger and Perkins, 1993 for feminist critiques of therapeutic cultures. See Barbara Ehrenreich and Deidre English (1978) for a feminist critique of assertiveness from this period).

At first, assertiveness training in the feminist movement was done in the context of a collective political movement rather than with a therapist and patients and fitted with the emphasis on social change through consciousness-raising groups (Cameron, 1995). As assertiveness training moved away from feminist groups in the mainstream, there was an increasing therapeuticisation of 'consciousness-raising groups' (Herman, 1995). Many feminists at that time were critical of these developments for co-opting some of feminism's ideas but not its political aims. This is something some feminists argue today in relation to therapeutic cultures as a whole.

The changes in assertiveness training illustrate this argument, as it has gone on to be 'mainstreamed, codified, professionalised and institutionalised' (Cameron, 1995: 180). This shift 'involves both an institutionalisation and a de-politicisation of the original feminist practice, turning grassroots self-help into top-down advice-giving' (Cameron, 1995: 179). Contemporary assertiveness training uses many of the same techniques and the rhetoric of 'empowering women', but the programmes are not run by peer groups but by paid expert professionals, and Cameron (1995) argues, an easy, cheap, and relatively unprovocative way for organisations to look like they are doing something about equal opportunities.

The changing nature of gender relations during the 1970s and 1980s gave rise to a huge increase in self-help books (Cameron, 1995, 2000b; Starker, 1989). In particular, this time saw the emergence of the success self-help book aimed at career women, which Deborah Cameron describes as 'the bastard offspring of feminist "assertiveness" and corporate "leadership"' (1995: 184). She also sees a rise in the relationship advice self-help books aimed at showing that women do have 'authority over domestic life and (hetero)sexual relationships', but should not rock the boat, and should 'adjust to masculine norms at home' (1995: 197). For Barbara Ehrenreich and Deidre English (1978), many self-help books aimed at women were concerned with pathologising traditional femininity itself. Cynthia Schrager (1993) writes that self-help books appear to be challenging traditional forms of femininity but in reality are upholding it in service of heterosexual relations.

Public selves

In more recent times, there has been a multiplication of different types of therapeutic cultures. From 'seminar spirituality' (Heelas, 1996: 58), 'Prozac nation' through to 'trauma culture' and what appears to be 'an insatiable public demand – in the print media, drama, films, and television – for accessible, entertaining information of psychological disturbances and psychiatric experts: "private ordeals" become a matter of great public curiosity and untiring investigation' (Seltzer, 1998: 110).

Part of this appetite has lead in Seltzer's view to a public sphere which 'represents itself to itself, from the art and culture scenes to tabloid and talk TV, as a culture of suffering states of injury and wounded attachments' (1998: 254). These therapeutic cultures are changing our notions of the relationship between inner and outer, public and private (See Brown, 1995; Berlant, 2000, 2001a, 2001b; Lury, 1998; Seltzer, 1998).

This proliferation of therapeutic cultures has brought different models of the self with it. In contrast to the optimistic self with the unlimited potential of the humanistic self, critics argue that the most prominent self of contemporary times is the wounded and imperfect self (Furedi, 2002, 2004; Wainwright and Calnan, 2002; Moskowitz, 2001; Eccelston and Hayes, 2009).

Twelve-Step

One of the most prolific of these 'trauma' therapeutic cultures is the 'recovery movement', which has incorporated what is known as the 'Twelve-Step movement' from Alcoholics Anonymous, which itself has 90,000 groups across the world (Miller and McHoul, 1998a). The model of Twelve-Step and the concept of addiction have now been applied to a whole series of activities including gambling, shopping, eating disorders, using the internet, having cosmetic surgery, having sex, and even reading self-help books (Miller and McHoul, 1998a).

The Twelve-Step recovery movement focuses very much on women's issues, women participants and women professionals and is circulated on daytime TV, TV films and recovery groups. Indeed for Elayne Rapping, 'recovery is indeed the dominant, official response... to women's suffering these days' (Rapping, 1996: 94). It took off with the publication of Robin Norwood's book *Women Who Love Too Much*, and Melody Beattie's book *Co-Dependent No More* started the move to create more and more Twelve-Step groups. In 1998, there were over 3,000 Co-dependents Anonymous groups through North America (Rapping, 1996). For many feminists, there are parallels between feminism and therapeutic cultures: personal anecdotes, confession, sharing, empowerment, liberation, but the main difference between them is that therapeutic cultures neglect the role of power relations and social structures (Rapping, 1996; Shattuc, 1997).

Redundancy counselling

As discussed earlier, the 1990s has also seen an increasing proliferation of therapeutic practices in the workplace. Traditional-style counselling still takes place in the workplace. Its forms have multiplied to include 'bought in' counselling such as stress counselling, redundancy counselling and employee assistance programmes, but also as a management technique used in performance appraisals and grievance procedures (Hollway, 1991). The contemporary organisational practice of intensifying work and reducing numbers of employees has lead to an increase too in redundancy counselling, mainly provided for managers, and the use of therapeutic terms like 'survivor syndrome' to describe the effects of these practices. In her analysis of the increasing use of therapeutic concepts in 'crisis management', Dana Cloud (1998) discusses the way that the multinational communications organisation AT&T dealt with the layoffs of 40,000 employees in 1986 when they were handed a pamphlet which advised employees to acknowledge their anger:

> Granted change can be painful. When it damages careers, emotions such as grief, anger, and depression come naturally.... Shoot for rapid recovery. Take personal responsibility for adapting to change. (cited in Cloud, 1998: xi)

Frank Furedi (2002, 2004) writes that blue-chip companies such as Whitbread and Cable & Wireless now provide therapy as part of the employment contract.

At the same time, there has been an increase in the types and forms of therapeutic practices in the workplace as discussed in Chapter 1, with individualised personal development practices such as coaching and mentoring on the increase, as centralised or 'sheep dip' training is seen as too passive and generalised and 'customerisation' of services is extended to employees. Rather than being seen as simply a remedial requirement, personal development is now seen as a significant part of work, especially for managers. Theorists of therapeutic cultures and of organisations have no doubt that there has been an intensification and proliferation of therapeutic practices and ways of thinking in the workplace (Cameron, 2000a, 2000b; Rose, 1989, 1996a, 1996b; Townley, 1994, 1995). These interventions may take the form of training courses, seminars, workshops and coaching and even management techniques such as performance review and performance coaching. Aimed at transforming individuals and teams so they will take up new ways of behaving and feeling, the substantive focus for the activities might be emotional intelligence, influencing, communication skills training, teambuilding, assertiveness or leadership.

Conclusion

This schematic history shows the breadth of influences on personal development in the workplace. In relation to this book, it surfaces themes to do with the power relations between therapeutic experts and clients, the interiority and depths of the self, cross-overs between the inner and outer and the public and private, and concerns about colonisation of the self by therapeutic practices. From this history, it can be argued that traditional ways of understanding work and therapeutic cultures are now problematic. So for example, orthodox divisions, such as between the inner self and private life, work as non-subjective labour versus the self as work, real life as seen as outside of work are made more unstable and complex. This raises questions about how well these influences outlined are represented in critical accounts. What kind of self emerges in practitioners' understandings of their practices? How do they see their relations given these different permutations? What level of the self is seen to be important in interventions? Having covered some of the historical accounts of the growth and extension of therapeutic cultures, Chapters 3 and 4 provide reviews of recent influential theories and commentators in the sociology of therapeutic cultures. Chapter 3 offers a detailed discussion of the work of sociologist, Anthony Giddens, James Nolan and Nikolas Rose in order to outline the lines of argument and axes of debates in the more macro accounts of therapeutic cultures. In contrast, Chapter 4 turns to cultural theory and more ethnographic accounts of participation in therapeutic cultures. These two chapters show the range of debates, the lines and axes of these arguments and potential conceptual resources for understanding personal development work and workers in later chapters.

3
Therapeutic Cultures: Practices of Social Control or Self-Creation?

Introduction

Having introduced the background to this book, and its aims, this chapter provides a detailed review of key ideas and positions within what I am calling the sociology of therapeutic cultures. In particular, it will review the work of Anthony Giddens, James Nolan and Nikolas Rose as these are highly influential sociologists whose writing on therapeutic cultures is shaping the field, albeit from different perspectives. They provide a range of critical perspectives with which to understand the rise and contours of therapeutic cultures across a number of social domains, including the workplace. Working at a more macro, theoretical perspective, each theorist offers a different take on the key features of therapeutic cultures and the potential politics effects of their growth and proliferation. In particular, these social scientists seen the therapeutic self as something influenced by large-scale changes in society. This chapter will be followed by Chapter 4 which focuses on more empirical accounts of therapeutic cultures, in particular accounts of self-help books, self-help book readers and representations of therapeutic cultures on television. These are important because they provide a more micro account of how people interact with therapeutic cultures, and reveal some of the complexities in these reactions in a way which the more broad sociological theories do not.

Therapeutic cultures and the reflexive self

The chapter starts with sociologist Anthony Giddens (1991, 1992) as his work is immensely influential in understandings of the self in contemporary times. In relation to this book, his work is interesting in relation to therapeutic cultures because he takes a less dim view of the turn to the self and the rise of therapeutic cultures than many other influential academics. As a result his work draws upon a number of case studies from therapeutic cultures, such as the AA, self-help books, and co-dependence which analyse therapeutic thinking in some nuanced ways and which have been neglected by recent writing on therapeutic cultures. Furthermore, his analysis of these different sites offers useful conceptual resources for understanding different types of self-work practices. In recognising the importance of therapeutic cultures as potential resources for the self that has to make itself, Giddens' work gives us a more sympathetic approach for understanding the participation of people in therapeutic cultures. His work also enables us to understand the complexity and even ambivalence of this participation than earlier critics such as Lasch and Sennett. Although Giddens argues that therapeutic cultures are 'morally stunted', and can lead to us being dependent on experts, his account differs quite considerably from the dominant view that therapeutic cultures are simply individualising, privatising and de-politicising (see for example Cloud, 1998; Lasch, 1980, 1985; Nolan, 1998).

Generally, he is much less scornful of the turn to the self and its emotions, seeing these changes as evidence of an important new form of personalised 'life politics'. Against this backdrop, Giddens sees therapeutic cultures as a significant supply of resources for our selves and our self-narratives in lieu of traditional sources. Therapeutic cultures, Giddens argues, are not as degenerate or dangerous as some critics have suggested, but do, in his view, lack overarching moral guidelines, and can be punitive when used in the context of mental health when they may be enforced on vulnerable people.

De-traditionalisation

Like other writers on therapeutic cultures such as Bellah et al. (1985), Rieff (1966), and Lasch (1980, 1985), Giddens argues that traditional sources of guidance on how we should lead our lives, such as religious authorities, local communities and our families, have become much less influential. Referring to this process as 'de-traditionalisation', Giddens argues that how we understand who we are, how we should live, and who should help us is being reconfigured in contemporary society. In essence, for Giddens, this means that the self is no longer given to us, but has to be made. This is where therapeutic cultures can be helpful, according to Giddens, since they provide both solace and resources for self-formation. Solace is needed in his view, because the modern self is much more insecure. Like Lasch, Giddens suggests that we experience existential feelings of bewilderment and loss caused by the reduction in prescriptions, routinised activities and rites of passage, all part of de-traditionalisation. In opposition to Lasch, Giddens believes that these existential feelings of 'ontological insecurity' can be ameliorated, rather than exacerbated, through therapeutic cultures.

The issue of therapeutic cultures as a fund of ideas for the self is central in the critical literature on therapeutic cultures. For many critics, such as Rieff (1966), and Lasch (1980, 1985), therapeutic ideas are impoverished resources for the self, particularly in their post-Freudian and non-clinical forms (See also Ian Craib (1994, 1998, 2001); Stjepan Mestrovic (1997); Simon Williams (2000, 2001) for similar views on the superiority of psychoanalytic therapy compared to post-analytic therapeutic cultures).

Selfing resources

Contrary to this argument, Giddens suggests that therapeutic cultures can be a significant supply for self-formation, bringing pleasure and anxiety reduction and offering a 'methodology of life-planning' (1991: 180). In this view, contemporary psychotherapy 'provides a setting, and a rich fund of theoretical and conceptual resources, for the creation of a reflexively ordered narrative of self' (Giddens, 1992: 31). As Toby Miller and Alex McHoul write 'self-help, like Freudianism, likes nothing better than a good story' (1998b: 148). Psychotherapy is not the only useful example of therapeutic cultures, as he notes that the self 'is a project carried on amid a profusion of reflexive resources: therapy and self-help manuals of all kinds, television programmes and magazine articles' (Giddens, 1992: 30). Therapeutic cultures, in his view, do not destroy the self, and its relationships, but make them.

One important view in social theory is that the self is produced through narrativisation. This is certainly the case for Giddens, for whom our identities are created through our developing a consistent, coherent biography of our self. Given that we are not what we are, but what we make of ourselves, this, he stresses is more than us getting to know ourselves, it is about us 'building and re-building a coherent and rewarding sense of identity' (1991: 75). Self-production for Giddens is not then a one-off project in which the self is made once and for all, but in need of constant revision, 'with more or less continuous interrogation of past, present and future' (1992: 30). This constant revision does not just affect our past or present selves but also our future selves, because these are dependent on the 'reconstructive endeavours' in which we engage (1991: 75). Transformation is built into self-narrativisation, for Giddens, 'constructed as part of a reflexive process of connecting personal and social change' rather than through traditional rites of passage which caused 'psychic organisation' in pre-determined patterns (1991: 33). In spite of these transformations and revisions, Giddens argues that we strengthen our sense of our selves as coherent and consistent rather than turning us into post-modern multiple selves. For Giddens (1991, 1992) then, the self is a project of creation, transformation and development.

Self-monitoring

The constant monitoring and revising of the self is viewed by many critics as an area for major concern. Whereas for Giddens, this self-monitoring is a form of reflexivity, for Lasch (1980, 1985), it constitutes narcissism. For Giddens, the process through which we constantly reflect upon, examine, and revise who we are, and what we do in the light of new knowledge is unavoidable because of the changes wrought by de-traditionalisation. Its aim is not unhealthy self-absorption in Giddens' view, but to install choice and consciousness into our habitual behaviours so that the present and the future become opened up for decision making. As Giddens writes, 'the reflexive project of the self must be developed in such a fashion to permit autonomy in relation to the past, this in turn facilitating a colonising of the future' (1991: 189). Drawing upon self-help books and case studies of addiction, Giddens argues that therapeutic cultures offer an important means for installing reflexivity into our lives. In this view, the reflexive self then is a rational decision maker, weighing up the pros and cons of a situation and making choices. As such, Giddens' model of the self also seems to involve a scientific view of reflexivity in which a pre-existing self cognitively appraises itself at a distance as if it were an object, and acts towards itself in a rational and calculative way (Adkins, 2002a; Skeggs, 2004). This view is reinforced by Giddens' emphasis on the self as a 'project' and therapy as a methodology for 'life planning'. This model appears to neglect other forms of reflexivity, such as 'aesthetic' reflexivity, which may be helpful in understanding the significance of emotions in therapeutic cultures and the roles of fantasy, and desire in self-formation (Lash, 1994; Adkins, 2002a). Overall, he seems to presume an instrumentalising voluntaristic self, when in reality much of our selves is constrained and given (McNay, 2000).

Expertise

Reflexivity also plays a significant part for Giddens in our relation with expertise. The increasing dominance of therapeutic expertise is one of the central themes in the sociology of therapeutic cultures. Taking a different position on this argument, Giddens argues that therapeutic expertise is always seen as contingent and provisional, as with all forms of contemporary expertise, because of individual and institutional reflexivity, where the 'terms introduced to describe social life routinely enter and transform it' (1992: 29). This leads Giddens to argue that whilst we are driven to seek out expertise, we are also more sceptical of the knowledge we find, believing that the outcomes of knowledge are risky and in some cases, very detrimental.

Summary

One of the contributions of Giddens' work is in the way he suggests a potentially more complex relationship between professionals, clients and expertise in therapeutic cultures. He argues (1991, 1992) that contemporary commentators and consumers have more of a critical take on therapeutic expertise, regarding it, as with all expertise, with more suspicion than is proposed by some critics such as Lasch (1980, 1985), Cushman (1995) and Craib (1994) and feminist lesbian critics Celia Kitzinger and Rachel Perkins (1993). His view that expertise has become relativised and pluralised may mean that therapeutic expertise is less dominant, more transient and more in competition with other forms of knowledges than many critics suggest (Rieff, 1966 and Lasch, 1980, 1985). By drawing our attention to the multiple sources for the self across different expertise and social settings, Giddens provides a less totalising account of the effects of therapeutic cultures.

Unlike many influential critics who do not focus on any specific therapeutic practices, Giddens gives a close reading of self-help books. By providing a closer reading of self-help literature, Giddens goes some way to providing detail on how the contemporary self is being conceptualised in therapeutic cultures. For him, self-help literature is 'a kind of on-the-ground literature of our reflexive engagement with our everyday lives' (Giddens and Pierson, 1998: 141). One of the limitations with this focus on self-help literature is that he is not able to convey the heterogeneity in therapeutic ways of thinking, and their subject effects. Whilst self-help books can tell us something useful about changes in the way we think about our selves, they are only one source of ideas within therapeutic cultures, and are encountered in particular ways. Different therapeutic knowledges will encourage different forms and foci of monitoring and transformation, and produce different subject effects. For example in relation to therapeutic approaches, very simply put, in cognitive therapy, we would monitor and revise our thoughts, in Rogerian therapy we would attend to and reconstruct our emotions, and in behavioural therapy, we would monitor what we said, and how we acted, and attempt to re-programme these. This means that he does not attend to the different narratives and their structures, which he imagines make up the project of the self.

Whilst his account gives an interesting take on the proliferation and pluralisation of expertise, it raises questions about the contexts in which people encounter therapeutic approaches. These contexts may affect their reception and power effects. For example, encountering therapeutic ideas at work through attending a mandatory training course on performance appraisal will have different relations of power and subject effects than electing to read a self-help book. There are questions here about the degree of choice on the recipient's part, the specifics of the knowledge encountered, and the power relations between therapeutic practitioner and recipient that are largely unaddressed in Giddens' work.

One of the questions that remains is how specific contexts affect the reception of therapeutic cultures, and the way that the self and power are understood within these contexts. This is important to this book because personal development is encountered in particular social spheres, and one of my arguments is that this inflects the types of meanings mobilised by practitioners. This next section turns to review an argument that state institutions are the main context in which we come across therapeutic ideas. It is of relevance as it extends the definition of therapeutic beyond self-help books and psychotherapy and begins to attend to the issue of power in therapeutic relations.

The therapeutic state

The previous section showed that whilst many critics are particularly scathing about the effects of therapeutic cultures, Anthony Giddens is more phlegmatic about its emergence and effects. For him, therapeutic resources can provide important guidance in an increasingly free-floating society. In contrast, this next section focuses on the argument that we are witnessing the rise of what has been called the 'therapeutic state'. The emergence of the therapeutic state, in this view, represents 'a shift from an authoritative to a therapeutic mode of social control – a shift that has transformed not only industry but politics, the school, and the family (Lasch, 1985: 47). To give an outline of this more pessimistic argument, this section will concentrate largely on the work of James Nolan (1998, 1999), a North American sociologist. His work builds on the work of Christopher Lasch (1980, 1985), an earlier influential critic of the rise of therapeutic culture. He has also produced the most recent, comprehensive and empirically based book on the practices of what he sees as the therapeutic state. Nolan's work then represents a more up-to-date critical stance towards therapeutic practices. Furthermore, his work is influencing a number of UK commentators such as Frank Furedi. Nolan's work is of particular relevance to this book because, unlike other critics, he clearly defines what he means by 'therapeutic', which I discuss more below. Furthermore, in analysing its use empirically, he clearly shows how therapeutic practices take particular form depending on the particular context they operate in. In so doing, he shows how therapeutic practices comprise a blend of complex cultural themes, some having developed over 200 years ago. Furthermore, his empirical work in state institutions shows the way that ideas about the therapeutic transmogrify to fit different contexts.

Nolan's work also provides us with one way of critically examining the politics of therapeutic cultures. By analysing the power dynamics of therapeutic ideas in state institutions, Nolan helps us to consider the coercive aspects of therapeutic practices by giving us a detailed empirical account of its interventions. In so doing, his work presents interesting implications for this book in terms of the dimensions of power in practitioner-client relations personal development, whilst at the same time, it needs to be remembered that the contexts in which he did his study are very different from those of this research. This section will mainly review Nolan's thesis but will also introduce other relevant social theorists to develop particular issues such as emotion and its expression.

Many of the critics of therapeutic cultures are concerned that therapeutic practices continue to proliferate and colonise new social spheres. In line with this, Nolan suggests that the 'therapeutic ethos' now informs all aspects of policy making (See Frank Furedi's work on what he sees as the therapeutics of New Labour and British social policy, 2002, 2004). Using a number of case studies based on the justice system, education in schools, welfare policy and political rhetoric, Nolan argues that the 'therapeutic worldview' has become a significant form of 'cultural capital' with 'a high exchange rate' in state institutions (1998: 19). Following on from Rieff (1966), Sennett (1986), and Lasch (1980, 1985), he criticises the way it is supplanting traditional moral codes and therefore transforming the conceptual foundations of public life (See also Herman, 1995 and Kaminer, 1992).

There is a question about the applicability of this very North American based argument. But I want to argue that it alerts us to the extent of the proliferation of therapeutic cultures in Britain because it draws attention to the diverse social and political spheres that the 'therapeutic' can infiltrate and the forms that it can take within these spheres. So Nolan writes:

> From the presence of psychological experts testifying on behalf of emotionally injured victims in the criminal justice system, to the feeling, self-esteeming emphasis in contemporary education, to the sentimentalised congressional arguments for state protection of the emotional well-being of children, to the use of therapeutic language in presidential rhetoric.... the therapeutic ethos... [is] clearly evident in the major institutions of the American state. (1998: 280)

Characteristics of the therapeutic

Of course, how critics define the therapeutic will determine how pervasive it is seen to be. Building on the work of Rieff (1966) and MacIntyre (1985) amongst others, Nolan argues that four main features define the therapeutic ethos:

- the 'emancipated self',
- the 'pathologisation of human behaviour',
- 'victimisation' and
- the 'emotivist ethic'.

I will briefly discuss each in turn. In the first of these, the 'emancipated self', the self is understood as intrinsically good, and therefore, the ultimate reference point, and moral arbiter of decisions and actions. According to Nolan, this view holds that it is society that constraints the self, and represses, or perverts its natural goodness. If the self is seen as intrinsically virtuous, Nolan (1998) suggests that this leads to a different conceptualisation of how therapy works, with Rogerian therapy advocating liberation not Freudian adaptation. The second feature for Nolan is the 'pathologisation of human behaviour'. In a similar way to other critics of therapeutic cultures such as Stanton Peele (1995), Nolan argues that we are encouraged to understand our actions in terms of health and sickness, rather than ethics such as rightness and wrongness.

Victimhood

This is related for Nolan to the third component, 'victimisation', an aspect of North American culture which has received much attention, and which Nolan defines as the increase in 'the tendency for individuals and groups to understand themselves as victims of abusive pasts or of the oppressive social environment that surrounds them' (1998: 15). (See Dineen, 1999; Lamb, 1996 and Sykes, 1992 on what they see as the rise of the category of the victim in North American cultures. Sykes puts forward a right wing argument that the rise of 'victim' politics has lead to an increase in unnecessary political correctness and has had a negative effect on democracy. See Brown (1995) for a more nuanced problematisation of politics founded on the figure of the 'victim').

Victimisation is a problem for Nolan because it means that blame is attributed to others and circumstance rather than the self, and replaces the stoical belief that 'pain, suffering, and injury were viewed as part of life, contributing toward the refining process that helped the individual to surrender self and grow in virtuous character' (1998: 15). Other commentators have argued similarly: for example, Wendy Kaminer (1992) suggests that existential unease and the complexity of life are seen as failures rather than inevitabilities and Lisa Blackman and Valerie Walkerdine (2001) discuss how failures are now seen as catalysts for self-improvement.

Emotivism

The argument that there is a growing public fascination with our own and others' emotions and that this is damaging our privacy, morality and politics is typical of critical accounts of therapeutic cultures (Craib, 1994, 1998, 2001; Williams, 2001; Berlant, 2000, 2001a, 2001b and Sennett, 1986). Nolan's claim that the fourth feature of the therapeutic ethos is the 'emotivist ethic' is representative of this argument. Drawing upon Alasdair MacIntyre's concept of 'emotivism', 'the dictum that truth is grasped through sentiment or feeling rather than through rational judgment or abstract reasoning' (MacIntyre cited in Nolan, 1998: 6), Nolan suggests that feelings have become the ontology for the contemporary self. In his view, emotions have become the foundation for making moral decisions, for understanding relations with others, and making one's relation with one's self. 'I think therefore I am' has been replaced by 'I feel therefore I am' (1998: 6). This valorisation of emotions leads to us believing that we need to learn how to identify what we feel, Nolan argues, and then express it to others in both the private and public spheres. Like other critics, Nolan's concern is the impact emotivism is having on civic society, epitomised for him in a quote by Jean Bethke Elshtain, 'The citizen recedes, the therapeutic self prevails' (1998: 6).

Politics of feeling

Whereas Nolan and Lasch (1980, 1985) are worried about the colonisation of private emotions by the state, sociologist Richard Sennett's (1986) main worry is the reverse of this. For him, the public sphere has been invaded, and as a result denigrated, by expressive personal relations usually found in the private sphere. Part of the problem for Sennett is the expressive forms that are encouraged by therapeutic cultures, which are imagined to reveal the authentic self due to the nature of their informal codes. Sennett argues that in the eighteenth century, expressions of emotions were not seen as spontaneous manifestations of an individual's uniqueness. Instead, they were highly conventionalised and artificial, and yet still viewed as real. In his view, therapeutic cultures today are encouraging us to conflate authenticity with informal relations, meaning that we now see formal, conventionalised, expressiveness as inauthentic.

Consequently, he argues, the boundaries between the public and the private, and the self and other are eroding. This is a problem for him because he believes that public and private spheres need to be kept separate by different forms of conventionalised behaviours and degrees of formality. A subset of this view is that democracy has become a 'politics of feeling' and citizenship, a 'category of feeling'. One of the most influential proponents of this view is Lauren Berlant, a North American cultural studies critic (Berlant, 2000, 2001a, 2001b). In her view, emotions are being used as a basis for politics, because of the commonly-held belief that 'the feeling self is the true self', and that people 'know what they feel when they feel it, can locate its origins, measure its effects' (2001b: 131–132). For Berlant, the view that our emotions are transparent to us and always knowable has been in doubt since Freud. In this new form of politics, Berlant argues that the use of feeling good as a litmus test for justice is an inadequate model for transforming society because it leads to the very social institutions that are the causes of oppression, such as the law, presenting themselves as the solution to people's suffering. In contrast to Giddens, for whom the turn to emotional intimacy is part of a new 'personalised politics', for Berlant, it represents a politics of personalisation, in which intimacy is wrongly seen to be the pinnacle of the good life.

Utilitarian expressivism

It is not just the expressivism of therapeutic cultures which worries Nolan. It is the combination of expressivism with utilitarianism, which in his view, in contrast to Giddens' take, gives the therapeutic ethos a 'unifying cosmology' (1998: 301). This means for Nolan that, rather than blurring the public and private, it integrates the 'cultural distance' between the 'highly rationalised, impersonal, and alienating public realm' and 'a private world of religious practice, "brotherly love", family, sexuality, and identity', making these separate spheres less 'cognitively dissonant' (1998: 18). In line with other critics, such as Philip Cushman (1990, 1995) and Christopher Lasch (1980, 1985), Nolan argues therapeutic thinking 'assuages many of the tensions' of modern life, offering a 'suitable antidote to the difficulty of life' in a highly rationalised, mechanistic and capitalistic world but without changing any of these tensions or the causes of these problems (1998: 19). In fact, for Nolan this combination of the language of utilitarianism – efficiency, productivity, and cost-effectiveness – in tandem with therapeutic language of self-actualisation, fulfilment, and human dignity has legitimatised the state's coercive reach into the private lives of its citizens. Apparently dissimilar, for Nolan, they both put forward a similar model of humanity's ability to control and re-create themselves, nature and the social world. He writes, in the therapeutic ethos, it is imagined that

> there are no limits to what we can make of our inner and outer worlds....One's understanding of oneself is not limited to references

> to things outside of the self. It is largely self-created and mutable to new creations. Again there are no limits. (1998: 285)

The therapeutic ethos, in this view, extends the logic of the self-made individual into a fantasy of autopoeisis in which the self is seen to be a self-enclosed and self-reproducing system (Lury, 1998).

Summary

As with Giddens' work, it is possible to point to certain limitations in Nolan's characterisation of power. His argument that the state is becoming increasingly reliant on therapeutic understandings of its citizens is an important one but is narrow in its model of power. His focus on state control and its coercive power means that he does not explore how legal claimants, school children, prisoners, drug users and politicians understand their use of therapeutic idioms. As Barbara Cruikshank (1993) writing on self-esteem policy notes, just because thousands of people understand themselves in therapeutic state terms does not mean that the state is all-powerful. What is under-explored in this kind of analysis is the response of recipients to therapeutic ideas and techniques. Hence their mobilisation of therapeutic techniques may be detached, partial, instrumental or tactical, and will be dependent on context, circumstance, and attendant punishments and rewards. Furthermore, Nolan's argument rests on the idea that to commit to therapeutic ideas in this context constitutes coercion and an encroachment on the inner self. For some critics such as Nikolas Rose (1989, 1996a), whose work will be examined in the next section, the proliferation of therapeutic understandings has less to do with what is 'done to us', and more to do with what we do to our selves in the name of freedom, rather than compulsion, and through which the inner self is produced rather than colonised (Hacking, 2002: 116). Of course, the contexts and classed and racialised dynamics of therapeutic encounters will affect the reception and operation of therapeutic ideas and practices.

Whilst there is no doubt that Nolan's definition of the 'therapeutic' is helpful in broadening our understandings of how complex a category it is, it is also open to the accusation of being too narrow and overly coherent. So, to take the example of emotivism as defined by Nolan (1998), his characterisation usefully draws attention to the assumptions and thinking that can underpin some of the ways that emotions are understood and performed in therapeutic cultures, and does so in more depth than many other critics of therapeutic cultures. However, there are many different approaches to emotion in therapeutic cultures which are not covered by Nolan's use of the term 'emotivism', which will be explored in Chapter 7. This chapter now turns to a different take on the power of the state in relation to therapeutic cultures, outlining a highly influential Foucauldian argument about the technologies of therapeutic practices.

Therapeutic cultures and the disciplined self

In the previous section, it was shown that a key question for critics of therapeutic cultures is the nature of the power relations between therapeutic experts, therapeutic expertise and clients in therapeutic cultures. As has been outlined, for critics like Nolan, the state uses therapeutic experts to operationalise a top-down coercive control of its citizens. Foucauldian theoreticians of therapeutic cultures, in contrast, provide us with a very different model of power. Studies of therapeutic practices influenced by the writings of Foucault are widespread (See for example Blackman and Walkerdine (2001), Newton et al. (1995) on stress management and employee-assisted stress counselling; Brewis (1996) on personal effectiveness in management education; Foote and Frank (1999) on the pathologisation and normalisation of grief; Townley (1994, 1995) on self-surveillance in management training practices and HRM practices; Cummins and Hoggett (1995) on counselling and the enterprise culture at work; Hacking (1995) on memoro-politics and the rise of multiple personality disorder).

For these theorists, we participate actively in controlling our selves rather than simply being manipulated, duped or bullied by someone else. As Ian Hacking in a discussion on self-improvement writes, some critics of therapeutic cultures when thinking about power:

> leave out the inner monologue, what I say to myself. They leave out self-discipline, what I do to myself. Thus they omit the permanent heartland of subjectivity. (2002: 116)

Nikolas Rose and the psy professions

This kind of analysis is exemplified in the work of the highly influential British sociologist Nikolas Rose. The work of Rose (1989, 1996a, 1996b, 2000) is useful for this book because he analyses the proliferation of therapeutic practices across a wider set of social institutions than Nolan, and focuses in particular on the workplace. Unlike other critics, Rose is interested in the technologies of self-transformation mobilised in therapeutic cultures. By analysing technologies and techniques Rose draws our attention to the practices of self-transformation in therapeutic cultures, and helps us to consider the variation in these practices, and the meanings and effects they produce. In addressing this aspect of therapeutic cultures, Rose begins to address a lacuna in the literature on therapeutic cultures, with its tendency to stay at the level of institutions. This kind of focus is especially important for this study, given its aim of examining personal development workers' accounts of personal development.

Drawing upon a Foucauldian model of power, he writes that the therapeutic ethos:

> achieves its effects not through the threat of violence, or constraint, but, by way of the persuasion inherent in its truths, the anxieties stimulated by its norms, and the attraction exercised by the images of life and self it offers to us. (1989: 10)

This is an important point because it draws attention to the lure of therapeutic cultures. Lasch (1980, 1985) also points to the enticement of therapeutic cultures but for him, these induce a form of false consciousness perpetuated by capitalism and the state. For Rose, the confluence of 'psychotherapeutics and political power reveal not the devastation of the psychic autonomy and security of the self but the fabrication of the autonomous self as a key term in the analysis of social ills and cures' (1989: 217). For Rose the 'true' self is produced, not hidden through therapeutic cultures as we 'become attached to the version of [our selves] that [we] have been led to produce' (1989: 247). The lure of therapeutic cultures for Rose is the means it gives us to produce ourselves as 'true'. Its attraction lies, he argues, in the way that it claims to help us become bigger and better citizens.

Subjectification

The relations between state, and other social institutions are not simply coercive, but take on many aims, 'not just to control, subdue, discipline, normalise, or reform' but also to make us 'more intelligent, wise, happy, virtuous, healthy, productive, docile, enterprising, fulfilled, self-esteemed, empowered' (Rose, 1996a: 12). This means for Rose that we are not 'incessantly dominated, repressed, or colonised by power (although, of course, domination and repression play their part in particular practices and sectors) but subjectified, educated and solicited' (1996a: 79). The essence of Rose's conception of this relation is that we are encouraged to undertake this government of ourselves 'in the hope of personal happiness and an "improved quality of life"' (1996a: 157).

Neoliberal ideals

For Rose, and contrary to Nolan, therapeutic ways of thinking 'do not have their origin or principle of intelligibility in "the state"' (1996a: 165). However, the ideals of therapeutic cultures are consonant with those of neoliberal democracy, and 'have made it possible to govern in an "advanced liberal" way, providing a plethora of indirect mechanisms that can translate the goals of political, social and economics' into a particular 'regime of the self' (1996a: 165). There is no controlling cabal making this happen, in Rose's view but symmetry between the ideals of political programmes of neoliberalism and therapeutic cultures. They come together in inciting us to relate to our selves as 'selves of a particular type' defined by 'autonomy, choice and self-responsibility' and 'equipped with a psychology aspiring to self-fulfilment, actually or potentially running their lives as a kind of enterprise of themselves' (1996a: 33).

Freedom to be myself

This enterprise of our selves has a number of similarities with Giddens' notions of the project of the self. Thus it represents the way that we use therapeutic expertise to help us 'shape a lifestyle' through working on ourselves. And as a result 'emancipating our true selves, maximising our powers, enhancing our autonomy, and releasing our potential' (Rose, 1996a: 157–160). Where Rose differs from Giddens in this respect is that he is less optimistic about our dependence on experts, the political implications and freedoms that this mode of the self brings. Rose changes the terms of this debate by arguing that we are 'bound to a regime of subjectification in which subjects are not merely "free to choose", but *obliged to be free*' (1996a: 17). In his view:

> we have been freed from the arbitrary prescriptions of religious and political authorities... But we have been bound into relationships

> with new authorities, which are more profoundly subjectifying because they emanate from our individual desires. (1996a: 17)

Our way of being free then is to do it in the terms and practices defined by experts. In this view, one way we are encouraged to get our freedom is through choice. For Rose, like Giddens, therapeutic cultures tell us that our choices make us who we are. In this way, contemporary therapies are, Rose argues, 'precisely, therapies of freedom' (1989: 257).

Self-monitoring is one practice central to these ideas of choice. It is a practice which worries some critics. Whereas Lasch (1980, 1985) sees 'narcissism', and Giddens (1991, 1992) 'reflexivity', Rose sees 'self-surveillance', which he defines as:

> An interminable hermeneutic and subjective relation to oneself: a constant and intense self-scrutiny, an evaluation of personal experiences, emotions, and feelings in relation to psychological images of fulfilment and autonomy. (1996a: 195)

In this view, in an attempt to realign 'what we are with what we want to be' (Rose, 1989: xiii), we internalise surveillance techniques, becoming our 'sternest and most constant critic' (Rose, 1996a: 239). Our imagined capacity for unlimited control of the world, in this view, gets turned on to our selves.

Work as life

Many writers on organisations see the workplace as a major site of control. Rose's analysis of therapeutic cultures in the workplace complicates this view as he shows that the workplace has become a site where expressivism and self-development come together with self-surveillance. Blurring the so-called division between the public and private spheres, Rose argues that increasingly work-life, rather than home-life, is seen as the means for self-expression and self-fulfilment, with personal aspirations believed to be tied to workplace goals. In this view, therapeutic practices in the workplace such as performance appraisal, 360-degree questionnaires, career development, management training become simultaneously, and paradoxically, techniques of both 'individuation' and 'individuality', in the sense that 'the exercise of self-surveillance.... is linked to, or indeed, rendered an aspect of, self-development or self-actualisation (conventionally part of the cultivation of individuality' (Lury, 1998: 11). For Rose, therapeutic cultures are central to the promotion of the self as an entrepreneur, and her or his self as an enterprise.

Therapeutic technologies

Techniques get scant attention in the literature on therapeutic cultures in comparison to the topic of expertise. Rose's work is particularly interesting because he emphasises the need for an analysis of both. In his view, the examination of mundane technical practices, 'selfing' techniques, and therapeutic technologies, defined by Rose as 'hybrid assemblages of knowledges, instruments, persons, systems of judgment, buildings and spaces', is essential because in his view, these are the very means by which we shape our selves (1996a: 26). One of the most significant of these self-shaping techniques for many Foucauldians is the 'confession'. (See for example Marie Heidi Rimke (2000) who examines the application of the confession in contemporary self-help books and suggests that three main forms are presented: priestly confessions to an authority, peer confessions and self-confessions, private self-examinations. See also Jo Brewis (1996) on the use of confession technique in a university post-graduate management course.) In Rose's view then, confessions, technologies and techniques are embodiments of expertise, organised to produce particular kinds of selves.

Technologies for Rose also include relations. One example of such a technology, for Rose, is the 'pastoral relation', exemplified by the relation of 'spiritual guidance between a figure of authority and each member of his or her flock' and 'embodying techniques such as the confession and self-disclosure, exemplarity and discipleship' (1996a: 26). According to Rose, the pastoral relation can take different forms: 'priest and parishioner, therapist and patient, social worker and client, and in the relation of the "educated" subject to his or her self' (1996a: 27). Like many therapeutic practitioners then, Rose sees the practitioner-client relation as a form of therapeutic technique.

The variety of these technologies means that for Rose the focus for technical interventions varies:

> What is acted upon?... Desires? Yes: undoubtedly one vector of our contemporary relation to ourselves passes through the flows of drives, phantasies, repressions, projections, identifications, and the impulses to speech and conduct... For the genealogist, desire is only one of the vectors... One would want to stress also the vectors that

> flow around the superficiality of 'behaviour' itself – the pedagogies of social skills and life-style... Perhaps equally significant... has been the new relation of self-to-self exemplified by the notion of self-esteem. (1996a: 195)

Different technologies, then, embody their own distinct 'presuppositions and objectives about human beings' (1996a: 26).

This emphasis on technologies and mechanisms means that Rose can show that therapeutic cultures are heterogeneous on a number of fronts. According to Rose (1996a), there are a number of dimensions against which therapeutic cultures can be seen as distinct from each other. One of these as we have seen is in terms of technologies. The other aspects include the types of problematisations – the definitions of what parts of the self are seen as problematic, and why; authorities – the experts who are seen to speak the truth about the self (1996a: 27); teleologies – the 'aims, ideals and exemplars' of the different practices; and strategies – ways to regulate people, families, employees which all linked to 'wider moral, social, or political objectives' (1996a: 28).

Autonomous selves

Unlike other authors, such as Nolan who do not examine therapeutic practices at this technical level, Rose can argue that it is this very heterogeneity which has enabled therapeutic cultures to expand and diversify. And yet in the end, Rose argues that the heterogeneity of technologies and relations all adds up to the same 'type of self':

> Overarching all of their differences, contemporary techniques of subjectification operate through assembling together, in a variety of locales .... in relation to psychological images of fulfilment and autonomy. In all these diverse machinations of being, in all these heterogeneous assemblages, a number of themes occur: choice, fulfilment, self-discovery, self-realisation. (1996a: 195)

Unlike other critics such as Lasch who are simply damning of the types of selves produced in therapeutic cultures, Rose is more ambivalent, arguing that the 'fiction of the autonomous self' brings with it 'ambiguous costs and benefits' (1996a: 17). In his view, when we realise that there is a huge gap between the reality of our selves compared to what we could become, we become anxious, and are 'impelled by the pleasures and anxieties in the gaps' to transform our selves (1989: 247). Seen in these terms, Rose's work suggests that our pre-occupation with our selves cannot be so easily dismissed. In his view we participate in therapeutic cultures because we want to improve our selves and our lot, and to prove our selves to be good workers, good professionals and good citizens. In so doing we commit ourselves to a particular version of the self, and of what freedom means, which are congruent with the ideals of neoliberal democracies.

Therapeutic work

This means that unlike many other critics, his analysis attends to the workplace as a source of therapeutic ideas and practices and also shows how these practices have re-conceptualised notions of work and the worker. By arguing that the private sphere and its aspirations are now produced in the workplace by very public techniques, Rose extends the argument of Sennett (1986) and Lasch (1980, 1985) that the public and private are being mingled. Rose's attention to the interface between therapeutic cultures and the workplace is particularly interesting in relation to this book because many of the personal development practitioners interviewed operate in the workplace.

This means that he does not denigrate people's attraction to therapeutic practices and provides a way of understanding people's relation to therapeutic cultures in more diverse terms. Rather than being totally dismissive of therapeutic cultures, Rose argues that he is ambivalent, recognising that they have costs and benefits. Although in the final analysis, Rose implies that there are in fact more losses than gains as we try to transform our selves into the shape of an impossible ideal.

Summary

In summary, Rose's work raises some important questions about the appeal of therapeutic cultures, the dimensions of power in therapeutic encounters, changing conceptions of work and the importance of therapeutic technologies in understanding therapeutic cultures. Like Giddens, Rose's analysis is largely non-empirical, and his aim is to understand the overall project of therapeutic cultures in relation to political systems, which means that unsurprisingly, questions about the reception of therapeutic cultures and different instantiations of therapeutic practices are left relatively unaddressed.

Rose's work does seem open to the accusation that there is a homogenising effect in his analysis. Although he writes that 'it is important to stress the heterogeneity and specificity of the ideals or models of personhood deployed in different practices', he argues at the end of the day that these all add up to one particular configuration of the self, that of the autonomous self (1996a: 28). Because Rose's analysis is largely non-empirical, and his main concern is the macro relays between the self of programmes of neoliberalism and the self of therapeutic cultures, he does not examine how the heterogeneous nature of therapeutic cultures, that he rightly identifies, may lead to different versions of the self, its contents, and its transformations. Like Giddens and Nolan, his focus is on a more macro examination of therapeutic cultures, and whilst it is not surprising that he does not examine the local instantiations of therapeutic practices, and the effects of context on therapeutic cultures, it appears that these accounts are limited as a result. A major question then remains for this research: how does the heterogeneity of personal development practices affect the types of selves and transformations conceptualised by practitioners interviewed?

One of the other difficulties with Rose's work is his model of the power of therapeutic cultures. Whilst emphasising our own participation in therapeutic cultures, he leaves us with a view that they are totalising, in the sense that we do not draw other cultural ideas on the self, that therapeutic ideals work upon all of us in the same ways, creating uniform desires and identifications in complete ways. This is in contrast to Giddens, who sees us partaking in therapeutic cultures more sceptically, more provisionally, with differing degrees of commitment.

Receptions of therapeutic cultures

This chapter has provided an overview of three influential arguments and the axes and lines of these. These offer a number of different resources and concepts for understanding personal development. As pointed out though there are limits to these given the macro focus of this work. The next chapter moves to a more meso and micro focus, reviewing theorists who examine cultural representations of therapeutic cultures, and how these may be recasting traditional thera-peutic understandings. In particular, it brings in feminist theorists who highlight the gendered dimensions and effects of therapeutic cultures. The chapter then examines how participants in therapeutic cultures – in particular self-book readers – actually make sense of therapeutic ideas and techniques.

4
Cultural Representations of Therapeutic Cultures

Introduction

In the previous chapter, I provided an introduction to key thinkers in the sociology of therapeutic cultures who work at the macro level, offering broad ideas of the emergence of therapeutic ways of thinking in society, the state and the workplace. This section examines the contribution of commentators who draw upon different theoretical and disciplinary backgrounds, such as Marxism, feminist cultural studies, and critical psychology. Many of these theorists carry out a range of close textual analyses of cultural representations of the 'therapeutic' in diverse cultural products including films, television programmes, self-help books and political rhetoric. Although varied in their evaluation of the effects of therapeutic representations, these writers enable us to see that the ambit of therapeutic ideas extends beyond the state and beyond social institutions to the cultural sphere.

In addition, their research emphasises textual analyses and interpretation and works at a more micro level. In so doing, this work demonstrates how the 'therapeutic' in cultural representations takes many different forms and has different formal qualities. For example, these include particular structures, and narratives. Thus, Ken Plummer (1995) suggests that there are some characteristic features of the therapeutic 'self-help recovery story'. This includes having a shameful secret, followed by public acknowledgement of the secret, then an overcoming of 'denial', transformation of the self and the path to recovery. He argues that these features mirror the classic generic plots of modern stories: suffering, the journey, contests, consummation and home. He also shows their similarity to the feminine genres such as gothic, romance and soaps, and how they are characterised by particular forms such as personal stories, authorial testaments, new labels for 'problems', checklists, personality profiles, diagnostics and solutions. In similar vein, film theorist Janet Walker proposes that there is formulaic 'collapse-therapy-cure' plot structure in many Hollywood films on psychoanalysis (1993: xxi). In an analysis of self-help books, David Gauntlett (2002b) suggests that there are three types of self-help books:

1. make your self-narrative stronger and more cohesive;
2. transform, ditch or rewrite your self-narrative;
3. accept your self-narrative by amending your perception of it.

This work provides a more close-up range of resources for understanding personal development work across a range of cultural sites and practices. Thus we can enlarge our understanding of the therapeutic moves across different domains. The second section examines how self-help readers interact with self-help literature. Drawing on a range of feminist and cultural theorists, this section offers feminist takes on the gendering of self-help and the relation between femininity, feminine culture and therapeutic cultures. Finally, the chapter introduces the empirical research discussed in the book, outlining the research design and presenting the personal development workers I interviewed.

Therapies as consolation

This section begins by looking at the work of Dana Cloud (1998), a North American sociologist because she present a strong anti-therapeutic culture stance. She also brings in a different analytic focus: therapy rhetoric in culture. Cloud positions herself in opposition to Giddens and even Rose, whom she finds, somewhat surprisingly too uncritical of therapeutic cultures. Building on critics who argue that therapeutic practices de-politicise its end users, such as Lasch and Sennett, Cloud proposes that therapeutic ideas are used to buffer modern capitalism from critique by pacifying us all. To argue her case, she draws upon a Marxist informed rhetorical analysis in a range of case studies across the whole political spectrum, including films, newscasts, and feminist politics. Her main argument is that therapeutic language has become hegemonic, being mobilised by politicians, managers, entertainers, feminists and neo-Marxists.

The reason for this dominance of the 'rhetoric of therapy', according to Cloud, is to defuse political activism during time of social crises. It does this, she argues, through promoting 'the private life' as opposed to a public or civic life. In addition, therapeutic rhetoric offers 'consolation rather than compensation, individual adaptation rather than social change' (1998: 3). By using 'personalistic and privatising explanations' of all forms of social reality such as 'war, women's oppression, racism, exploitation, and poverty' we are all encouraged, she argues, including the left, to reject 'structural critique and public struggle' (1998: 158).

Therapeutic lexicon

In contrast to Nolan (1998), for whom the therapeutic is comprised of certain themes to do with the self, for Cloud it is characterised by a particular kind of rhetoric. For Cloud, this rhetoric is drawn from 'psychotherapy's lexicon – the conservative language of healing, coping, adaptation, and restoration of a previously existing order' (1998: xiv). This kind of language, she argues, neutralises our disappointment and anger, by offering us 'psychological ministration for the ills of society' (1998: xii). For her, this rhetoric has an intentional political function.

The politics of therapeutic cultures is a central theme for many writers. In contrast to Rose's view of a loose confluence between therapeutic cultures and neoliberalism, Cloud sees a more deliberate relation. For her, therapeutic rhetoric is the 'political strategy of capitalism' (1998: xiii). It has, she argues the uniform purpose of channeling 'oppositional political currents back into the mainstream' (1998: 16). This way of dealing with political conflict, according to Cloud (1998), is inherently conservative, in that the existence of suffering is acknowledged, but the status quo is not changed. In this view, radical critique becomes domesticated by therapeutic-speak.

Family therapy

To trace the rhetoric and its political effects, Cloud draws upon a number of examples, including film. Her main focus is the way that ideas such as privatisation and consolation are used. So she examines the use of 'family values' in political speeches and films such as *Boyz N the Hood* (1991) and *Menace II Society* (1993), arguing in these that the family is positioned as the antidote to poverty, and oppression. In news reporting of support groups during the Gulf War, she suggests that the metaphor of the 'family' was used to domesticate public dissent against the war.

Moving onto more radical cultural projects, she criticises what she sees as the idealism and implicit therapeutic individualism in what she calls the 'New Age politics' of neo-Marxists such as Ernesto Laclau and Chantal Mouffe. These, she claims, deny social causes and solutions (1998: 159). For her, the central tenet of the 'personal is political' of feminist consciousness-raising has also rendered feminism therapeutic. She sees this exemplified in the film *Thelma and Louise,* which she sees as a 'therapeutic text'. This is because it 'constitutes a feminist subject with nowhere to go and nothing to do but express herself' (1998: 123). For Cloud (1998) these cases illustrate the proliferation of therapeutic ideas, and echoing Lasch (1980, 1985), their profoundly de-politicising effects.

Summary

Cloud's work is helpful in that she questions the wider political effects of therapeutic ways of thinking. She shows that we need to look at therapeutic motifs in cultural products as well as in their more traditional forms if we are going to be able to reflect on the consequences of therapeutic cultures. The trouble with Cloud's account is that she uses a very narrow definition of the therapeutic, which means that she misses other potential manifestations of it. She also presents representations of the therapeutic as highly deterministic as if they have one effect or reading. Furthermore, Cloud does not address the reception of these representations, arguing that cultural studies academics' suggestion that we may read self-help books or television chat shows in counter-ideological ways is itself a manifestation of the therapeutic ethos, avoiding what she sees as 'proper' political activism.

Helping the self

There are other approaches to representations of therapeutic cultures that provide analyses of why we are drawn to therapeutic ideas. One example of this type of approach is cultural feminist, Cynthia Schrager's analysis (1993) of the power relations of self-help in the best-selling self-help books from the 1980s and 1990s. These books include *Women Who Love Too Much* by Robin Norwood (See Cath Jackson (1989) and Sara Scott and Tracey Payne (1984) for more negative criticisms of Norwood's book). Contrasting *Women Who Love Too Much* to Freud's case study of Dora, Schrager (1993) suggests that self-help promises to set up a different relation to knowledge and authority, replacing the hierarchical division between analysts and analysand in Freudian psychoanalysis. It does this by offering the 'tools of interpretation' to the reader so that she can 'self-author her own narrative of addiction and recovery' (1993: 179). She also notes that:

> whereas Freud addressed a specialised audience of male colleagues, relegating Dora to the position of subject (or, if you like, object) of medical scrutiny, Norwood addresses a community of women, a 'we' to which she herself professes to belong... This democratic and non-hierarchical nature of the self-help rhetoric is codified in the tenth and final step of the WWL2M recovery programme: 'Share with others what you have experienced and learned'. (1993: 179)

Safety valves

In spite of these reconfigurings of the expert-client relation, in the end, Schrager argues that self-help is an extension of 'patriarchal discourses and practices' (1993: 180). Like Cloud (1998), Schrager sees the book as a form of consolation, not a radical challenge. For her, it exemplifies what Lauren Berlant calls the 'female complaint', a genre of 'self-containment' that 'allows the woman who wants to maintain her alignment with men to speak oppositionally but without fear of her position in the heterosexual economy', and acts as a 'safety valve' for surplus female rage and desire' (Berlant cited in Schrager, 1993: 184). In Schrager's view, self-help books borrow from feminism. But politically they 'work against its fundamental tenets' (1993: 177). Whilst offering new terms for practitioner-client relations, this means for Schrager that the wider project of self-help books is to sustain the status quo, particularly for women.

Many critics of therapeutic cultures do not see self-help books as a source for challenging the status quo. But the difference with Schrager is that she acknowledges the success of self-help books, and attributes some of this success to the way they have addressed issues in our subjective lives and have appropriated feminist principles (See also Hochschild (1994) on this point). If feminism is going to transform women's lives, then in Schrager's view, it needs to analyse the appeal, success and precepts of self-help books and offer its own politically informed notion of self-making. In their current form, though, for Schrager, most self-help books do not challenge wider power imbalances in society.

Feminine culture and self-transformation

Exemplifying the kind of feminist cultural readings Cloud might criticise, a number of authors provide a more sympathetic reading of representations of therapeutic cultures. At the same time, they do recognise the politics of therapeutic cultures while at the same time questioning what constitutes 'the political' in social theory. The first example in this section comes from the work of feminist cultural studies academic Hilary Radner (1995). Although Radner's analysis is based on feminine culture, rather than therapeutic cultures, her work is pertinent because she examines the processes of self-production and self-transformation, which are very relevant to this research. She also draws upon self-help books, as examples of feminine culture, to illustrate her claims.

There are some resonances in her work with Cloud and Schrager. Like them, she suggests that self-help books can operate as a form of containment in that they appear to satisfy their demands but do not fundamentally change social relations. On the other hand, Radner also argues that there is more going on in women's participation in feminine culture. For her, women know that feminine culture is a 'conflicted' set of practices, and so their involvement in it should be understood as:

> a process of investment and return, of negotiation, in which the value of a given articulation of pleasure is always measured against its costs, the inevitable price of an invitation that is never extended freely, never absolutely, the terms of which change from day to day, place to place. (1995: 178–179)

In seeing women as both embracing and rejecting the ideals of feminine culture, she is suggesting that they are more reflexive and active in their negotiation with feminine culture, and by association, self-help books, than is usually acknowledged. This does not mean that the terms in which they produce themselves are intrinsically empowering. Like Rose (1989, 1996a) Radner is concerned about the idealised terms that impel self-transformation, but she is suggesting these are simultaneously denied, questioned, and renegotiated (1995: 177). Thus the terms of engagement are complex and not completely deterministic. Furthermore, she argues that feminine culture is heteroglossic, its practices used in tandem with other cultural practices amplifying the hybridity and bricolage in feminine culture use. Women move across different social spheres, mobilising different discourses as they go. Consequently, she proposes that we cannot understand feminine culture as a monolith, or its effects as singular or static.

For many critics, the ultimate effects of therapeutic cultures are quite clear and consistent. This is not the case for Radner (1995), who like Rose (1989, 1996a), analyses the category of 'autonomy' and shows how its conceptualisation varies across three different self-help books: Susan Price (1984) *The Female Ego*, Gloria Steinem (1993) *Revolution from Within*, Sue Llewelyn and Kate Osborne (1990) *Women's Lives*. Two of the books offer tactics to women readers which in the end, Radner (1995) argues, discipline women to behave in traditional ways in heterosexual relations, and feminise the idea of autonomy:

> This ethos of autonomy and self-control differs from that usually associated with the masculine subject because, rather than emphasising external accomplishment and public recognition, private happiness [is seen] as the source of satisfaction for women. (1995: 41)

Disregarding economic and social conditions, they offer role models who are returned to 'a private interior, ultimately silent, silenced space', a space which both writers suggest offers a happy ending through heterosexual monogamy in which self-fulfilment is psychologised and interiorised (1995: 44). In contrast, a self-help book written by two feminist therapists, Llewelyn and Osborne, she argues, offers women more transformative possibilities, paradoxically not through a story with a 'happy ending' but with 'a story of survival in which there are costs as well as benefits' and in which autonomy is achieved through the price of a narrative of 'reconstruction not reconciliation' with a 'provisional cure', no 'redemptive moment' and no true inner self (1995: 50). The endpoints and structures of therapeutic categories cannot always be recognised in advance of a detailed analysis of them.

Although Radner's focus is on feminine culture, I want to argue that her approach enables us to understand the relationship between therapeutic cultures, and their users in more complex ways. In presenting this relation as one of negotiation, in which the terms, costs and benefits of the negotiation shift, she raises interesting questions in relation to this book about the agency of participants in therapeutic cultures. Through her attention to the practices of self-cultivation and our active and deliberate engagement in these practices, she shows how we need to question what we mean by the political. Thus she argues that we need to 'displace the political from its position as part of a metacritical discourse onto the minute decisions of a contingent day-to-day practice in which absolute categories cannot be maintained from moment to moment' (1995: 178). Like Rose, she also focuses on the technologies of self-transformation, but in opposition to him, sees them as more negotiated and fragile than perhaps it could be argued he does.

Therapy TV

Having examined Radner's analysis of representations of transformation in feminine culture, this section turns to discussion on representations of therapeutic cultures on daytime television. Unlike Schrager (1993), who suggests that self-help's reconstruction of power relations in therapy promises more than it delivers, Mimi White (1992) and Jane Shattuc (1997), in their studies of the therapeutic and television, argue that therapeutic relations are being reconfigured in potentially politically challenging ways.

Confessing

For many critics, the 'confession' is the defining therapeutic practice. Mimi White (1992) shows how the confession has migrated to television, being deployed in soap operas and chat shows, and through these representations, it takes on a different structure and different terms. Typically, the structure of the confession is seen as a linear, progressive, redemptive self-narrative, but this is disrupted by what she calls 'non-transformatory redundancy', a form of redemption which is only temporary because in soap operas, or serials, different characters, or the same character, have to confess time and time again. In this way, the confession is figured, she argues, as both transformative *and* repetitive. The repetition of everyone confessing over and over again to everybody else on television, White suggests, also means that ideas about the authenticity of the confessional voice is being transformed. For White, these repetitions suggest that it is the processes of fantasy, desire, identification and the 'recognition, acknowledgement, and confession of these problems – even to oneself' that attracts us to therapeutic processes rather than just the final, redemptive cure (1992: 12).

Expert truths

The operation of power is central to many discussions on therapeutic cultures. There seem to be two dominant views in circulation, one that therapists or therapeutic ideas subordinate us and second, that we willingly consent to our own self-regulation. For Shattuc (1997), the issue is made more complicated by daytime television. On daytime television traditional Freudian therapeutic power relations are problematised, according to Shattuc, by the amount of people who can claim therapeutic expertise, including the host, guests, audience and viewers. The influence of humanist therapy, self-help and feminism means that the 'patient' is seen as more of an expert on her self, and is represented as active, and activist, as a rational thinker with the 'capacity to think and disagree' (1997: 136). At the same time as being experts in therapeutic expertise, host, guests and audience are also shown, in line with Giddens' (1991, 1992) argument, as being sceptical toward therapeutic authorities.

For many critics, the authority of therapeutic cultures comes from its perceived privileged access to the 'truth'. In opposition to this, Shattuc argues, in similar vein to White (1992), that traditional therapeutic practices such as the confession and emotional expressivism are not always seen as performance of the 'truth'. Furthermore, the nature of this truth is being reconfigured in the way the confession is being replaced by the public testimonial:

> No longer is the therapeutic a matter of secrets pried from the unconscious. Rather therapy is an ideology based on the power to affirm the survival of emotional weakness, repression, and subordination – all sensibilities derived from feminist therapy. (1997: 113)

Representations of therapeutic cultures problematise notions of truth and who has access to it.

Summary

Whilst the analyses of Radner (1995), White (1992) and Shattuc (1997) must be understood within the particular context of television and the social relation of reception, their interpretations of the conceptualisation of power, truth and cure in therapeutic representations are in stark contrast to other critics such as Cloud (1998) and Nolan (1998). They show how these terms are produced within representations of therapeutic cultures in particular, contradictory ways. Their work is important in relation to this research because they challenge the assumption that the 'therapeutic' has singular meanings, representations or effects. Their focus on the micro and the textual means that details such as narrative forms and structures, and contradictions can be seen, details which are not visible when a more macro view is taken.

Their work also breaks out of the deterministic optimistic/pessimistic binary in relation to the politics of therapeutic cultures by drawing attention to the ambivalences, costs and pleasures of our engagement in them.

One of the limitations of this form of analysis is that it does not ask what people think and feel about their participation in therapeutic cultures. Although these textual analyses increase our insight into the mixed messages of representations of therapeutic cultures, we still know very little about how practitioners and participants in therapeutic cultures construct and understand therapeutic practices and their meanings. This next section begins to address this question by mapping out the work of three theorists who undertake empirical work with readers of self-help books, and other participants in therapeutic cultures, in order to understand what sense they make of certain therapeutic practices.

Participating in therapeutic cultures

In contrast to more macro studies of therapeutic cultures, ethnographic accounts focus on what people think and feel about therapeutic ideas and practices. These studies are motivated by recognition that therapeutic cultures are a complex mix of ideas and practices, which are encountered in different contexts, and read in diverse ways by different people. While not in any way denying the significance of more macro social conditions, their emphasis is on how we interpret and relate to therapeutic cultures. Moving away from the view that meanings of therapeutic cultures on people can simply be read off texts, these researchers undertake interviews, focus groups and qualitative surveys, and participant observation studies of therapeutic practices such as self-help groups (Rapping, 1996), and cyber self-help groups (Denzin, 1998). As with the textual studies discussed in the section above, most of these studies focus on self-help books, although their emphasis is on the readers of self-help. There are some exceptions to this, such as Wendy Simonds, who also interviews the authors and publishers of self-help books and Deborah Cameron (1995, 2000a) and Liz Bondi (2003), and Liz Bondi with Judith Fewell (2003), who interview practitioners in therapeutic cultures. However, apart from Bondi (2003), the main subjects are not, in these cases, practitioners.

Self-help readers

A leading example of this kind of study is North American sociologist Wendy Simonds' account of women's self-help books (1992, 1996).

One of the first major studies of its kind, it draws upon interviews with readers of self-help books, their authors' and their publishers, together with textual analysis, and has been very influential in critics' understandings of self-help reading, and other therapeutic cultures.

Her work problematises the widely-held notion that end users in therapeutic cultures believe everything they are told. As Simonds writes, 'those who use self-help books... do not merely uncritically, unthinkingly, slurp up what they find within its pages' (1996: 26). She concludes that what readers come away with depends on their reading of both the books and of their own situation and that overall, the women 'did not believe everything they read' (1992: 28). In fact, as Giddens' account of the increasing scepticism towards expertise suggests, the readers she interviewed evaluated and criticised books on a number of counts: for being too facile, for overselling the promises delivered on the covers, for being sensationalist, and for over-generalising.

The quick fix

In essence, Simonds suggests that participants looked to self-help books 'for validation of how they already felt... for inspiration, for comfort, for explanations of situations they could not understand' (1992: 7). Countering many critics' abhorrence of the quick fix, Simonds shows that the women liked the books because they offered 'tools for accomplishing specific goals', 'quick fixes' and 'pep talks', which in their view enabled them to accomplish goals faster (1992: 31). They also described them as comforting in times of stress, isolation or pain, and 'spoke of their books as friends' (1992: 48). In summary, Simonds suggests that readers do not necessarily turn to self-help books because they expect the books to deliver all they promise but because they hope to find some comfort, some insight, and some information in self-help literature. Contrary to some critics, Simonds shows that readers are able to reconcile the technical with the emotional.

Like Rose, Simonds is also interested in what kinds of ideals about the self are circulated through self-help books. Her focus though is the 'ideal womanly self' (1992: 6). In spite of her argument that readers respond to self-help books in a variety of ways, she discerns an ideological coherence in the self-help books. She writes:

> Self-help ideologies proffer ways of procuring good selves. In self-help books, readers are all cast as damaged merchandise, as

> potential insatiable consumers of new and presumably better identities, but also as redeemable within. We can become who we *truly* are and achieve the good self with training, practice and techniques that self-help advisers teach us. (1996: 15)

Seeing self-help books as part of a wider set of cultural prescriptions aimed at women, she argues that 'self-help books, magazines, television, and advertisements all encourage women to see ourselves as mutable, correctable' (1992: 224). For Simonds, these prescriptions are part and parcel of a set of technologies of the self that help 'to make ourselves into objects to be scrutinised, worked into shape, remade (into whatever ideal is prescribed)' (1996: 25). Simonds (1992) conjures up here a very different sense of the experience of reflexivity and the project of the self than Giddens and one bases in contemporary notions of femininity and feminine lack.

Fantasy selves

Some critics have noted that technologies of the self create material practices for the self. In her analysis, Simonds shows how they also create fantasies, in particular fantasies of the instant, and yet, fundamental transformation:

> The imperative to self-promote, to do interior re-modeling, conjures up images from girls' and women's magazines. Take limp, stringy, greasy hair, add product X and make it full bodied and luxuriant. See the transformation of a grubby, fat woman – via diet pills or exercise machine – into a slender fashion plate. Self-help literature offers 'a psychic makeover'. Take alienated self-hood – pernicious negativity – read a book, and achieve glorious, beautiful, even world-changing, true identity. (1996: 26)

Although interested then in examining the different responses of her self-help book readers, Simonds (1992, 1996) concludes that the core message is quite damaging.

Some critics, such as Cloud (1998) and Lasch (1980, 1985), see clear links between therapeutic cultures as being in the service of capitalism. Simonds (1996) agrees quite vehemently with this position, particularly in her later work, arguing that therapeutic cultures encourage us to commodify our selves. She writes, 'through consumption, we take action; we buy ourselves better selves.... Self-help teaches women marketing strategies to use on ourselves' (1996: 25). For Simonds then, self-help books have an ideological message that over-rides any readers' tactics.

Winking at self-help books

There is another influential study of self-help books which emphasises reader ambivalence. North American sociologist Paul Lichterman (1992) argues that his readers 'wink figuratively' at self-help books, both trusting and discounting them at the same time. Believing that books provide new psychological ideas which will validate or label their own issues, he claims that overall his readers had a 'shared understanding' that 'these books can be read and adopted loosely, tentatively, sometimes interchangeably, without enduring conviction' and that they may only provide a temporary understanding of their issues, and in his view, resorted to buying them 'in the absence of other easily accessible, legitimate source of help' rather than eagerly anticipating them (1992: 441).

In line with Giddens' notion of the pluralisation of expertise, and at odds with many critics' view of the dominance of therapeutic thinking, Lichterman (1992) argues that the readers he interviewed 'draw on the books in ongoing relation to portions of more formally elaborated cultural frameworks, and in relation to mass-mediated images of personal life', using the ideas and concepts from the books in conjunction with other 'frameworks of meaning' such as feminism or religion or rules of thumb from media images, teachings and ideas from other sources (1992: 441). Accordingly he argues that self-help reading is a 'thin culture' because 'it does not support a deep commitment from readers... The reading functions as a loosely adopted and partial source of self-definition for even avid self-readers' (1992: 427). At the same time, it offers temporary solace and advice.

Summary

Simonds' and Lichterman's research enables us to see that readers engage with self-help books in a much more ambivalent way than may have been imagined in some of the more macro studies. This argument suggests that we may read self-help books in a tactical, partial way. This appears to be more in line with Giddens' (1991, 1992) view of our scepticism toward expertise than Rose's (1989, 1996a, 1996b) proposal that we act as disciples of therapeutic experts and see therapeutic ideas as a form of unquestionable wisdom. That said, self-help books are one particular form of therapeutic culture, and encountered in specific reading practices and contexts. The question of how different our responses may be in other cultures still remains.

The trouble with Simonds' analysis is that she constructs the ideological content of these books as unified and powerful in spite of her position that women take away different readings. This raises questions about the extent to which contemporary therapeutic cultures do project a unified ideal self, and if they do, the extent to which users identify with these. Furthermore, she does not make it clear how she sees her readers responding to the incitement to make themselves over into better selves, whilst at the same using the ideas in their self-help books in tactical, fragmented, targeted ways for particular problems or times in their lives.

The makeover

This section now turns to studies that relate to my research in terms of its focus on personal development. Drawing upon case studies of assertiveness training and communication skills training, the British feminist linguist Deborah Cameron's work (1995, 2000a, 2000b) explores the relationship between therapeutic cultures and the workplace, in particular, she focuses on the way that how we speak is now seen to be the 'cause and remedy' for many problems. These problems, in her view have little to do with talk (2000a: 182)!

Unlike many other studies covered so far, Cameron is interested in the understandings of practitioners and how they encounter therapeutic practices. Although her main concern is the increasing number of prescriptions regarding how we speak, she interviews practitioners involved in running assertiveness training and communication skills training, as well as self-help book readers, and participants attending assertiveness and communication skills courses.

Like Simonds, Cameron (1995, 2000b) sees parallels between feminine culture and therapeutic practices. In particular, she focuses on the connection between 'the makeover' and self-help advice. A technology of femininity, in its original form in women's magazines, the makeover's attraction, Cameron argues, originally started with the fantasy that cosmetic changes will somehow lead to a larger transformation in women's lives. In her view, the makeover has now expanded. It has moved away simply from appearance to include a range of idealised selves: 'how to be a better wife, mother, lover, daughter, friend and employee' (1995: 172). Feeling deficient, motivated by desire and guilt, Cameron, like Rose, argues that we go to experts to be 'taught how to perform particular identities by replacing established ways of acting with new and allegedly more desirable ones' (1995: 169). In this view, the makeover becomes the dominant technology of transformation in self-help books.

Banal advice

Unlike other critics, Cameron does not see our preoccupation with self-transformation as the problem. For her, it is 'the banal and stereotypical images in which the pundits and experts of the self-help industry would like us to be transformed' (1995: 210). As with Rose and Simonds, Cameron argues that these images take on a moral function, circulating ideas about 'what it means to be a "good person"' (2000b: 4).

And yet, in talking to her readers, Cameron found that readers derived most pleasure from the banality and recognisability of anecdotes in the books, rather than their overall message of how to self-improve. Furthermore, advice is contradictory and conflicting, according to Cameron (1995). This she sees as a symptom of the unstable, uncertain, and contradictory nature of femininity today. This is especially marked in the differences between public and private sphere femininities for Cameron. And represents the competing ways in which women are addressed.

Both/and

One main criticism of therapeutic cultures is that they de-politicise people. They do this, it is argued, by re-privatising problems and solutions and encouraging people to focus on themselves, which is not seen to be the proper content of democratic politics. Cameron is more ambivalent in her analysis of the politics of self-help. She argue that 'self-help is powerful *both* as a tool of the oppressive "regime of truth" that tells women who to be, *and*, potentially, as a stimulus with alternative possibilities' (1995: 210). They can do this, she argues, by providing a 'fiction of empowerment', which may enable women to make changes in their lives, however limited these maybe politically (1995: 210). In regard to the anti-communal tendencies seen by some critics, Cameron counters this by suggesting that:

> Self-help books rarely recommend socially oriented solutions, yet they don't kill off readers' hope for connection, either... this

> genre... allows them to tap into a community of sort; they 'feel less alone' when they read. (1995: 227)

Abduction of feminism?

Nevertheless, like other feminist critics such Schrager (1993) and Rapping (1996), Cameron finds the appropriation of feminist ideas worrying. As does Arlie R. Hochschild who refers to the 'abduction of feminism' by self-help literature (1994: 17).

In contrast, Elayne Rapping emphasises how self-help can be seen to be a form of feminist politics in some forms. Thus she writes, 'It could be argued that self-help now fulfils what were once prime functions of feminist politics: it takes women's experience seriously, it gives voice to aspects of that experience that make many women unhappy, and it says that something can be done'. She also argues that 'The recovery movement, in taking feminism more seriously than the current Left, offers women something which we cannot so easily dismiss because we have nothing, at the moment, to replace it' (1996: 11).

One of Cameron's main concerns about the appropriation of feminist tenets is the way that the meanings of 'power', 'choice' and 'freedom' get re-conceptualised in psychological ways (2000b: 212). This results in women 'taking comfort' in weaker forms of power and traditional notions of gender, and self-help addressing 'persistent gender troubles without actually getting rid of gender in the forms we know it' (2000b: 216). Cameron writes:

> What it does not provide, however, is a coherent political analysis of the present, a clear alternative vision for the future, or a self-consciously oppositional community in which proposals for change can be put into practice, and alternative values can become collective norms. (1995: 210)

In contrast with several critics, for Cameron (1995), the political effects of self-help books and assertiveness training are complex and not monolithic, and need to be understood in the light of users' meanings and lives.

Summary

In conclusion, these more ethnographically inspired accounts outlined here offer a different way to understand therapeutic cultures. They show that we participate in more detached and provisional ways than is implied in some of the macro studies. At the same time, they begin to explain what we find appealing about therapeutic cultures apart from the lure of ideals and fantasies. Much of this literature also focuses on the relation between self-help, feminism and femininity. The emphasis in these studies though is emphatically on self-help books. This provides us with a limited sense of how people participate in other practices such as training courses or coaching, although it provides a useful set of conceptual resources for thinking about negotiation, ambivalence and self-politics. Their focus, however, is predominantly on clients of therapeutic cultures, rather than practitioners, which means that the views of a considerable group of people central to the proliferation and reproduction of therapeutic cultures are still largely missing. Although Cameron (1995, 2000a) does interview assertiveness and communication skills trainers, this research does not form the main part of her analysis, and so practitioners' conceptualisations do not come to the fore. This leaves us with a number of questions on practitioners and their views still unanswered which I explore in the following chapters based on my own empirical study. I describe this briefly below.

Research approach

As I showed in previous chapters, therapeutic cultures have been heavily criticised. Seen by many critics as reproducing inadequate versions of the self, variously described as narcissistic, emotivist, morally self-referential, and individualistic, therapeutic cultures are believed to be a major problem. This is because of the extent to which it is believed that the ideals, beliefs, language and practices of therapeutic cultures have proliferated and expanded into many different social spheres, and the influence they have on the ways we understand our selves and our lives. So, therapeutic cultures are defined as a new and extensive form of social control reproduced by powerful social institutions such as the government, schools, the judiciary and the workplace. In these debates, therapeutic cultures are presented as both the result of fundamental social changes such as de-traditionalisation, and also the catalyst of new social changes such as the de-politicisation of politics and the emotionalisation of the public sphere.

Whilst accepting some of the broader implications of these arguments, I see three main problems with these conclusions. First, these approaches overlook or misrepresent people who participate in therapeutic cultures, and their understandings of what they do. Secondly, there is a lack of differentiation in the theories between distinct types of therapeutic ways of thinking and practising, and the different social sites in which these might be encountered, and the consequent social, cultural and political effects of these specificities and particularities. Thirdly, many of these accounts present therapeutic cultures as denoting a unified, universal type of social change. This is what Kevin Hetherington in his analysis of new social movements calls the 'denotation problem' (1998: 9) in which certain local practices are seen to 'denote the development of an *n-society*' (1998: 11). This is a move, he argues, in which social theory 'loses sight of the specificities and locatedness' of what it is researching, and ignores or trivialises what these practices might connote (1998: 31). It is this attention to specificities and locatedness I wanted to bring to my own research project.

Empirical work

My main point is that some of these problems could be addressed if more empirical research were carried out on participants in therapeutic cultures. Overall, in spite of the breadth of critical commentary on therapeutic cultures, there has been very little empirical research undertaken, especially in Britain. As this chapter has discussed, there have been a number of sociological and cultural studies on self-help readers. There have been a few studies on management training and spiritual management development but these have not focused on practitioners. In a recent paper, Nikolas Rose (2000) acknowledges the lack of empirical work done on psychotherapy. Referencing his own critique of therapeutic cultures, he writes:

> Now, it would be nice to say that these rather abstract remarks could be confirmed by empirical evidence on the actual practice of psychotherapy. But unfortunately we lack detailed ethnographies of the way in which the psychotherapies work. If one could observe in practice the ways in which the psychotherapies work it would be possible to support or even to deny the kinds of approach that I have tried to outline about the way in which certain kinds of things are brought in to existence in the therapeutic situation. (2000: 12)

By undertaking detailed qualitative work and ethnographies, we could begin to understand how therapeutic cultures manifest themselves locally. We could see what difference it makes in which contexts therapeutic cultures are encountered; how therapeutic practices are changing with changing ideas of the self, and work; and the different ways in which practitioners and clients relate to therapeutic ideas and practices.

It is against this set of debates and questions that I began to develop my own research project. This chapter gives an account of this research process: what methods were used and why, who the informants were, why, and how they were recruited, and what they were asked in relation to the research aims. It also discusses how the data was analysed, and what theoretical and interpretive frameworks were drawn upon.

Defensive project

One of my main aims in the research was to understand practitioners' conceptualisations of their practices. Given the relative lack of empirical research on therapeutic cultures in sociology, I turned to anthropological and cultural studies ethnographies, as these seek to understand cultural practices which might seem counterintuitive, illogical, unpalatable, or fantastic to us on the local members' own terms and treat participants' meanings respectfully.

At the start of the book, I mentioned that one of my aims was to counter the largely hostile and dismissive accounts of therapeutic cultures in the critical literature. Although my research project was partly what the soap opera cultural critic Charlotte Brunsdon (2000), calls a 'defensive project' in that I was motivated by wanting to show practitioners in a less dismissive light, my research aim was not to recoup therapeutic cultures unequivocally but to represent the significance of personal development for practitioners seriously and thoughtfully.

The primary research aim became then an ethnographic informed one of wanting to understand therapeutic cultures through the definitions and interpretations of a sample of practitioners in personal development in Britain. Although I have used the term 'ethnographic', it needs to be recognised that there are many forms of ethnographic research, and that purists talk of ethnography proper as involving lengthy fieldwork and participant observation (Seitler et al., 1989). I saw this research working with 'ethnographic intentions' (Gray, 1992: 32).

In order to gather accounts of personal development practitioners and their conceptualisations of their practices, it was necessary to choose a research method, which would enable the detail of what they said to be seen. To do this, I chose to undertake qualitative in-depth interviews as it gave me the best chance of getting at what practitioners thought about what they did, and to access the diversity of their conceptualisations, which I saw as missing from much of the literature. I worked with a semi-structured interview format, so that I could guide the interview around particular themes which fitted with my research aims, whilst at the same time allowing for the generation of new topics by myself and the interviewees.

Practitioner focus

I decided to work with practitioners as opposed to clients on a number of counts. First, as cultural intermediaries they are seen as central to the dissemination of therapeutic cultures in much of the literature on therapeutic cultures. Secondly, they are represented in largely dismissive ways as politically self-serving (Rose, 1996a), or in condescending terms as well-meaning but naïve dupes (Cloud, 1998; Nolan, 1998; Rose, 2000). I wanted to give practitioners the opportunity to convey some more positive aspects of their work as an antidote to the pejorative account of their work in academic discussion. Thirdly, because I had had experience of being a practitioner and working with other practitioners, I wanted to make sense of my own experience and understandings. Practitioners believe that most of what they do helps people transform in meaningful and sometimes profound ways. Interviewing practitioners I hoped would enable me to examine these intensities.

My own experience also suggested to me that practitioners do not necessarily have a fixed position in relation to their practices. Friends who are practitioners and I would mock some of our own idioms and techniques, as we were aware of academic and popular critiques of therapeutic thinking and practices, and our own clients' potential cynicism in the context of the workplace. So, for example, we used to put on silly voices to mimic certain phrases that personal development practitioners in the workplace say such as: 'Does anyone want to share anything at this point?' 'How does that make you feel?' and 'Say "I" not "we"'.

This made me think that practitioners move in and out of their practitioner identities, whilst at the same time, being able to believe at different moments, that what they do is important, helpful and meaningful. In the critical literature on therapeutic cultures (Nolan, 1998; Rose, 1989, 1996a), it is clients, not practitioners, who are seen to vary in the degree of participation in particular practices, so some are seen as hobbyists, part-time or tactical (Feltham, 1995; Heelas, 1996). These issues raised questions for me about how practitioners saw themselves in relation to their practices and how practitioners' models are modified to pre-empt critical or popular critiques.

Research themes

My research design and interpretation was influenced by the ideas and debates outlined in Chapter 3 and Chapter 4. Thus, I wanted to test out some of the claims from the more macro studies of Giddens, Nolan and Rose. Their work shows how understandings of the self, its relations with the past, and its power to act upon itself, and the world, are being reconfigured. What we need to examine in more detail is how the specifics of personal development, and its interface with the workplace, are inflecting models of the self, and ideas on how the self can be changed.

In particular, I wanted to explore how practitioners presented their expertise and their relations with clients? Is power and influence one-way in favour of the practitioners? Are the ideal selves understood by practitioners the 'reflexive' 'enterprising' or 'emotivist' selves the critics suggest? Does Nolan's account of the therapeutic self and its valorisation of emotion fit with practitioners' understanding of emotion?

I also wanted to extend the textual analyses undertaken by Radner, White and Shattuc to personal development. In particular, I wanted to focus on the structures and forms which underpin practitioners' models of the self and its transformation. I was also interested in how practitioners present their work and the politics of that work.

Sample

For the research study, I chose to undertake an in-depth, intensive set of interviews with a selected sample of twelve practitioners, fourteen including a small pilot. Whilst a wider sample of practitioners could have been interviewed, the primary research aim of producing detailed ethnographic accounts meant that fewer but more comprehensive interviews were more appropriate to provide the specificity that was missing from most academic accounts on therapeutic cultures.

The sample consisted of fourteen practitioners, who were representative on a number of levels: they came from a number of important, prominent, contemporary therapeutic approaches such as assertiveness, and NLP; they worked in a range of sites such as universities, the workplace, private practices; four of the practitioners are employed full-time by their workplace, and the rest are self-employed.

My criteria for my choice of interviewees was that they were 'thoroughly enculturalised' in personal development, actively involved in practising as personal development practitioners, were reasonably articulate and able to give a thoughtful, clear account of their practices (Plummer, 2001: 136). The sample was made up of two types of practitioners which I felt would give accounts congruent with the research aims: first, more well known, influential figures who had disseminated widely on their practice particularly through writings, media appearances and teaching; second, a tranche of less prominent, more conventional practitioners, who were chosen for their ability to present accounts of specific types of personal development practices and had some experience of working in organisations or with explicit organisational work issues. I also thought that they might be more eclectic in their practices as they were less publicly aligned with a practice, and perhaps had switched to more contemporary versions of practices.

Interviews

The interviews took place in the practitioners' houses, often in their counselling rooms, sometimes in their offices at work, and also in hotel rooms where they were staying whilst working on workshops. In Jack Routledge's case, we went to a room with no chairs but filled with cushions, where Jack sat most comfortably whilst I bounced around precariously trying to balance body, microphone and credibility, perched on the edge of a large cushion. This meant that the schedule was demanding and travelling was quite tiring, particularly whilst working full-time myself. After the initial social niceties, I then started the interview using a prepared schedule which began with general questions around the practitioners' professional history and therapeutic approach, and then moved onto their views on other practices and criticisms of therapeutic cultures. The interviews typically lasted for two to three hours. Some parts of the interview were tenser than others, particularly around the critiques of therapeutic cultures. Some questions generated less interesting responses than others, with this varying from practitioner to practitioner. I asked for, and got permission to tape record all interviews, and subsequently, had the tapes transcribed for me.

The semi-structured format was as follows:

1. Could you say a bit about how you came to be involved in the practice that you now do?

2. How would you sum up the purpose of your therapeutic approach?
3. What would you say people 'get' from participating in your therapeutic approach?
4. What reasons have led you to adopt this approach?
5. Describe which clients you think your approach is most and which least suitable for?
6. Where might someone encounter your approach?
7. Are there therapeutic approaches which you do not practise yourself but you consider worthwhile?
8. Are there therapeutic approaches which you consider misleading or harmful?
9. What reservations, frustrations, doubts or disappointments do you have about your own approach?
10. Do you feel your approach is misunderstood? How, and by whom?
11. Who have been the people who have most influenced or inspired your practice?
12. What would be your ideal work scenario?
13. How has your practice changed since you first started?
14. Critics of therapeutic approaches argue that therapeutic ideas are de-politicising – what is your view on this?
15. Critics also suggest that therapeutic practices are on the increase in many different spheres. Do you agree with this? And if so, how do you account for this increase?
16. Do you think the ways in which we understand our selves today is different from how our grandparents saw themselves? What role do you think therapeutic ideas have in this?

Interpretation

After fourteen interviews, I decided to start the process of interpretation proper. Jennifer Mason (2002) warns about undertaking too many interviews because they can be time consuming to organise, and difficult to analyse. After fourteen interviews, I felt I had enough data to allow for a detailed textual analysis of a range of practitioners' conceptualisations across a number of themes, and which would enable me to meet my research goals. In relation to interpretation, there are of course many debates about the status of interview data. There are those who see the interview itself and the organisation of talk as the substantive research topic (Silverman, 2001). There are others for whom the data provides a source of people's psychological motivations or unconscious processes (Hollway, 1989; Hollway and

Jefferson, 2000). These did not fit with my research aims. I did not want to get 'inside their heads' (Mason, 2002) nor probe for the people 'behind the ideas' (Brunsdon, 2000). Instead, the focus for my research was how the practitioners' conceptualised what they do, which I saw based upon more widely circulating ideas about the self, personal development, therapy, self-improvement and emotions.

Textual features

Understanding meanings to be partly produced through what Charlotte Brunsdon calls the 'materiality of the telling', I was interested in analysing some of the textual features of the interviews such as the key terms, structural features, particular forms and tropes of language mobilised by the practitioners. Having said that, my first concern was analysing the interviews on their own terms, sifting through the data, and seeing what themes, questions and puzzles emerged, and how representative these were. At first, much of the data seemed all too familiar to me as an ex-practitioner. This is a problem Emily Martin describes as feeling 'at home like a fish is in water in which the problem is to find a way "to see the water" in which you have lived all your life' (1994: 11). Once I turned to a more detailed, close textual analysis, examining key definitions, metaphors, images, things started to grow more unfamiliar. Clusters started to emerge which now form the basis for the themes of empirical chapters, and their subsections.

Politics of interpretation

Analysis and interpretation of qualitative data are seen to be the time when the researcher has the most power in relation to those being researched. Feminists argue that in making choices about which themes or quotes to select, and applying theories to the data, researchers are engaging in political processes. These can result in representing those being researched and their ideas in particular limited or imposed ways. These ways can be problematic for some feminists because the researcher is forcing her own views on the data and this can lead to the distortion, misrepresentation, or dismissal of what people say. For example, Annie Opie writes that analysis and interpretation can lead to the 'textual appropriation of the researched' (1992: 53). In response, researchers such as Jackie Stacey (1995) and Caroline Ramazanoglu and Janet Holland (2002) argue that there is no innocent language in which to represent accounts. In line with this, cultural studies academic Ien Ang writes:

> because interpretations always inevitably involve the construction of certain representations of reality (and not others), they can never be 'neutral' and merely 'descriptive'. After all, the 'empirical' captured in either quantitative or qualitative form does not yield self-evident meanings: it is only through the interpretative framework constructed by the researcher that understandings of the 'empirical' come about. (1989: 105)

For Stacey and Ramazanoglu and Holland, it is possible, and often politically important, to take accounts seriously, for example in listening to people whose views are marginalised. At the same time, it is important to show how people have certain assumptions and conventional views in order to understand how particular meanings are produced and sustained. In this view, interpretations should be presented as provisional and situated. In relation to my own research, my interpretation has been motivated by an attempt to counter dismissive and totalising claims about therapeutic cultures. It is derived from my own to-ing and fro-ing between the data and theoretical ideas and has drawn from an eclectic mix of theories. So I used theoretical interpretive frameworks from a wide range of inter-disciplinary sources: anthropology, feminism, sociology, religious studies, cultural studies, and organisation studies to shape and structure the research. In particular, I have drawn extensively from anthropology and cultural studies as these provided different perspectives with which to understand the practitioners' meanings and their significance in ways which differed from the dismissive or patronising tone of much of the critical literature on therapeutic cultures. I have also used literature from the sociology of therapeutic cultures, as these are highly influential, but have used my material to challenge and extend ideas in the literature.

My procedure in the next three chapters is to present an analysis by theme not by each interview, together with close textual analysis and interpretation. The data is offered as long quotes, so that the practitioners' conceptualisations are clearly on view, and provide some context for my interpretations and conclusions. I have selected the quotes which are most illustrative of, or significant in relation to, the main themes of the research. Some extracts are discussed at length, whilst others are compared to these and examined in less detail.

Brief introduction to interviewees (all names pseudonymised and specific biographical details anonymised).

Dennis Fournier is a freelance Neuro-Linguistic Programming (NLP) trainer and runs training courses on NLP for the general public. Dennis is also a therapist, working mainly with married couples. He has recently co-written a book and published a number of articles on NLP in NLP journals and the gay press. He is also a fellow of the Society of Neuro-Semantics, a North American association for a particularly linguistic-based approach to NLP. NLP is a highly popular practice, originated in North America, which has become popular in Britain in the past fifteen years. It is a form of psychotherapy, accredited by the British Association of Counselling, but also a set of ideas and practices used in many organisations in coaching, sales training, interpersonal training and in therapy. Drawing upon cognitive psychology, linguistics, cybernetics and Gestalt therapy, it claims to offer a range of techniques which are said to enable its users to change their mental strategies. Sometimes called 'Design Human Engineering', it has been critiqued for an over-emphasis on techniques rather than core values (Tosey and Gregory, 2002). *The Element Dictionary of Personal Development* (Waters, 1996) defines NLP as 'the study and practice of human excellence'. It goes on to add:

> As a phenomenon, NLP is remarkable. In spite of an unpromisingly technical title and the fact that it is riddled with jargon, it has undoubtedly been one of the major success stories in the world of PD (personal development). And the story is far from over... How can we account for its appeal? The brief answer is that 'it works'. At least, NLPers would say that it offers them practical, highly specific ways to achieve rapid, sometimes radical and often lasting results. (1996: 144)

Richard Brown is a freelance management development consultant and also an associate lecturer within a department in a British university, which offers Masters qualifications in Human Resource Development and Learning. He does not align himself with any one particular practice, but was trained in T-groups and other humanistic practices in the 1960s. Freelance management development consultants are typically used by private, and increasingly public sector organisations to run training workshops in interpersonal skills, organise 'team-building' events and solve problems seen to be of an interpersonal nature such as conflict between departments or individuals. Although there are some management development consultancies, which may have between 20–100 employees, many consultants work on their own or in loose networks with other independent freelance consultants. Their fees can range from £300–£2000 per day depending on the nature of their client, their perceived expertise and the type of work that they do.

David Charles is a freelance management trainer and life coach. He mainly works with clients in the private sector running training courses on topics such as influencing skills and presentation skills. David has a range of men and women coaching clients in the voluntary and private sectors, most of whom are senior managers. David works closely with Suzanne Madeley, one of the other interviewees. He is currently finishing a programme of coaching training himself, which lasts over two years and is run by the Coaching Institute in North America. Life coaching is another practice growing rapidly in popularity within both private and public sector organisations, and also paid for privately by clients. Coaching can take place face-to-face or over the telephone. It can be used with private individuals or within a business environment. Life coaches can specialise in particular areas such as time or stress management or offer a more general service. They are usually contracted by the hour and typically charge more than traditional self-employed counsellors, and are paid from £50–£200 per hour. A number of university accredited courses specifically on coaching, going up to Masters level, have been developed by universities such as the University of Wolverhampton and Oxford-Brookes University.

Annette Dobson is the UK author of a number of self-help books over the past forty years published by Quartet, Piaktus, Kogan Page and HarperCollins. Annette is a leading figure in feminist informed assertiveness training. She is a trainer in assertiveness skills, emotional awareness and communication skills training.

Jude Britton is a leading well-known psychotherapist, psychotherapy lecturer and advisor. She has her own consultancy that provides therapy, counselling, supervision training and organisational consultancy mainly from a Gestalt perspective. She has written drama for radio and the theatre. She is an author of a number of books on therapy and group work.

Andy Knight is the head of a management development department in the head office of a large British bank, and an NLP Practitioner. As the head of management development, it is his role to design, organise and run management training events and personal activities for both staff and managers in the bank. His main role is not providing the activities himself, but employing self-employed personal development practitioners. As with many management developers, he started his working life as a manager, in his case, as a bank manager.

Suzanne Madeley works as a management developer and life coach. She has run a management development consultancy in partnership with David Charles for ten years, undertaking interpersonal skills training and some coaching. She was trained in assertiveness training, and is also undergoing the Institute in Coaching's training in how to be a coach. She is also being coached by one of the institute's members as a paying client. The institute based in North America, is classified as a charity, and is expanding its courses to Britain. Suzanne's coach is based in North America and uses telephone coaching with her.

Paul Patterson is senior lecturer in a British university, based in a department which offers Masters qualifications on transpersonal psychology and consultancy skills for management development trainers. Paul is an NLP practitioner but also draws upon other therapeutic traditions in his work at the university. He has published a book and several articles in academic journals on management development, and chapters on therapy, emotion and management development practices in academic and practitioner books.

Peter Pope works as a Gestalt therapist and trainer where he runs courses for social workers, teachers and managers from the public sector. He also undertakes one-to-one therapy sessions for publicly and privately funded clients, and runs Gestalt groups. He has published a number of books on Gestalt and groupwork.

Jack Routledge is a practising psychotherapist in a private practice. He is also a teacher and supervisor in psychotherapy in London, and a well-known writer on humanist psychology and its applications in psychotherapy and education. Jack is a key figure within the Association of Humanistic Psychology and a member of a radical men's group. He has written over twelve books mainly on psychotherapy.

Jade Simon is a well-known author of self-help books, who has written over twenty-two personal development self-help books and cassette tapes. She is a trained psychotherapist, a personal development coach for individuals and an interpersonal skills trainer for groups. She writes for magazines and makes radio and TV appearances as a personal development expert. Her books are published by Thorsons, an imprint of HarperCollins, described on its web page as bringing 'together the world's diverse strands of spiritual and magical traditions, together with ideas for well-being in health, mind, body and spirit'.

Sally Thompson works as an organisational development consultant, business psychologist, coach and Gestalt therapist. At the time of the interview, she was a partner in an organisational change consultancy. She now runs her own practice working with private clients, organisationally funded individual client, and groups, undertaking management development training courses, and coaching. She undertakes her Gestalt psychotherapy as a private practice. Gestalt therapy is primarily based on the work of an American, Fritz Perls, by all accounts a highly controversial and charismatic figure, working at the end of the 1950s and early 1960s, and a key protagonist in the Human Potential Movement at that time. Often seen by its practitioners as an existential and phenomenological approach, it focuses on 'authentic experience', which means practitioners asking clients to discuss what they think and feel in the present, and like psychodrama, it involves enacting experiences, feelings and events, either individually or in groups. It has a reputation for being a more confrontational style of therapy than other approaches because of its belief in authentic experience. Gestalt therapy had a substantial influence on organisational training practice in the 1970s and 1980s, was displaced by NLP, but is now experiencing resurgence as management consultants look for ways of credentialising their practices.

Jane Vincent has just finished an MA in Paul Patterson's department. She runs personal development growth groups for private paying clients and has done so for over twenty years. She started her career as a civil servant in South Africa, moved to Guernsey, where her activities as a growth group facilitator and civil servant caused some local scandal, and so she left the civil service to become freelance. She is just about to start training in NLP.

Violette Turner works as a volunteer for MIND, the mental health charity, and is a trained psychodrama therapist who has her own private practice working on psychodrama workshops with groups made up from the general public. Psychodrama is defined by the *Dictionary of Personal Development* as a 'method of dramatic (re-) enactment of human encounters... using part of the therapy room as a stage area on which the specifics of that person's life are represented' (Tosey and Gregory, 2002). It was developed in the 1930s and is seen to be distinct from role-play in that it is less about practising behaviours and more about performing and analysing aspects of one's life. Psychodrama can be run as a group and individual practice, and is also incorporated as a more limited brief technique on some interpersonal skills training courses.

One of the main debates in qualitative research as discussed above is around the power relations between researcher and those being researched. A similar debate takes place in therapeutic cultures. For many critics, one of the problems with therapeutic relations between practitioners and clients is that there are asymmetrical power relations. This is because as cultural intermediaries practitioners have more 'expertise', cultural authority and are in a position to define the client and their problems in their own terms. In my research, understandings of power between practitioners and client relations were more complex and this next chapter examines how else we might understand practitioner-client relations.

5
Expert Relations

The authority of expertise

> I think there has been a democratisation right through and it's hit the therapy world. People are not prepared to just subject themselves to something that they don't understand, not be in control, sit and have somebody say 'mmmm mmmm' and not say a word...

This quote is taken from an interview I conducted with Jade Simon, a well-known author of self-help books. Jade's view that clients are challenging therapeutic authority confirms one side of the debate on the status of expertise as exemplified by Giddens' argument (1991, 1992) that all forms of expertise in contemporary society are being subject to scepticism and disputation, as referred to in Chapter 3. The other side of the debate, exemplified by Rose (1989, 1996a), suggests that therapeutic expertise is insulated from much of this critique, and is in fact gaining credence across many social spheres because of its claims to truth and to be doing 'good'. So how representative is Jade's observation amongst the personal development practitioners interviewed? The aim of this chapter is to take up this question in order to address the meaning of therapeutic expertise in personal development. It will examine how issues of power between practitioner and client inflect notions of expertise because power relations between practitioners and clients is one of the main ways in which practitioners spoke about how they understood the work of personal development. Given my emphasis on the particularities of personal development practices, and the specific context in which the practitioners interviewed work, this chapter will also analyse how these shape their conceptualisations of practitioner/client relations in ways relatively unexplored in the literature on the sociology of therapeutic cultures.

In order to attend to these aims in depth, this chapter will begin by explaining the key terms of the debate on therapeutic expertise. It will do this by focusing on the issue of power, as the problem with therapeutic expertise is not simply the plausibility of its content, but the politics of its use. By covering the main arguments in this debate, it will enable a clear comparison to be made of the practitioners' accounts and to show how their conceptualisations endorse, differ from or test influential academic claims. The chapter will support this comparison with a detailed analysis of the practitioners' descriptions around four themes: equality, abuse of power, conversion and finally, charisma. These clusters capture the most significant and pervasive ways in which practitioners spoke about their relations to clients.

State of expertise

Returning to the debate, on the one hand we have an argument about our ambivalence toward expertise and on the other hand, we have the view that expertise has been strengthened and extended, rather than contested and narrowed. Therapeutic practitioners, in particular, therapists and counsellors, and academics in counselling studies, are equally concerned about the power relations between therapists and clients, and have various ways of theorising the nature of this power, its effects on clients, and means to re-address asymmetrical power relations (see for example Bondi and Fewell, 2003; McNamee and Gergen, 1992; Feltham, 1995, 1997, 1999).

According to one view, represented by Giddens, expertise is about laying 'claims to specific knowledge or skills which the layperson doesn't possess' (1994: 84). It is this 'imbalance of skills and information' between expert and layperson which accords authority to the expert (1994: 84). However, he argues, this authority is temporally and spatially finite due to the fragmentation of social 'fields of action', meaning that being an expert or layperson is a matter of social context (1994: 84). Furthermore, although we feel we have to draw upon expertise, we trust it less, approaching it with a 'mix of reverence and reserve, approval and disquiet, and enthusiasm and antipathy' (1991: 7). In Giddens' view, we treat therapeutic expertise as provisional, and context-dependent even though at the same time we may find it a useful and helpful resource. We do not, in this view, see therapeutic expertise as omni-competent, omniscient or omnipotent.

Self-help ambivalence

Empirical research on therapeutic cultures bears out some of these claims as indicated in Chapter 4. In studies on self-help books, readers are shown to question the authority of therapeutic ideas in self-help books, seeing the advice on offer as temporary or limited (Simonds, 1992, 1996; Lichterman, 1992). Research on the representations of therapeutic cultures on television suggests that the traditional model of the all-powerful authoritative therapist is being recast (White, 1992; Shattuc, 1997). In this view, daytime talk shows relativise the position of expert as the audience becomes 'an educator and an authority for others' and everyone becomes an expert (White, 1992: 46). This blurring of the expert/client/audience unfixes traditional positions of the 'person in the know' and the 'person to be cured' (Shattuc, 1997).

This unfixing is also encouraged by newer therapeutic models. Approaches based on humanistic or cognitive behavioural methods, according to Shattuc (1997), bring new models of the client as experts of themselves, diminishing the cultural authority of psychoanalytic models with their unequal relations between therapist and client. Of course, humanistic and cognitive behavioural therapies are critiqued for their models of the client and power dynamics: See for example Miriam Greenspan (1993) and Betty McLellan (1995). For them, even newer therapeutic models such as Rogerian counselling, self-help, and the recovery movement, which see themselves in opposition to the hierarchical 'practitioner knows best' models, are seen as perpetuating oppressive conditions for women and encouraging self-regulation against impossible therapeutic ideals.

Self-help is an example of one of these newer therapeutic models (Schrager, 1993; Shattuc, 1997; Rapping, 1996). With its roots in feminist consciousness-raising, self-help encourages the sharing of knowledge between clients, holding up a promise of empowerment by 'bypassing' the authority of practitioner (Miller and McHoul, 1998a). Somewhat cynically, Toby Miller and Alex McHoul write that we 'enter into a dialogue with ourselves, a therapy without a social worker or shrink, where we come pre-shrunk, ready to read ourselves' (1998a: 105). In these contexts, it is argued that expertise is mobile and that the layperson can be the expert.

Therapeutic power

On the other side of the debate, epitomised by Rose, therapeutic expertise has monopolised both commonsense beliefs and professional beliefs about the self (see also Nolan, 1998). Like Giddens (1991, 1992), Rose suggests that there is a crisis in general professional power. Where Rose differs from Giddens though, is in his argument that the demise of general expertise has led to the simultaneous expansion of therapeutic expertise into many social spheres. One of the factors responsible for this, Rose argues, is the way that therapeutic expertise is seen to provide the 'truth' about our selves and our lives, and scientific instruments to access this truth. According to Rose, a myriad of assorted practitioners, such as social workers, managers and psychologists, amongst others, replenish their dwindling stock with therapeutic expertise, providing practitioners with an ethical justification for their practices. In this view, they can take the moral high ground because they can assert that they make us better people, better workers and better citizens, and we believe them. As a result, for Rose (2000), therapeutic authority has become authority itself.

Self-regulation

Becoming better in these ways, Rose argues, requires us to engage in new relations with practitioners. In his view, we are taught by practitioners to participate in our own self-regulation, motivated by our anxiety and desire to reach the idealised selves on offer in therapeutic cultures. Our complicity is not coerced or commanded, according to him, but developed through relations of discipleship, exemplarity, seduction, captivation and in particular, conversion (Rose, 1996a; Miller and Rose, 1994).

In her Foucauldian analysis of self-esteem, Barbara Cruikshank describes therapeutic experts relations as 'simultaneously voluntary and coercive' (1999: 72). Drawing upon the 'self-regulating capacities of subjects', these newer forms of pedagogical relations mean that 'the plausibility inherent in a claim to scientificity and rationalised efficacy binds subjectivity to truth, and subjects to experts' (Rose, 1996a: 156). Bound to experts, we are at the same time positioned as free to choose.

This means that relations take the form of assistance, for Rose, but are simultaneously relations of subordination and dependence. This is the case for Foucauldian theorists, even when the therapist strives to be egalitarian, as 'relations of empowerment are in fact relations of power in and of themselves' (Cruikshank, 1999: 70). In this view, therapeutic practitioners have the upper hand on many counts: to paraphrase Rose (2000), they are in charge of the pace, direction, structure, etiquette, and language of the therapeutic encounter, authorised by a combination of institutional, professional and expert power. In this view, they have a 'priestly power' in which we confess and they don't. Furthermore, they are a person of knowledge and we aren't. They supply the classifications and techniques, and we attempt to become someone through their regimes of truth. In therapeutic cultures, according to Rose, empowerment is a form of discipline, freedom an imperative, and autonomy, neo-liberal social control.

Questions

It is in the context of these debates about the changing social and cultural character of professional power and expertise that I shall turn to my interview data. These debates raise the following questions: Do practitioners see themselves as having expertise, and if so, what kinds of expertise do they draw upon? Do practitioners see themselves as 'doing good' and if so, in what terms? How do they conceptualise the nature of their power in relation to their clients? Have relations of seduction and conversion replaced models of mastery and pedagogy, as Rose suggests? How does the specificity of the personal development movement affect practitioners' views on power and their relations with their clients? In exploring these issues in depth, this section will turn to analyse the concept of 'equality'. This was a significant theme across all the interviews, albeit on different terms, and was central to the way that the practitioners interviewed understood their practices.

Living the good life

This section examines the concept of equality as defined by the practitioners interviewed, as this emerged as a significant theme. As we have seen so far, critics see the power relations between therapist and client as complex, and in some cases, view it as a significant cause for concern. The issue of equality is an important one in a context where several critics believe us to be in the midst of an advice explosion with expertise seen to be taking over all parts of our lives, in tandem with the state or in service of capitalism. As we have seen from Rose's model of practitioner/client relations, equality between practitioner and client is impossible on a number of counts. In contrast, many of the practitioners interviewed see the concept of equality between themselves and their clients as central to their work. Not all the practitioners would refer to their recipients as clients; for example Annette Dobson who runs assertiveness training for women, simply refers to them as 'women'.

The way that this equality is conceptualised varies with the different approaches and practitioners, and in some cases, practitioners, like Rose hold that equal relations are impossible, or even undesirable. Of course, it could be argued that practitioners would say that they have equal relations with their clients because they are disguising their self-interest or are deluded. Some social theorists suggest that the idea of equal relations is not limited to therapeutic cultures but espoused across many social spheres, being seen today as a more suitable way of handling power than naked power plays (de Swaan, 1990; Miller and Rose, 1994). For de Swaan, equal relations at work and at home are characterised by a shift to 'negotiated consent' and away from forms of command (1990: 159). In line with this, Norman Fairclough (1989, 1992) argues that people with institutional power such as managers and teachers reduce the overt markers of power differentials by trying to appear more informal and friendly. For many social theorists then, equal relations can hide real imbalances of power.

Academics studying counselling provide a different perspective on the issue of equality. In their research on voluntary sector counselling, Liz Bondi and Judith Fewell (2003) argue that the origins, institutional context and theoretical ideas used in therapeutic practices are important in understanding forms of equality mobilised by practitioners. Personal development has a complex history and context, as discussed in Chapter 2. One of the most striking particularities is that many clients become practitioners themselves. So most of the interviewees first encountered personal development as a user and after trying one or more practices became, or trained to become, a practitioner of one kind or another. Many practitioners also continue to participate in practices as clients. In the more traditional therapeutic forms of personal development, practitioners may be in 'supervision', a form of counselling relationship with a more experienced counsellor in which professional problems are explored. Others try new practices to extend their knowledge of their own practice by participating in the next 'level' of the practice. One of the practitioners I interviewed had just finished a counselling course and was moving on to do a 'coaching' course; another had just finished a Masters in Change Agent Skills and was booked to do a short course in Neuro-Linguistic Programming.

Expertise is seen as 'in progress', with an endpoint that continuously shifts out of reach, and one's identity as a practitioner can be seen as always 'under construction'. Parallels of this client-practitioner mobility can be found in other contexts. In education a pupil may become a teacher, a student may become a lecturer, and in complementary medicine, a client of reflexology may go on to become a reflexologist. But what these shifts in identity require, and different from personal development, is that the person lose their apprenticeship status. Being a teacher means that you are no longer a pupil.

This dynamic brings a distinction to the power relations between practitioners and clients compared to other power relations, and begins to cast a different light on the critical literature on the power and inequality of this relationship in therapeutic cultures as discussed in the previous chapter.

This dynamic has some similarities in the field of complementary medicine. In her research, Ursula Sharma (1995) shows that practitioners often have had the illness that they then go on to cure in others. However, they do not draw upon their former identities as patients as a means of identification with their clients. Neither do they present their own suffering as giving them the means to heal. Instead they state that their illness enabled them to encounter different medical practices. In my research, practitioners refer to the idea of client mobility in ways that differ from the model described by Sharma (1995), often drawing upon models of identification and equality between themselves and their clients, as will be shown in this section. We might approach the interviews with a view to understanding the complex interplay of power here which is not theorised by critics of personal development.

Being sorted

This section begins by exploring Jade Simon's conceptualisation of equality in relations with their clients. Jade's quote is a good place to start as she is representative of practitioners who relate equality with client mobility. In this quote, Jade is discussing her personal philosophy towards clients:

> I was very, very keen on the clients directing the show and the client moving on from...it's always been a very important factor ... clients moving on from being clients to therapists if they wanted to be, and that was an integral part of the way I worked right through. And that's what Mind [the mental health charity] had great difficulty with. I know now that they have changed.

Jade Simon presents the movement of clients becoming therapists as *the* success story, the happy ending for self-improvement. In this model the practitioner is seen as more 'sorted' than the client. Yet in spite of this, Jade holds onto a notion of equality by claiming that this superiority is seen as the means by which the client can achieve parity with the practitioner. Authority comes from the practitioner having 'been there', but having got out through improving herself. This dynamic enables future client-practitioners to claim that they too had 'been there', but had now moved on. Expertise comes from knowing how to do this.

Refusing expertise

In contrast, Annette Dobson presents an approach in which the practitioner is not seen as the example of the success story. Annette is the author of a famous and influential book on assertiveness, entitled *A Woman in Your Own Right*, first published in 1982, and which has been re-printed over seventeen times. Annette is also an assertiveness trainer. In this quote Annette, is explaining how she first started working as an assertiveness trainer in reply to me asking how she became interested in assertiveness:

> I started running groups for women: sexuality groups for women. And found quite early that basically I was up against a brick wall because the women had so little? I am saying 'they', but I know it's 'we', and I include myself in this? but just looking at sexuality, women had so little idea of who they were in terms of the rest of their lives... So it was then that I thought, well really what I have got to do is start off with the assertiveness and I thought then... because I am fundamentally an educator, I am committed much more to education than I am to therapy, because of the equality of the role. I... I... there is something about the equality of teaching that appeals to my soul so much and I wanted, I started off the first evening class.

For some people the idea of educator/student relations would not symbolise equality. Teachers are often seen as having the power to control, observe and discipline their pupils, so how does Annette see teaching as enabling equality? The core part of her model of equality here is that she has common ground with her women clients, based on a shared subjection to societal norms that oppress women. This commonality provides a platform for more equal relations between teacher and women clients. However, Annette makes it clear in the next excerpt from her interview, that she does not see all models of teaching as facilitating equality. She is responding to my question about how to account for the popularity of assertiveness training:

> You had a combination of an awful lot of people setting themselves up as trainers, not using my model of assertiveness. And you had an awful lot of people setting themselves up as trainers and teaching assertiveness badly... or in a very limited way... because they hadn't been through it themselves... And so there were a lot of people, I mean really doing their best as trainers, but they'd had no training themselves and without any experience of doing any role-play, without ever having been themselves in the position of their own role-plays, and their own situations, had not the first idea about how to handle role-play in others. So therefore, role-play would be dropped, and the thing would become completely based on the person being the expert, the trainer being the expert, giving a lecture, being the expert...it would then become a discussion, and people would give advice and consultation. But the whole self-help, the whole role-play, to me which is the utter essence of this, was completely gone, because they couldn't cope with it, because they had not done it themselves, so they had no idea of how to make it safe enough. And so with the role-play gone, the fundamental teaching of assertiveness went.

Annette's model of equality requires a refusal of expertise by the teacher. This is because equality for Annette comes from the shared experience of vulnerability between the teacher and the women on the programme. See Liz Bondi and Judith Fewell (2003) for a discussion on the way voluntary sector counselling can be seen to mobilise a redefined relationship to expertise, an 'inverted kind of expertise, in which they are "experts in not being expert"' (2003: 5). For Bondi and Fewell, this is because of the way that counsellors define expertise, as both content and relational practice, and it is in the former which they see themselves as 'layperson', and therefore equal to their clients, and the latter in which they see themselves as more expert.

Role-plays

In Annette's discussion, role-play acts as the mechanism that best enables equality because it allows women to learn from themselves and their peers rather than from the teacher. Role-play played a central part in my own training to become a trainer using Annette Dobson's model of assertiveness. We learned to practise being assertive through role-playing our own difficult situations in small groups, usually of three, in which one person role-played herself in her situation, another played her respondent, and the third person was an observer. At the end of the role-play, each person would give comments on what the role-player did well, and what he or she could do to improve. The assertiveness trainer herself was not allowed to be part of the role-play. When we were training to be assertiveness trainers ourselves, we were given very clear guidelines on how to set up role-plays within groups, which involved showing the group how to set up a role-play and giving our experiences of how difficult we found being assertive to the group. Teaching the group how to set up a role-play was seen as empowering the group to run role-plays without our help.

For some people, Annette's definition of equality would be unusual as equality is often defined in terms of mutual respect, and access to shared power or resources. In this next excerpt, Annette continues her discussion on expertise in response to me asking about why she withdrew from assertiveness training for a while:

> The more in a sense my reputation grew, the more people would look up to me as an expert regardless of the fact that I wasn't. I am not remotely interested in being an expert, and I still don't believe it. And what makes me such an excellent teacher is that I have never ever ever lost sight of how difficult it is to be assertive. I always remember someone saying in the feedback at the end of a course that she'd only just realised that I really did mean it when I said about the importance of being vulnerable when you are teaching... You really cannot teach assertiveness as a lecture. And you are never going to do the role-play until you feel safe, and you're never going to feel truly safe with somebody if they are the expert, because you're never going to identify with them enough. You are going to say, 'my God she knows this', but you're never going to have the safety until you know that this person also does really actually know how hard it is.

Annette is adamant in these discussions that she did not want to be seen as an expert. This was evidenced by the vigour with which she spoke of the importance of equality and the length of time she devoted to this topic in the interview. This is in spite of her being the author of a popular and famous book on assertiveness in Britain. Annette is very well known as the leading British assertiveness expert and almost a 'cult figure', so we have to understand Annette's desire for equality as an aspiration, and one to which she was committed because she sees the relation between the assertiveness trainer and her trainees as one of mutual identification. Mutual identification for Annette is based on a shared gendered experience of finding it hard to be assertive. This claim of identification only works with a particular version of gender, in which identification is something which has the power to allow women to see across their differences, including the differences between Annette and the women on the courses. The idea of gender as a process not an endpoint allows her to conceptualise her own relation to femininity as an ongoing struggle. This model of 'I've been there and still find it tough' enables Annette to claim equality between herself and her trainees in spite of her fame.

In contrast to Rose (1989, 1996a) and Nolan (1998) for whom expertise provides a new form of authority for practitioners, for Annette the powerlessness of the trainer is the source of authority and equality. In opposition to Jade Simon's model of clients *moving on* to become practitioners, in Annette's model, the trainer and the women being trained are all together in the same boat as a collective, in which there is no successful endpoint, only repetition and mutual recognition. Annette's model is one of 'emotional equality' defined in terms of shared emotion and mutual recognition. The idea of emotional equality enables Annette to hold on to an aspiration of equality whilst at the same time as being famous and seen as an expert. Emotional equality is unusual because it is based on disappointment and failure. For Rose (1989, 1996a) and Blackman and Walkerdine (2001), failure to achieve idealised therapeutic versions of the self leads us to return back to therapeutic cultures for more advice, tips and techniques. In contrast, for Annette, failure builds community.

Mutual fallibility

Like Annette, Peter Pope, a Gestalt therapist, has a strong belief in the ideal of equality. In this excerpt, Peter is responding to me asking whether he agrees with certain critics that therapy is a substitute for religion:

> Something which is very important to me is that I look back at my life, back at things that I've done, and I try not to assume that with a client that if I was in the same situation I would have done any

> better. So any approach which assumes they know how to lead a better life worries me.

For Peter, as for Annette, equality is based on a model of commonality between practitioner and client based on mutual fallibility. In Peter's model, however, equal relations between therapist and client are not based on gender or shared oppression. Furthermore, Peter does not explicitly reject a view of his current self as 'sorted', unlike Annette. The ideal of mutual fallibility is based on a deliberate identification of his past self with the client's current self, 'I was like you and would have done no better either'. But in contrast to Annette, Peter presents himself as able to look back and identify with the client and indicate that he would do better now. Peter continues his discussion:

> Peter: The most important thing is that therapists don't see themselves as priests. That isn't what we are. We have no special links to God, so I think that is important.
>
> Elaine: So people might have a blueprint for what a good life is, is that what you mean?
>
> Peter: Well, I have no objection to people having a blueprint. I think life is bigger than a blueprint but I don't in itself have any objection to blueprints so long as they say 'this is my blueprint rather than God's'... It puts the therapist in an unequal position... we mess up as well... once you have separated yourself from being like other people then you are a much less useful therapist.

Peter's model of equality is not compromised by the therapist having a blueprint for living, so long as it is relativised by the therapist and not seen as special or authoritative. Rather than being a refusal of expertise, as is the case for Annette, this is more of a model of pluralisation of expertise. This move is necessary so that the client does not take the therapist's blueprint as his or her own. In this model of equality, there is an onus on the client to find their own answers in terms which echo Charles Taylor's discussions (1989, 1991) on the contemporary imperative for our selves to be themselves through being unique. This means we have to work hard to show ourselves as individuals, by demonstrating our difference from other people.

Unlike Annette, who draws upon an analogy of teachers to symbolise her practice, Peter uses the image of priests with which to juxtapose his own position. Priests can symbolise transcendence and this does not fit with Peter's model of equality through mutual fallibility. Interestingly, none of the informants draws upon a model of doctor/patient to represent their relations with clients. The doctor/patient model has too many connotations of hierarchical power and expertise, and patient passivity, in which the professional distance is seen to help the patient. For doctors, getting emotionally involved would detract from the detached reason needed in scientific diagnosis and surgery.

For Annette her ability to help her clients is not based on traditional expertise, but on the therapist and client being alike in terms of their shared vulnerability. It is this shared emotion that brings equality. What emerges from this research is that Annette does not see her authority coming from her being special or superior in relation to the client. Jade Simon's model is based on the practitioner as special because of her success in improving herself, and any failures being clearly a thing of the past. For Annette, failures are points of mutual identification based on fallibility between practitioner and client. Struggle is very much a thing of the present, and the future. For Annette the desired end-goal for clients is not seen to be achieved via the practitioner or to be 'inside' the practitioner or the client, but out there, out of reach of practitioner and client.

Skills exchange

I now turn to a practitioner interviewed who holds a different view of equality from Annette. Violette Turner is a psychodrama therapist and also works on a part-time basis for the mental health charity, Mind. In this next quotation, Violette is responding to my asking how directive a role she takes in psychodramas:

> They [the psychodrama clients] are basically directing the psychodrama but like any leadership thing, it is not that simple, is it? Because people who have got skills or have got training, it is not equal is it?... Although if you are in an on-going psychodrama group, you pick up all the techniques so it might become more equal but I don't think there is any way that you can be equal. You see, it is this 'tele' business as well. Because the director and the protagonist are having a relationship, so hidden things are being communicated that aren't necessarily obvious.

Echoing Rose (1989, 1996a), Violette believes that there is an imbalance of power between the therapist and the client. Equality is an impossibility in her view and nor is it an aspiration. Some of this gap can be closed to some extent as clients learn certain skills. For Violette, the real inequality between the two though, differentiating her practice from Jade's model of clients 'directing the show', lies in the transference between therapist and protagonist. This parallels the transfer of skills from therapist to protagonist. In Violette's model, a conscious exchange of skills does not overcome the asymmetrical power dynamics inherent in the unconscious exchange of emotions from client to therapist. In order for the client to make progress, the client has to submit to unequal relations, in which s/he replays other unequal relations from her past. Unlike Annette and Peter's model of identification through shared emotions which leads to equality, Violette's model is characterised by inequality, unconscious identification and distance between practitioner and client.

Along different lines, in this next example, Jade Simon suggests that the therapist can act as a role model, and still preserve equality. In this excerpt, Jade gives her views on the differences between therapist and client in response to my asking why she prefers self-help to traditional therapy:

> The other thing is, what I found is that clients more and more nowadays want to know about you and so the model of therapy is 'to keep yourself out of it' and 'keep yourself blank'. And I don't think I was ever very happy with that. I wasn't happy with it when I was a client either. I think it is fair enough for the client to want to know that you're OK, you're not perfect, you have had problems maybe, and that you have actually worked through them and that really you have got it together.

Progress narrative

The model of the therapist operating here is one of therapist as the hero in a 'progress narrative'. The progress narrative is a dominant cultural form, based on an evolutionary upward curve of self-improvement, in which we gradually and continually perfect our selves through life's experiences or our choices. The upward curve may have some low points, which help make us what we are, but these are never as bad as the start (Nisbet, 1969; Stacey, 1995). This narrative shapes how we understand our individual lives, and our futures, and our collective history and potential. It can be seen as a 'genre', with a particular structure and set of conventions.

In the context of Jade Simon's view of personal development, the progress narrative consists of a slow trajectory of self-betterment achieved through the overcoming of obstacles, each of which provides increasing and accumulative self-improvement. In her discussion of religious origins of psychoanalysis, Suzanne Kirschner (1996) argues that the sources for the overarching idea of human progress are the Bible, the Enlightenment and evolutionary theory, and that the cultural form underpins disparate academic disciplines such as politics, developmental psychology, and sociology. The progress narrative's design, she suggests 'assumes the inevitable progress of mankind towards a stable end point of well-being and moral perfection... Theoretical frameworks [in politics, sociology and developmental psychology] partake of such features as its basic linear design, its prospectivism and future orientation, and its function as a means of explaining, and offering the hope of amelioration of, the imperfections of the human condition' (1996: 105).

The end-point of Jade's narrative is not the perfect self, but a wiser, more 'sorted' self. In contrast to Annette and Peter though, she is further along the path of self-improvement than her client. Equality comes with Jade's model of 'I've been there, done that and now you can too, if I show you the way'. Although she is a role model and hero of her progress narrative, equality is still offered through a double point of identification. This double point of identification comes with the two positions of 'me as I was when I was like you' and 'me as I am now having moved on'.

Jade explains her approach in more detail in this next excerpt:

> When all is said and done what actually is most helpful is actually me standing back and looking at the way I've developed. It's helped me personally, and it's what's helped the clients that I have worked with in my work practice.

Like Annette and Peter, Jade Simon sees her own experience as important to her practice but unlike them, this experience is not based on fallibility but accumulated know-how, which can then be transferred to the client. In Jade's approach, it is the therapist's understanding of her own past that has therapeutic benefits rather than the client working through their own past, as would be the case in psychoanalysis. In this next quote, Jade draws upon a different analogy to explain how her practice works:

> In many ways, it isn't a lot different from adult education classes that would teach people how to put up a shelf and so on, and be empowered as a result of that. And I like to see it like that, and I

want to demystify it. What I say to people is 'Look, this is just my business. I just happen to be somebody who has learned all the stuff, read all this stuff. What I am doing is putting you a short cut really. You may well want to actually go back to the drawing board yourself and you may not have time'.

Short cut

Jade Simon presents her expertise as the ability to offer a 'short cut'. In her model, she can offer a short cut because she too has been there, had success and as a result knows where the client wants to be and how to get there. Unlike Peter, who argues that the therapist should relativise the blueprint s/he offers and present it as her/his own, for Jade her short cut is universal. In Peter's view, a blueprint lays out the therapist's guide for living but still requires that the client take time and make the effort to put the blueprint into operation, whereas the short cut is a means of saving time or effort. The short cut enables her clients to speed up what is usually seen as a gradual process of accumulating skills and wisdom. In contrast, the quick fix is severely criticised by writers on therapeutic cultures: see for example Ian Craib (1994, 1998); Cath Jackson (1989); Ken Plummer (1995). See Stjepan Mestrovic (1997) and Simon Williams (2000, 2001) for discussions of short cuts and quick fixes as a form of McDonaldisation.

In the model of exchange that Jade Simon conceptualises, she transfers skills not self-knowledge to her clients. And these are not abstract skills and knowledge but ones cultivated through Jade's experience and enlightenment. This contrasts with Jackie Stacey's (1997) view of practitioners in contemporary healthcare medicine for whom the knowledge that cures is self-knowledge. It also differs from Ursula Sharma's research (1995) on complementary medicine, in which practitioners limit what they share with their patients in spite of their claims to equality. They did not exchange their diagnostic skills or their therapeutic techniques with their clients. Equality in these practices is based on the clients sharing their self-knowledge of their condition and in return practitioners explaining some of their medical understandings. In Jade's model, equality comes with the transfer of skills as well as knowledge. This is in contrast to Violette, for whom transference rather than skills transfer brings progress.

The concept of skills transfer is seen by some critics to be disempowering rather than egalitarian as in Jade's view. Discussing the idea of the transferability of skills, Norman Fairclough (1992) suggests that skills are seen in two contradictory ways in contemporary society: as prized, active individualising attributes and as passive, normalising and de-individualising. They are de-individualising because they are seen as transcontextual, suitable for any context, occasion and user (Fairclough, 1992). For some critics, the idea of skills transfer derives from behavourism, in which the self is seen as a composite of learnable skills (Cohen, 1985; Rose, 2000). In Stanley Cohen's (1985) view, in a discussion on social control, the focus for intervention is what people do, not what they feel or think, constituting a shift from actor to act. This emphasis on external behaviours away from internal causes is seen as proof of therapy's superficiality and instrumentality (Cohen, 1985; Rose, 2000).

In contrast for Jade, her skills are parts of her self which then educate the client. Her past becomes the means by which someone gets a new future. Their connection with her is important, so although they are detachable, and transcontextual, as Fairclough (1992) suggests, they are effective because they belong to her. Her individuality embedded in her skills becomes the basis for the client's expression of individuality.

Client power

Staying with Jade Simon, this section turns to the issue of client power which was mentioned several times by her. This is in contrast with many critics such as Rose (1989, 1996a) and Nolan (1998) for whom the client's influence over the therapist is not discussed. In this next excerpt, Jade refers to this power in responding to my question about why she prefers self-help to therapy:

> Jade: I feel very, very committed, I got more and more committed to self-help as the years have gone by... the whole concept of it. And I have found that I'm often feeling alienated with the world of therapy... it's often very empowering...the process is empowering for people and quite restricting sometimes for the therapist and the way they work.
>
> Elaine: In what sort of way would you say it was empowering and restricting for therapists?
>
> Jade: What happens in the concept of therapy, clients go along and although a counsellor or therapist will talk nineteen to the dozen about how they're just a vehicle... clients cannot see the way out because they're in a very desperate position, they are feeling very de-

> powered. Therapists are in a very powerful position. I think what happens is that the client somehow kind of seduces the therapist into a role that is actually quite a powerful role. It has a lot of influence and seduces advice out of the therapist. What I would rather is be up front about that and say 'Look here. This is my wisdom that I've gained. This is how I manage my anger or I found useful to manage my anger. These are the guidelines. Take them or leave them. Adapt them, try them out, if they don't work, try your own thing out'.

In this excerpt, there is a stark reversal of power. This contrasts with Rose's model (1989, 1996a) in which it is the therapist who seduces the client. For Jade, client empowerment is based on an avowal of expertise in opposition to Annette's refusal of expertise. To hold onto the notion of self-help whilst also giving advice, which some people might see as contradictory, Jade presents her expertise as conditional, provisional and customisable. This idea confirms Giddens' view (1991, 1992) that expertise is seen as fragile and partial, and suggests that some practitioners incorporate this understanding into their practice.

Summary

In this section, I have shown that equality is a defining component in practitioners' understanding of their relations with clients. This aspiration to equal relations is unexamined in much of the theoretical literature, and where it is discussed, it is seen, as in the case of Rose (1989, 1996a, 1996b) as an impossibility, or as in the case of de Swaan (1990), a cover for the imbalance of power between practitioner and client. Although there is a shared concern by the majority of practitioners interviewed for achieving equality with their clients, we have also seen that they conceptualise equality and its achievement, in diverse and often contradictory ways. For example, in Jade Simon's model of equality, the practitioner's giving of advice to the client reduces the asymmetry between practitioner and client, by enabling the client to 'catch up' to where the practitioner is. For both Jade and Peter, the practitioner's advice is seen as equalising because it is grounded in identification between the practitioner and the client, in a recognition of 'I used to be like you and so I understand', rather than any objective abstract knowledge. In Peter's case, equality is best achieved by a relativisation of this advice, with clients coming to their own aspirations without too much imposition by the therapist. For Annette, the refusal of advice giving by the practitioner, and the shared feelings of oppression experienced by practitioners and clients engender equality, defined by Annette as emotional equality. Having analysed the way that practitioners conceptualise equality, this next section examines the abuses of power by practitioners because for both critics and practitioners, there is a serious concern that therapeutic practitioners can unduly influence their clients and even exploit them. For some of the practitioners interviewed, the area of the abuse of power was a significant topic for understanding how their practices had improved or changed.

Against or with their will?

For some of the practitioners, the abuse of power by practitioners was discussed explicitly and seen to take particular forms. However, this did not mean that abuse was always seen as leading to inequality. In the literature on the sociology of therapeutic cultures, some of the worst abuses of power amongst the multitude of negative effects a therapist can have on a client, are numbing their feelings of resistance to the status quo, and luring them with impossible ideals. There are many debates on the abuses of power by therapists in the counselling literature, and by feminists. These often focus on sexual and mental abuse. See for example: Janice Russell (1993), Miriam Greenspan (1993) and Betty McLellan (1995). In T.M. Luhrmann's (2001) ethnography of psychodynamic psychiatrists, much of their training focused on the different types of harm a therapist could inflict on a patient. Much of the focus was on unconscious or accidental harm.

Like many of the critics, Richard Brown, a self-employed personal development consultant and university associate, is worried about the ways that practitioners influence clients' options. In this excerpt, Richard is discussing the changes in therapeutic practices over the years:

> Richard: There has been quite a growth in structured, instrumental approaches to personal... called personal development...you know 5,681 different questionnaires you can fill in that enable you to put yourself in a box. 'I am an A'. I think it is to do with control. Even the personal growth stuff which is still acceptable I think is heavily structured and controllable. And I think the looser forms are less controllable.
>
> Elaine: So controlling what people think and how they perceive themselves?

Richard: Yeah, and being able to put bounds on things. You know being able to bound, what, how far they explore alternative selves I think.

Elaine: You have liked group process work because it is in a way a blank canvas and anything can happen?

Richard: Well yes. The hesitation is in terms of how the person or people with power behave or work with that blank canvas. Because I still think it is possible for people to say, 'Here we are, we have a blank canvas and I have experience of working with a blank canvas so I will tell you what the picture looks like'.

Endpoints

Richard's model sees clear endpoints as disempowering because they constrain what the client can become. Part of Richard's beliefs here is that some practitioners get power over clients by imposing ideals on them, and will do so even when a technique is open-ended. This model of Richard's fits with the form of expressivism that Bernice Martin (1981) describes in her analysis of the institutionalisation of the counter-culture movement in the 1970s and 1980s. For Martin, this form of expressivism involved an attitude which was anti-structure in educational practices. As with some popular models that suggest that therapists want to put ideas or stories into clients' heads, for Richard the use of short cuts is an expression of domination. This is in opposition to Jade for whom short cuts were a means of equality. Embedded in this model is a commonly-held view that therapists have a desire for control, and can exercise a powerful influence over the client in what they should become. In his model, the best kind of self comes freed of constraints and is open to new possibilities and potentials.

Jack Routledge

Working from a different perspective, Jack Routledge, transpersonal counsellor and leading humanist psychology author, talks about the explicit use of harm in this next example. Jack is responding to my question about the ways in which therapeutic practices have changed over the last thirty years:

I mean one difference that is very clear is a much greater appreciation of the way in which therapists can do harm. In the seventies... a

> group leader, as long as he was being what he would say was authentic and straightforward and so forth, could do anything. If he wanted to get angry with someone in the group, he would get angry with them. If he wanted to throw them out of the room, he would throw them out. If he wanted to go to bed with the best-looking women in the group, he would do that. And as long as it was from the heart, as it were, and done expressively, and overtly, with no bullshit, it was fine. Now I think today, we recognise that group leaders and therapists have a lot of power over and above their personality and they have to be careful not to abuse that power and not to abuse their clients or their members. And so a lot of things which seemed OK then don't seem OK now... I think that's a big difference, being aware of the client as a suffering human being who might not be completely equipped with all their existential marbles, and who might need a bit of looking after, care, nurturing, a bit of respect for their vulnerability...in the seventies we treated everybody as if they were strong and in some ways that was good.

Violent authenticity

For Jack, dominance of the client by the practitioner is a technique. In his view, it can bring more equal relations than a technique of nurturance. Jack represents these two styles of naked dominance and nurturance in gendered terms, in which the former is coded as masculine and the latter seen as feminine. This is, however, not the masculine model of cool, detached rationality epitomised in some models of psychoanalysis (Greenspan, 1993) but a model of hot-blooded lability. The approach described is an 'ego trip', in which the use of violence and dominance are deemed legitimate because they signify authenticity. Authenticity in this case is manifested by the wilful expression of desire, overthrowing the shackles of social convention. This relates to Charles Taylor's discussion on the Nietzschean notion that authenticity is defined in opposition to social conformity and morality. According to Taylor (1991), this meant that for Nietzsche, self-making is 'quite incompatible with the Christian-inspired ethic of benevolence' (1991: 65–66). This view, Taylor writes, has been 'followed and exceeded by various attempts to champion the instinctual depths, even violence, against the "bourgeois" ethic of order' (1991: 66). (See Ralph Turner (1976) also on the contemporary view that the ideal self is unconstrained by social norms or institutions, and

Charles Lindholm (2001) for a condensed historical account of beliefs about authenticity).

In this model, everyone is fair game because clients are treated as if they were equals. Although Jack recognises the dangers associated with this model, he suggests that treating clients as if they were equals involves seeing them as strong, autonomous, and masculinised. Authenticity in this model does not come from dependence on others.

In a more critical vein, Jane Vincent, a growth group facilitator, refers to the violence in some groups she attended:

> It started off by being quite militant... in contrast today it is incredibly gentle and very spiritual. I suppose as trainers have learnt that people still get the profound experience... Let me explain what I mean. When I did it, the first training had quite a jackboot style to it. There was a lot of shouting and screaming and 'You will be here on time!'... People's faces were stern and seventeen years later, people smile, they are warm and it is okay. They have learnt that people will still have this profound experience and a far healthier experience if all this stuff is removed. Similarly on 'essence', I remember on my training, it was quite violent. I did my training with my ex-husband and he punched me. That would never be allowed today. Violence was almost incited at that stage because they believed that that worked. Well it did work for me from the point of view that it was profound. But people's experience is equally profound today.

Violence is seen in this model as guaranteeing authentic change. As with Jack Routledge, Jane Vincent presents the two styles in gendered terms in which the earlier style is presented as masculine and again the second one as feminine. The sadistic model sees the use of cruelty as a technique that reaches a depth in both therapist and client. Depth is associated with authenticity, as if the further inside of the self you go, the further you get away from the acculturated, false self, and the nearer you get to the authentic true self. Both Jack Routledge and Jane Vincent's examples suggest that the deeper the therapeutic interventions go into the self, the more traumatised the client may be, and the more practitioners need to be aware of their power, but the more effective the techniques will be. In these examples, the client's will is seen as an instrument of change.

The previous examples have mainly focused on the use of power and its effects on clients. The next two differ in that they discuss the effects of power on practitioners. This first example from Richard Brown also relates to the theme of violence as a therapeutic technique:

> And I went to things that I had no intention of doing myself. And actually some of the attack therapy-based ones, I actually thought were outrageous. I could possibly see their role in their origin, which is very harsh drug addiction units. But they are a funny sort of business. I am not saying I didn't have some gain from it. A sense of danger and personal power. Touching the fascist in me really, and I am not sure touching the fascist in people, particularly the way it was worked, is necessarily a good thing.

In this example, Richard presents the sadistic control of clients as having an erotic charge. Getting a kick from this form of control, the practitioner's identity is transformed as well as that of the client's. Like Jack, Richard is ambivalent about the use of brutality, suggesting that much tougher measures are justified with certain clients. This relates to Giddens' suggestion (1991, 1992) that addiction in therapeutic cultures is seen as a lack of reflexivity and autonomy and that therapeutic technique can replace habits by implanting choice back into the self. In Richard's example, it is as if violence can wake up the will by reaching down to the deep self, going beyond the surface habitual self.

This next quote moves away from violence as a technique but still focuses on the issue of the potential dangers in practitioners' use of power. The quote is taken from the interview with Peter Pope, the Gestalt therapist, at a point in which he has just finished discussing the idea that therapists should not claim to have superiority over their clients:

> Peter: The same is true of NLP where I think concepts like truth, honesty and authenticity disappear. I've got a moral objection to NLP.
>
> Elaine: Because they disappear? Does that mean you don't think it works, or that it is amoral, or immoral?
>
> Peter: I think it works alright but in as much as it works. I think the main thing is that people who practise it get taken over by it. They lose a sense of what they want for a sense of what would be a powerful statement.
>
> Elaine: Do you mean by that that they are able to use some of the NLP techniques to appear powerful?

Peter: To be powerful at the expense of knowing why they want to be powerful, or why they want to have power over other people, or what they might be doing if they weren't trying to have power over other people.

In Peter's view, lack of self-knowledge in the therapist can lead to an abuse of power. If the therapist is unreflexive about their own desire for power, they get captivated by the techniques to such an extent that the techniques become the self. In this way, for Peter the problem with NLP is its effect on the practitioner not its efficacy in relation to the client. The writing in the sociology of therapeutic cultures rarely addresses the problem of therapists who are dominated by the practice rather than their clients. In this description, the therapist becomes the mechanism for the technique.

Summary

This section has shown that the practitioners interviewed are concerned about the uses and abuses of power in their relations with clients. As with some critics, they are worried about the ways in which practitioners can control what clients think and what they do. Their accounts differ from many of the critics in that they are also troubled by the power of therapeutic techniques on themselves, and by their own lust for domination. Concerns about power are also related to the imagined potential for trauma which is seen to be connected to the depth that practitioners' interventions go. As shown in Chapter 2, the notion of the self having an interiority has emerged historically over the past 200 years. In that time, it has been conceptualised as having different contents, which have been differentially distributed by gender and race (Pfister, 1995; Pfister and Schnog, 1997). The idea of interiority has also been understood through a metaphor of 'depth' (Taylor, 1989, 1994). The idea of 'depth' has been used in various ways, but is most often associated with our most private, asocialised and core self. In this view, privacy is seen to be a part of the self which should remain untouched by the state and other non-intimate others.

In their discussion on the authority of therapeutic experts, Peter Miller and Nikolas Rose (1988) discuss the privileging of self-control by practitioners as a way of getting into people's depths without breaching this imagined private space. The practitioners interviewed also reproduce a notion of the self in the depths as the most private, core self but also where transformation can be most successfully, if somewhat dangerously made. In this model, practitioners use the client's will, seen to be buried in the depths of the self under layers of socialised behaviours, as an instrument of change. For these practitioners, power comes from bending the will of the client in a coercive way. This is seen to be attractive and dangerous, leading to a lust for power verging on megalomania. In contrast for Jack, traumatisation can be a mechanism for achieving equality with clients, because it reaches the parts that other techniques do not, parts that are needed to be reached to achieve real transformation.

The road to Damascus

Having looked at the ways practitioners conceptualise equality in their relations with their clients, and described the ways that equal relations can turn into abuse and abuse can turn into equal relations, this section looks at conversion. Conversion was central to practitioners' understandings of their relations with their clients, and how they presented their identities. Although Rose (1989, 1996a) and Miller and Rose (1994) refer to the importance of conversion as a key mechanism for shaping the self, they do not examine how conversion is seen to operate, and how conversion relates to the relations between practitioners and clients. See Peter Ackers and Diane Preston (1997) for an interesting study of conversion in management development practices. In contrast, anthropological literature on conversion in religion examines it in close detail, and as a result, shows conversion taking many forms, undergone in acutely different ways, involving different stages and caused by a range of practices (Heelas, 1996; Lofland and Skonovd, 1983). Drawing on these general ideas on conversion, this section examines how conversion was seen by the practitioners as a mechanism for equality and exchange.

Andy Knight

I begin with a quote from Andy Knight, an NLP practitioner and head of a management development division in a bank. His view is representative of several practitioners interviewed in the sense that conversion is viewed as a means to give to a client. In response to my question on how he became involved with NLP, Andy explains in the following way:

> I did a session with Geoff and Colin, who work for me, on NLP and its spelling strategies within education. And we invited fifteen,

twenty teachers and parents along to it, including a couple of sceptical headmistresses and we did a morning's work for them... We did this session and it worked really well and one of the headmistresses rang me back the following day and said, 'This NLP stuff, we have just tried it on the most difficult kid in the school'; and I thought, 'Oh my god'; '...and it works, total breakthrough. When can you come and work with me?' I said, 'I can't. I told you I wasn't selling anything. This was just a bit of community spirited stuff in the community'. So I put her in touch with one or two people and she is a real convert now, and this was at a special school for dyslexic children.

In this example, Andy presents his practice in terms of philanthropy. But his generosity does not mean that he does not present himself as powerful as shown through his ability to convert. The strength of his power is demonstrated in the extremes that he has broached – the most difficult pupil and the most sceptical headmistress. As literature on conversion shows, conversion has a structure in which a 'before' is contrasted with an 'after' (Ackers and Preston, 1997 and Lofland and Skonovd, 1983).

Before and after

In this case there is a condensation of time between the 'before' and 'after' as in the archetypal 'road to Damascus' experience in the immediacy of both cure and conversion. The 'after' is also constituted by a renunciation of the 'before'. In this example, the headteacher replaces her scepticism of NLP with zeal to spread the word. Through the conversion, Andy is able to bring equality to people through his techniques and yet still present himself as powerful. Andy's sharing of techniques is not seen to depreciate his power, but augment it, in contrast to critics like de Swaan (1990) who suggest that the appropriation of expertise by clients, or 'proto-professionalism' reduces the authority of the expert.

Passing it on

In a similar example of conversion as a kind of a gift, Jane Vincent, the growth group facilitator, discusses her ability to convert people to her growth group:

I have introduced, I don't know, a couple of hundred people to it over the years easily, my entire family, my mother, my family, my

> best friends and I have had my old girlfriend from school. We were fourteen at school in Cape Town and we were best mates in Cape Town, and now we live half an hour away from each other in England. And she went and did it this weekend. I just bawled my eyes out because she just, she cried and she said 'Thank you'.

Whereas Andy Knight underscores the extent of his power to convert through his transformation of extreme examples, i.e. the most difficult pupil, and the most sceptical headteacher, Jane Vincent demonstrates her power in terms of the quantity of her recruits. Jane does not perform the conversion directly, but acts as someone who passes on the good word and how to access it. The conversion takes a weekend, slightly longer than in Andy's case. In return Jane Vincent receives intense gratitude and recognition as her best friend acknowledges her indebtedness.

The media

From a different angle, Jade Simon, self-help book author and personal development therapist, describes a process of conversion through the use of mass media:

> I used to sneer at the media constantly... I used to hate doing it because they'd want me to put everything in quick fix sound-bites. And I have learned to respect the power of the media which is phenomenal, and respect people's need for that quick fix sound-bite, respect for the fact that a lot of that is all that a lot of people will get. And if I was to come and sit and do some therapy with people, I would maybe help a couple of hundred people at the very, very most in about a five-year period, whereas through the media, through writing articles, women's magazines, doing quotes, appearing on TV, I'm giving something to millions, and through the books as well.

In this example, Jade Simon draws upon a fantasy of the power of effects: that of her own in tandem with that of the media. Although the sound bite is not ideal, for Jade Simon it enables her to provide access to her ideas, and therefore acts as a mechanism for equality. Unlike for Andy Knight and Jane Vincent, she does not need face-to-face contact with people, or demonstrate the efficacy of her techniques to convert them. The power of her ideas is enough to convert millions.

Even though the mass quick fix and the proselytising spirit of therapists are despised by critics, for Jade Simon they are democratising. In contrast, for many critics the quick fix is the quintessential instrumentalising technique.

As Charles Taylor (1991) writes:

> The dream of the quick fix is present [in therapeutic cultures]... in spite of the fact that from the very beginning, and still today, the goal of self-fulfilment has been understood as antithetical to that of mere instrumental control. A quick-fix technique for letting go is the ultimate contradiction (1991: 60). (See also Ian Craib on what he calls 'formulae for living'. (1998: 166)

Helper's high

On a different tack, returning to Jane Vincent, the growth group facilitator, she recounts her own conversion from being a client to becoming a practitioner in response to me asking why she became a practitioner:

> Maybe I was a closet helper... I discovered that I could give...The rewards are enormous, the joy. The work is hard. We work long, hard hours. If the training is sixty hours over five days, we are probably there for eighty to ninety hours. And here I was managing director of my own companies and I was scrubbing toilets. The rewards are enormous: the humility, the learning, the relationships, the fun. But I got hooked on it. I got so much fun and I got off on seeing people shift in their lives. And I think it awakened the healer in me because I didn't even know the word 'healer' and I didn't know I could do that stuff. So it was a kind of validation of me. Valuing me. And feeling I have a place on this planet. And that I can give. And it is not just writing a cheque or buying someone a present.

In this example Jane Vincent not only transforms others but also transforms herself. In this model the practitioner's self is produced through the ego validation she gets as reciprocation for her gift of healing others. Her giving acts to extend her self into something more ideal. For Jane Vincent, this mode of exchange is to be contrasted with commodified forms of exchange, representing a bigger order of things to which she is party. There is an equality here between the therapist and the client achieved through the reciprocal relations of the exchange in which Jane Vincent derives what Miller and McHoul call the 'helper's high', pleasure and recognition and the client gets healed (1998a: 114). This emphasis on equality is reinforced by Jane Vincent's taking on of menial work ('scrubbing toilets').

Summary

In this section, I have examined how practitioners imagine the process of conversion as a means through which clients can achieve equality. For Miller and Rose, conversion is the most 'potent' means for a practitioner to shape a client's self (1994: 35) and the practitioners interviewed confirm this. For Rose (1996a, 2000) a key way for practitioners to do this is through claims to truth, and technical efficacy. Although the practitioners' models are based on the 'ur-structure' of conversion – the 'before' and 'after' – their forms do vary. The different models can be placed on a continuum from intense, instant, individual conversions performed by the practitioner in close proximity at one end, which are more explicitly recruitist, and more rational, diffuse, collective conversions set in motion by the practitioner and performed at a distance at the other end. At the intense end is Andy Knight's model of the 'miracle' which instantaneously converts the sceptic headteacher because of its power and proof. The headteacher is not presented as someone in search of conversion, but someone who is transformed passively as a result of Andy's miracle. She, in turn, learns the techniques of miracles herself and goes on to convert people herself. At the other more rational and diffuse end, is Jade Simon, for whom conversion is less mystical and comes through providing expertise to people, which will change the way that they behave. There is no one emotional turning point for an individual but instead, Jade Simon is working with a model based on a large scale spreading of rational techniques through the media. In the middle of the continuum come Jane Vincent's models. In one of these models, conversion is slightly more gradual, and less dramatic than Andy's. It is intense, and like Andy's, is based on one single transforming event, but does not involve Jane Vincent herself performing the conversion. In Jane Vincent's other model, she herself converts gradually over a period of time, and presents this as an awakening of what was already present but hidden in herself, rather than a 'born again' experience. In this latter model, Jane Vincent's conversion has a moral aspect in that she presents herself as a 'better' person. In conclusion, these practitioners do allude to Rose's notions of truth and technical efficacy as forms of authority but with different emphases and to different degrees. So Jade Simon sees technical efficacy as key. But for the others, their allusions to special powers required to convert people suggest that their understanding of truth is predicated less on psychological expertise, and more on their ability to access 'a bigger picture' at work. In their work on management training, Peter Ackers and Diane Preston (1997) relate growth of the 'conversion mindset' in contemporary management thinking to a revival of charismatic forms of authority in organisations in the form of gurus. In a related way, in this last section on data analysis, I analyse how the concept of charisma operates in the practitioners' accounts and how this relates to issues of power and expertise.

Close encounters

The previous section showed how practitioners allude to aura and mystery in their accounts of conversion. Although Rose (1989, 1996a) mentions 'discipleship, exemplarity, seduction, captivation' and Giddens (1991, 1992, 1994) 'reverence' to describe forms of relations between experts and laypeople, Rose and Giddens' main focus is on how therapeutic practitioners mobilise expertise in the form of 'scientific knowledge' and 'techniques'; consequently neither of them goes into depth on these type of relations. One way for us to gain insights into practitioners' allusions to magic and special powers is by using Max Weber's typology of authority (1978), and in particular, his discussion of charisma. Writing at the end of the nineteenth and into the start of the twentieth century on changing forms of organisation, and religion, Weber is often seen as one the founders of classical sociology, and one of the founders of the sociology of religion. Discussing the means by which people legitimatise their exercise of power over others, Weber introduces a three-fold model of authority types: traditional, rational and charismatic (1978: 215–216). Traditional authority rests on a belief in long-standing wisdom, folk custom, simple and 'natural' convention. Rational authority claims to be legitimate because it is based on rules, procedures, and appeals to impersonality, exemplified by bureaucracies and scientific knowledge. It is this kind of authority to which most social scientists refer when they discuss therapeutic authority. In Weber's third model, certain individuals exert influence over others through the possession of 'charisma'. Charisma refers to special gifts of body or mind, such as a magnetic personality or unusual skills, making someone 'out of the ordinary', superhuman or even supernatural in some way (1978: 241). Examples of such charismatic individuals for Weber (1978) include hunters, leaders, shamans, priests and warriors. The possession of charisma gives a person a hold over others, in ways that are different from persuasion through expertise or wisdom, or the rational efficiency of the scientist. The effect of the charisma on us is emotional rather than rational, leading to us feeling excited, awed, vitalised and consequently devoted. For Lindholm (1992, 2001) emotional identification is essential to charismatic relations. So how does this discussion of charisma operate in practitioner accounts? What kinds of response does it engender in its recipients? How does the use of charismatic authority relate to the theme of equality?

Dennis Fournier

This section starts with a quote from Dennis Fournier, a neuro-linguistic programming trainer and therapist, because he introduces the concept of magic, a common theme amongst the practitioners:

> People say NLP is magic. But no, it's not. It's just a sufficiently advanced technology. And the wonderful thing about this is that I can work with a client, and they can make weird and wonderful changes. And I know what I've done but I'm still touched by the magic.

In this quote, Dennis both refuses and claims the significance of charismatic power in his approach. Debunking the naïve view that there is something mysterious about what he does through a reference to the rational authority of science, Dennis suggests, at the same time, that the effects of NLP are also arcane to the layperson, from whom he distinguishes himself. His charisma derives from his being on top of these complex and other-worldly techniques. Unlike Peter Pope (in an earlier section) who was concerned that NLP techniques overpower the practitioner so that the technology becomes the self, for Dennis, the technique is charisma.

Special gifts

In a similar vein, Jade Simon, self-help book author and therapist, talks about the magic of her group work skills:

> Often when people work with me, particularly in a group situation, I do have what seems like, even to me, an uncanny ability to get in there and say the right thing, and suggest the right thing. And it

> does feel uncanny at times. It feels like it just comes out. I don't prepare it. And it would be very easy to think that I've got some special gift or power. A lot of people would say I have, but I honestly think that that's just my brain working quite efficiently in that situation really.

In a strikingly similar way to Dennis Fournier, Jade Simon also refuses the claim of charisma and yet again undermines this by hinting that there is something supernatural in what she does in the eyes of others. As commentators on charisma note, charisma has to be repeatedly attributed to charismatics by their followers, and so is in the eye of the beholder. By invoking her clients' validations of her charisma, Jade is able to show that she does have special powers for the ordinary person. Whereas for Dennis, the technique is charisma, for Jade, charisma takes the form of her individual special perceptive powers.

Sunlight

On a different tack, Jane Vincent suggests a different way of understanding charisma in this next excerpt in which she is talking about what happens when she has finished working on a growth group:

> Every time I go and assist on one, I beam for days after. I walk along the street and I smile and people smile back at me and I think I am bringing some sunlight into the world.

In using the metaphor of sunlight, Jane Vincent draws on clichés of harmony, natural goodness and the collective good, but also Christ-like allusions of bringing light to the world to symbolise the extent and power of the effects of her charismatic power. Jane's charisma is embodied in her self, rather than coming from technique or special interpretive abilities. Like Jade Simon, she shows how her charismatic powers are validated by others, but in Jane Vincent's example, their validation is evidenced by their copying of her actions, symbolising their followership. In drawing upon religious imagery, she alludes to something greater than her, with which she is in touch, and can mediate with on behalf of us and disperse to us.

Charismatic fascination

The next two quotes suggest a different angle to charisma than mentioned so far by the practitioners. They refer to the intense emotional relations engendered by the practitioners' use of charisma. In this first quote, Sally Thompson, a Gestalt psychotherapist and organisational development consultant, is talking about herself as a client and describing her experience of Mary, a group therapist who facilitated a group of which she was part:

> She impressed me enormously. She was strict about boundaries and she was very, very intuitive. She was very good at working at issues in a way which was very holding, so people were safe but that got to the heart of the issues. And that means people were complete in the work that they were doing – she didn't leave people hanging. She was a very graceful woman.

The effect of Mary's charisma on Sally Thompson is one of fascination and admiration. Sally presents Mary's charisma through the combination of opposites and the reference to intuition, a form of knowledge popularly seen as opposite to scientific rationality, and viewed as mysterious. In spite of Mary's talismanic power, Sally shows her to be fair and balanced, not abusing her effects on others. The effect on Sally is a sense of adoration and a desire on Sally's part to be like Mary.

With a more intense model, Suzanne Madeley, a life-coach and management trainer, describes her relationship with her own coach. Having discussed her coach's special ability to know what Suzanne is feeling before even she does, Suzanne then goes on to explain how it works:

> Suzanne: I do feel like I have a relationship with my coach.
>
> Elaine: What words would you use to describe that relationship?
>
> Suzanne: Erm. I would say that it's intimate in a strange kind of way. In that obviously she knows an awful lot about me. It's not face-to-face intimate... When I first saw her again... I remember saying to her on the phone 'I feel a bit strange. It feels like a blind date. Like we've been chatting on the phone but we don't really know each other face-to-face. I'm not sure how to be'. So there's that. So there's an intimacy I think the phone affords you even more so than face-to-face... It's very, I feel, very, it's very affirming, kind of loving almost. She does make me believe that I can have what I want... It really feels like she's mine. She is the way she is, for me.

In this model of charisma, Suzanne presents her relationship as an intense homoerotic bond. Like many contemporary models of intimacy, Suzanne sees self-disclosure and recognition as what creates the bond as her intimacy with her self brings intimacy with her coach (Jamieson, 1998; Giddens, 1991, 1992). The strength of Suzanne's feeling is conjured up by the repetition of the word intimacy, and in that she is not sure how exactly to define it. Unlike Sally, who desires to be like her therapist, Suzanne describes an erotic pleasure based on a desire to possess her coach.

Summary

As discussed at the start of this chapter, critics such as Rose are concerned about the power that therapeutic expertise gives practitioners over clients. Charisma is conceptualised in opposition to notions of expertise as defined by Rose in relation to therapeutic cultures. It is not seen to be simply about psychological authority, or scientific techniques. In some contexts, charisma may be seen as a dangerous form of power. It is sometimes seen to disempower, or overpower 'convertees' because of its irrational or magical nature and due to the devotion that is given to the charismatic individual in return. These examples from my interviews show that the use of charismatic power is seen not as something that leads to abuse but as something that has its place in bringing about equality. Charisma enables practitioners to present themselves as bringing benefits and special abilities to the relationship which empower the clients without them being seen as deliberately distant, superior or different, as might be the case with experts and expertise. In Jane Vincent's case, charisma is in a form which can be dispersed from her body through to others in a purposeful, directed way. For Dennis Fournier and Jade Simon, their charisma brings special transformations to their clients which would not otherwise be available. In these examples, the charisma of being a good practitioner is not dispersed but instead the charisma of being better selves like the practitioners is. In Sally and Suzanne's examples, the charismatic encounter elicits awe and adoration which are seen by Weber as typical responses to charismatic individuals, and for Sally and Suzanne, bring transformational effects in and of themselves, along with the techniques being used by the practitioners.

Although the practitioners discuss the achievement of equality in their clients through charisma, this does not mean that practitioners do not at the same time present themselves as having special powers, such as the power to convert and the power to heal. However, some practitioners refuse self-promotion and suggest that it is their clients who mark their power as special, not them. Charisma also enables a way for practitioners to talk about the non-rational in their work, getting around the difficulty of defining what they do and the effects it has, meaning that instantaneous, radical transformations can be explained. It alludes to their having access to things outside of rationality, almost unspeakable and transcendent aspects of life. To conclude, the mobilisation of charisma allows the practitioners to legitimatise their authority, marking them out as special in the eyes of others, but it also enables them to present their relations as equalising.

Conclusion

In the introduction to this chapter, questions were raised about how practitioners see their power, expertise and relations in personal development. It was argued that relatively few sociological accounts of therapeutic cultures detail the different conceptualisations practitioners have of their power relations and the meanings of these. Assumptions are made that their expertise is based predominantly on 'scientific' knowledge and that this form of expertise is central to their authority. In relation to power, for many critics, there is always an imbalance of power in the practitioners' favour. Although mention is made of the variety of the types of relations between practitioner and client, as in the work of Nikolas Rose (1989, 1996a), these relations are not particularised, meaning that we do not know how they operate. In contrast, the practitioners present highly detailed, complex and contradictory models of their relations. They see their authority coming from a number of sources: personal experience, their success, their exemplarity, special qualities and skills, and proof. This does not mean that they do not allude to scientific knowledge, techniques or efficacy but that these are seen as secondary and used in tandem with the other sources indicated above.

Their power is evidenced in a number of ways. For some practitioners it takes the form of the power to convert, for others it is encapsulated in a fantasy of the effects they can have on millions and others in the form of charismatic effects. For others, it is confirmed by the ability to go 'deep' into the client, whilst for many it is the ability to transform clients whilst not going deep.

There is also differentiation between the practitioners in the ways they understand their relations with their clients. The nature of the relations is derived from their knowing where the client's object of desire is, and how s/he can access it. In some examples, the practitioner embodies the object of desire. In others s/he can show the client where it is. In some models the client has to go via the practitioner in order to get it. In others, the practitioner holds up a kind of mirror to show the client that it is inside of them. In order to access their object of desire, the client will be expected to do particular things. So some practitioners such as Andy Knight and Jade Simon see themselves in possession of what the client needs. And for both of them the object of their desire can be quite easily and painlessly transferred to the client if they convert. To get to where you want to be you have to go via Jade Simon because she has what you want. She does not see herself on the same level as her clients but sees herself as empowering them. In her model, the client does not need to be shaped at any depth nor develop any self-knowledge, as all they need is what she has. In opposition to this, for Richard Brown, the object of desire lies outside of the client and any attempt by the practitioner to share his or her own solutions will influence the client's sense of ideal self. Whereas for Annette Dobson, neither the practitioner nor the client has the object of desire, as it is always out of reach of both. However, this is the source of community. A key part of Annette Dobson's model is that the practitioner does not impose her will on her clients in any way.

These models also bring with them different notions of how the practitioners see their identities. In Jade Simon's model, she sees herself as a role model of a 'sorted out' person but the relation is one of enablement. Whereas in Jack Routledge's model, the ideal practitioner is an exemplar of a free spirit, encouraging authenticity through non-comformism and spontaneity. The relation here is one of traumatisation in which you can only get what you want if the intervention by the practitioner goes deep and shapes your will. In quite the opposite case, Annette Dobson does not see herself as a role model and refuses any claims to special powers or expertise, seeing herself as an ordinary layperson, with whom clients can identify from a position of emotional equality. In Annette Dobson's model, the relation is one of mutual identification based on an aspiration to emotional quality and recognition. In a model that contradicts the idea of the practitioner as layperson, Andy Knight, Jane Vincent and Dennis Fournier imagine that they have special powers, which enable them to shape others but without the domination seen in Jack Routledge's model.

The gift

Given all of this, how can we understand the practitioners' accounts in a way which gets at the symbolic value of the exchanges and the ways that these help them produce a sense of self? One answer would be to draw upon the anthropological model of the gift as an analogy for their relations, as it involves the production and transformation of identities (Mauss, 1990; Godelier, 1996). The model of the gift has been used in the context of voluntary sector counselling by Liz Bondi and Judith Fewell (2003) and AA counselling by Jacques Godbout and Alain Caille (1998) and Lewis Hyde (1999). My use of this model in the context of personal development builds on this work as a way of understanding power and authority, and in particular, charisma in the practitioners' accounts. A brief overview will be given here before discussing its main themes in the light of the interviews.

The classical model of the gift is described by Marcel Mauss (1990). Its basic structure involves three stages: the giving of a gift, the receiving of the gift, and the repaying back of the gift. The gift can take many forms, such as jewellery, rituals, women and children, as in Mauss' anthropological work, or blood donation (Titmuss, 1971), care (Fox, 1993), or the support given to alcoholics by the AA (Hyde, 1999), in more contemporary accounts. In my material, the gifts included the gifts of 'empowerment', 'recognition', 'renovation', 'betterment', 'love', and 'equality'.

So why do people give gifts? In essence for Mauss (1990), the donor gets two kinds of return: the first being an improved status and the second, a countergift. The improved status comes with the way donors acquire power, initiate relationships, create new identities for themselves and the donee, forge alliances and get to attribute rights and duties (Berking, 1999). In relation to the practitioners interviewed for this research, Andy Knight helps several needy clients and in return takes on the identity of philanthropist, constructing himself as a true professional in comparison to others who charge for their services. For Jade Simon, writing self-help books and articles in magazines enables her to give her tips to what she imagines are millions of readers. This allows her to see herself as having great power, but also as using this for benevolent ends.

The gift also imbricates the recipient in giving in return. The gift also imparts prestige on the recipient, as well as the donor, but consequently obligates her/him to reciprocate the gift in some way, shape or form (Mauss, 1990). This does not mean that the donor can demand or require a return, although they may unconsciously or consciously want one (Testart, 1998). Instead, the obligation to return the gift is freighted into its structure. The gift exchange sets up social ties between the giver and recipient in which the gift-giver is seen to gain the upper hand through their act of giving. Until the gift is returned in some way, the recipient is burdened with a sense of inferiority as there is seen to be a lack of equilibrium in the distribution in duties and rights (Berking, 1999).Thus, Jacques Godbout and Alain Caille (1998) suggest that instead of seeing the gift as a straight line or arrow, we should instead imagine it as a boomerang.

The counter-gift can take many forms. It may be material in nature, but can also take the form of recognition, acknowledgement, compliance, docility, and status-giving (Fox, 1993). In this view, gift-giving is intrinsically unequal. It embodies asymmetrical power relations and this is why it can be seen as an act of generosity but also an act of violence (Mauss, 1990). The gift then has its dark side (Godbout and Caille, 1998). In the context of personal development, one of these could be seen as the fee between practitioners and clients. Lewis Hyde (1999) suggests that even when fees are paid to therapists, the 'spirit' of the gift can rise about the financial exchange.

The structure of the countergift fits with many of the examples given in this research. To accept the gift is to accept the terms of the gift. By accepting the practitioner's gift with its promise of equality, clients are expected to take on new selves. To accept the gift is to accept a new self, or a healed self. Embedded in the notion of what we could call the 'equalising gift' is the wish of the practitioner that the client be transformed (Fox, 1993). This means that the return gift may involve some kind of labour of self-transformation. So for example, whilst Jade Simon transfers tips to her clients, she expects that they will do their bit in using the tips to transform. They are obligated to change. In his account of the power trips of some group therapists, Jack Routledge sees ego trips as a form of 'gift of authenticity' that bestows equality, and in return the practitioner needs recognition. In Andy's model, in return for the 'gift of conversion', the headteacher returns with admiration and also passing on the gifts to other through her work as a convert. The practitioners interviewed do not simply see their gifts as self-sacrifice, but as based on the returns they derived from giving. For example, Jane Vincent talks with great intensity about the rewards she derives from running a growth group. In her case, she receives a 'gift of recognition' in return, which enables her to produce a new self. The gift exchange is two-way in its production of new identities.

There are exceptions to this model of the gift in the practitioners' accounts. For Annette Dobson, there is no gap between those who give and those who receive. She refuses claims of superiority, and in so doing her gift to her clients does not create differentiated relations.

As with accounts of people in the AA, the gift is seen to be exchanged between equals (Godbout and Caille, 1998). In her case, the gift is a 'gift of identification', providing the means to build community.

The analogy of the gift allows us to understand practitioners' relations in fresh ways. It brings together some of the critics' concerns about the power of practitioners, together with the conceptualisations of practitioners and their genuine belief in their ability to change people for the better. By drawing on the model of the gift, we can move beyond simply seeing practitioners' relations with their clients in terms of market exchange, and to build on Rose's (1989, 1996a) view that therapeutic practices enable practitioners to claim to be 'doing good'. Although the practitioners interviewed do not conceptualise their practice in terms of economic rewards or fees in these interviews, one practitioner, Suzanne Madeley, when talking about herself as a client did, because it meant that she had to perform what she saw as the usual emotional labour involved in personal relations: 'I didn't want to feel obliged to her. That very clearly is what I get from counselling, is that I don't owe them anything. So if you went and did an hour of listening to me about something, then we bank it in some way. It's not conditional...I would have said "How are you?" And sometimes I think "No. I need to take, totally take here, and not have to give anything"'. Relatedly, Wendy Simonds (1992) argues that one of the reasons women enjoy self-help books is that they encourage them to take a relation of care to themselves. By attending to the specifics of the practitioners' accounts, we are able to develop our understanding of the different ways in which doing good is seen. It enables us to see the practitioners as being both self-interested and generous, as self-aggrandising and enriching of others.

In spite of the differences in these models, there is an understanding of what I would term 'charismatic exchange', in which the key gift across these different relations is 'charisma' itself. In the idea of charismatic exchange, the special qualities of the practitioners are imagined to be dispersed in ways which bring equality to the clients. The gift of charisma enables the client to overcome problems, be empowered, take action, make changes, become transformed after contact with the practitioners. In return, the practitioners have their charisma validated. There are, though, different versions of charismatic exchange operating here. Annette Dobson, for example, may fit this description, in spite of her denial of her being 'sorted out'. Charisma is positioned outside of traditional expertise and this form of expertise is something which Annette herself refuses. It is this refusal of expertise combined with the extent of her fame which 'charismatise' her, enabling her to be the one who offers herself as a 'gift of identification'. In Jade Simon's model of charismatic exchange, 'bits' of herself are passed along to the client, charismatising them, enabling them to better themselves. For Richard Brown, and Peter Pope, the charismatic exchange involves the practitioner in withholding their own charisma, not imposing their own versions of the world on their clients, and in so doing, bestowing the 'gift of empowerment' on their client, allowing the client's own charisma to come through.

One of the reasons for this might be the interface with the workplace in which practitioners work. Unlike therapists operating on behalf of the state, these practitioners operate in the private sector on freelance contracts, often working with people with more institutional and financial power. Practitioners are also likely to be sensitive to critical conceptions of their practices and to their lack of perceived accredited body of knowledge, or in Weber's terms, rational authority. By drawing upon charismatic authority, they hint at something bigger, something powerful, and transcendental and to which they can give access. Instead of professional knowledge or vocational qualifications, they have charisma which gives them a 'state of grace' (Giddens, 1994: 89). This affords them a status that is portable across several social spheres rather than being tied to certain contexts like other forms of expertise that come with the division of labour.

6
Transformations of the Self

The previous chapter examined the ways in which personal development workers discussed their relationships with their clients. In particular, it examined how they imagined their power relations with their clients and the nature of their expertise in relation to their clients. This chapter turns to the theme of transforming the self.

Revealing, revamping and making-over the self

> With personal development work, people become more authentic. So people are more themselves, and don't need to put up a screen.
>
> Sally Thompson, Gestalt therapist and organisational consultant

> I don't think there is such a thing as a false self... It's expanding their choice and options. So there's no false self. There's just limited awareness and the options we have at any one time... It's not false, it's out of date. So they just come for an upgrade. My job is to create an upgrade of their life that is structured in such a way – if I use that computer metaphor – that it will have an inbuilt self-updating ability.
>
> Dennis Fournier, NLP practitioner and counsellor

These two quotes taken from my interviews with Sally Thompson and Dennis Fournier illustrate the different ways in which personal development workers understand the self and its transformation in their practices. Sally draws upon a complex notion of development not as a transformation to a new self but a return to the true self. Drawing upon a popular model of the hidden self as the more authentic self, for Sally transformation is a form of unmasking of a self, which has some unity over time. In contrast to Sally, Dennis explicitly mobilises a computer analogy to present the self as something that should not be constant but needs to be always changing and improving itself. In his model, transformation is understood as a 'revamping' process. This involves him in implanting a mechanism into the client so that their self can keep up with the times.

'Confess self'

These contrasting examples of the self and its transformation in personal development approaches raise questions about the way that some critics have presented the 'self' and its transformation in therapeutic cultures. For Rose, and others, the ideal self of therapeutic cultures is the model of the 'enterprising self', and its main technique of transformation, the 'confession' in its various guises across many different social and cultural spheres including the workplace and television. In this vein, Liz Stanley has described the self-expressive imperative of modernity as 'speak self, confess self, make self' (2000: 43). Workplace examples include Jo Brewis' (1996) account of the confession in management education, and the way a struggle by an individual in telling their story renders it more valid and honest and Barbara Townley (1994, 1995) on confession practices in human resource management in the workplace.

The confession is structured by a process of the renouncing of the past self to bring forth the new self. For some commentators, the confession has been replaced by testimony as the transformational technique of therapeutic cultures. In contrast to the confession, the testimony involves an affirmation of the self that has come through.

'You too!'

The other main transformatory technique referred to by writers on therapeutic cultures is the 'makeover' (Cameron, 1995; Simonds, 1992, 1996). The makeover is structured differently to the confession, around a narrative of 'before' and 'after' in which the gap between the two is extreme but closed almost instantly. In a discussion of the extension of makeovers to television, Rachel Mosley (2000) suggests it also has an element of 'Look! You can do this too!' – a sense of the accessibility and achievability of its 'after' for everyone. The makeover suggests a qualitative break with the past self, or parts of the past self, as this past self is seen as deficient or defective in some way.

Questions

In terms of techniques of transformation, how central is the 'confession' to personal development? Are there other techniques in operation that are less discussed by critics? What are the defining features that confirm that the change has taken place? Is it seen as easy to bring about? Is transformation incremental, a breakthrough or a 'big bang'? The 'makeover' produces questions about how the gap between ideal and self are closed. If the old self is replaced by a new self, then what happens to the old self? What parts of the self are seen as in need of the 'makeover', and how would these parts be integrated with the existent self? How is the new self seen to be an 'improvement' on the old self?

The actual forms of transformation techniques are under-examined in the literature on therapeutic cultures. An exception to this is Kenneth Plummer (1995) who examines the structures of the recovery story, suggesting it is made up of a staged template consisting of the journey, suffering, secrets, contest, transformation and coming home. Does this structure apply to the way the personal development workers interviewed describe transformation?

Teleologies

Therapeutic cultures also draw upon the metaphors of cure, healing, and growth. Each of these brings with it different temporalities and teleologies: cure and healing suggest a return to a former improved state; growth, the unfurling of the self from its nuclear state to a wiser, more able self, or the metamorphosis of the self into something very different, but much better. The term 'personal development' appears to reproduce a Darwinian sense of ongoing evolution, in which transformation proceeds 'gradually, cumulatively, and irreversibly, through a kind of unfolding of internal potentiality' (Nisbet, 1969: 3). In this way, it seems to contain a 'telos in which the process culminates' (Freeman, 1993). Is this how the personal development workers conceptualise development? If so, what is the direction, or the endpoint of personal development? Another key metaphor of self-improvement in contemporary cultures is that of the journey. This is seen to involve the accumulation of the self as it faces obstacles. These various models point to different kinds of temporality and in particular the nature of the past and its influence on the present and future self. They also raise questions about whether it is believed that you become someone new or who you are (Stacey, 1997). In this vein, I want to argue that the transformation techniques described by critics have particular forms, which give rise to particular understandings of the self, its relations to the past and future, and its ideal endpoints. So are these the same as those used by the personal development workers, and if so, what meanings do they have for the personal development workers?

In beginning to address these questions, this chapter now moves on to examine the accounts of the personal development workers interviewed, and first, investigates the theme of authentic change. This is a useful place to start because critics and personal development workers both worry about the authenticity of self-transformation in therapeutic cultures, but the personal development workers' concerns are based on different issues from those of most critics.

The real thing

Much of the critical literature on therapeutic cultures is concerned with the inauthenticity and inadequacy of transformation in therapeutic cultures. Underpinning critics' anxiety is a model of therapeutic transformation as a mass production line in which people are individuated but de-individualised. Ian Craib refers to some therapeutic processes as the 'cutting out of gingerbread people' (1994: 1). For many of these critics, these ideals programme the future self and its future too closely. Sidonie Smith and Julia Watson (1996) argue that current contemporary culture encourages a commodification of self-authentication and an imperative to find the true self whilst fetishing 'touristic identities' or 'throwaways' (1996: 6). In this section, I look at how personal development workers see the true self, authentic transformation and 'touristic identities'. How do the personal development workers conceptualise transformation? Which forms of transformation are seen as more legitimate? Do personal development workers worry about the 'throwaway' or the mass-produced self?

Heroic epics

I start with a quote from Jude Britton, a well-known Gestalt therapist, author and Gestalt therapy lecturer, because she outlines a model of transformation which is representative of understandings of transformation in the personal development workers' accounts. In this excerpt, she is recounting how she transformed from being a client into becoming a practitioner.

> But the net effect was that if you could stand the heat, you got an amazing training in that part-time course. And I could stand the

> heat. A number of us could. Jack Routledge... all sorts of people went through that and emerged battle weary...

Jude Britton's example is reminiscent of heroic epics, with her mobilisation of imagery like 'heat' and 'battle'. It is representative of a common theme in personal development workers' accounts of self-transformation through trial. Transformation is only achieved by people who are seen to be heroic enough to be put through their paces, take some punishment but come through. In this model, the successful transforming of the self means that it is already in them to survive. But what they need is to be tested to the limit for this better quality to emerge. This is a self, which is reminiscent of Anne Cronin's discussion (2000a, 2000b) of potential as something, which both pre-exists this moment of transformation, and at the same time, is in need of development. In this example, the transformed self can claim to have transformed through retrospectively acknowledging that she stayed the same, in spite of duress.

Real selves

In a similar reference to suffering, but again drawing upon a model with complex notions of the self, Jack Routledge explains how therapy offers different transformatory possibilities from other practices:

> Elaine: How do you characterise therapy as compared to aromatherapy and other alternatives?
>
> Jack: I think in this field, and in so many fields, there is a left-hand path and a right-hand path. If you want change, if you want really to change your personality and character, you have to deal with all the things that you are. You have to wrestle with all the things that you think are problems. You have to really go into the shit and be prepared to get dirty and be prepared for pain, to work through that pain and come out on the other side. Whereas the right-hand path says if you get down amongst that stuff, you stay with that forever, so we have to rise above it. You have to fix your mind on what is good, what is true, what is fine, what is to be admired, model yourself on that. Don't give any energy to all these negative things, painful things. Simply withdraw your energy from those and put it into all what counts, what is highly desirable, what you really believe in your heart that you should be focusing on... and this left

> path, and right path, as it were are very prevalent in all kinds of different fields. It's a permanent tension and is a permanent tension inside a lot of people. I know a lot of people who say to me I don't know whether I should do therapy and go off into groups or whether I should try meditation and rise above it.

For Jack there are two models of self-transformation, both with religious undertones, which underscore their significance and 'big picture' nature. The models are: suffer to redeem your self, or model yourself on spiritual ideals. In the first, therapeutic change involves an intense struggle, a dark night of the soul, reminiscent of repentance, in which you have to face up to who you really are before you can change who you are. In this model the bits of the self that are hidden and degenerate are your 'real' self. As with Judaeo-Christian models of redemption, suffering provides the means with which to overcome fallenness, and the self-deception involved in denying the self's flaws. Lauren Berlant writes on the way pain is seen to produce clarity, and suffering a sense of 'having lived a life' in testimonial cultures (2001b: 133). In order to enable self-transformation, there has to be a remembering of and a rapprochement with the 'real' fallen self in order to stop it falling apart. In his allusion to going through shit, Jack suggests that we are forged out of our bad experiences, and in particular, past experiences of which we are ashamed. Jack's real self does not fit with James Nolan's (1998) idea of the emancipated self as naturally good and innocent, as outlined in Chapter 3.

In Jack's second model, transformation of the self involves forgetting the 'real' self, and identifying instead with moral ideals external to the self, but ratified by an inner true self. In this model, the future self is not to be found inside of the self, but outside of the self. The ideals mentioned by Jack seem more in line with traditional Western morality than the enterprising self that Rose and others suggest populate therapeutic cultures. To continue with Jack's discussion:

> Elaine: What's your answer?
>
> Jack: You really want to have both. The image I have is of a spiral staircase, on a mirrored floor. So that every step upwards on the staircase is a step downwards in its reflection. So the more primal work you do, the more it frees you up for spiritual exploration, the more spiritual exploration you do, the more ready it makes you to deal with your primal stuff. So I think they go very well together,

> they're not either/or. It's more of a case of adjusting to the whole range of who you are as a human being: you have the heights and depths. If you just go for the heights, you're not a whole human being. And if you just go for the depths, you're not a whole human being. You want to extend both.

More human

For Jack, personal development is about becoming more human. For him, being human involves perfection and imperfection, as he reproduces a popular model of humans as both animalistic and impulsive, and rational and civilised. It involves braving the 'real' fallen self and clearing out some of the self's history – to make more room for creating the future self. As the present self becomes more like the future self, then more of the real abject self can be uncovered. The larger the distance created between the abject real self and the future self of ideals, the more authentically human we become. Becoming properly human also means extending what a human is. Although Jack draws upon a trope of self-improvement as movement, this does not involve a straightforward linear stepping forward, but an ongoing shuttling back and forth, between suffering and idealism. Jack's model also echoes the Romantic progress narrative, which consisted of strife and suffering so Romantics could be seen as experiencing conflict and alienation, crisis, despair, and dejection, making them appear more complex and successful (Kirschner, 1996).

In a discussion on psychoanalysis, Roy Schafer (1980) argues that the key narrative in Freudian psychoanalysis is an ancient story of suffering, defeat and triumph. In essence, for him, the psychoanalytic story is of a child who is like a beast that becomes domesticated but is always contained within the self. The story involves a lifelong transition from fear and irrationality, lack of self-definition and instincts and drives to stability, mastery, adaptability, rationality, self-definition. The models of authentic transformation suggested by Jack draw upon the trope of suffering but do not reproduce the progressive narrative suggested by Schafer in which the shameful part of the self is domesticated or hidden away.

Commitment

In this next example, Peter Pope distinguishes between authentic transformation and more superficial transformation in different terms:

> Elaine: Now it seems that there is an increase in terms of professionalism, would you say that is accurate?

> Peter: I think it is accurate. I think it is not as positive as all that because I think that one of the things I note is that for all of its faults that middle period – 70s and 80s – people were willing to risk themselves, were willing to put themselves on the line. People wanted to grow. And we are now getting some people who are doing the training, who want to go through the motions, and want to end up with a Masters, and have fun doing it, but unwilling to commit themselves to what is personally quite demanding.

Like Jack Routledge and Jude Britton, Peter suggests that authentic change comes with challenge. But for Peter this is less about suffering and more about bravery. Growth is not, in this example, the natural evolution of the self, but something that takes courage. As with Jude, the self is transformed through testing itself but in Peter's example, a key transformatory moment is the person demonstrating that they are willing to take risks with themselves. This is not a model of an essentialist self unfurling. It is a model in which the self is willing to take risks, acts as a core self, and through this process, can lose some other parts of itself or gain new parts through therapeutic practices in order improve itself. For Peter, commitment is needed for authentic transformation and is shown through submitting oneself willingly to dangers.

Journey to the centre of self

In a different model of danger, Violette Turner explains how the technique of psychodrama works:

> You will be given the beginning, the middle and the end. You will be going from the periphery to the core, and then back to the periphery. And it is taking the person on a journey into depth, and then bringing them out again... they dip into the depths and then they go out into the world again. There is a bit, when you are a protagonist, when you start at the beginning, and come all the way round and then come back to the beginning. It is quite possible that you have no awareness of where you have been... It has been likened to a bit of a trance state... You can be doing all these things but at the end of it, it is possible not to remember except that you take it in because it is a journey and progression.

Like Jack Routledge and Peter Pope, Violette sees psychodrama as a potentially dangerous journey. However, Violette's model involves a journey in which a return is made back to the beginning, rather than to a different ending. Rather than working its way through the depths and coming out at the other side, as in Jack's model, the self dips in and out of the depths. These aspects do not mean that progression has not been made but that the self cannot give an account of its journey and has no memory of the journey. Up to now, all the techniques and processes for transforming the self have implied a self that is conscious as it is being transformed or transforming itself. But in this model, Violette invokes spatial metaphors, not like Jack who used heights and depth to convey different moral parts of humanity, but images of depth, centre and margins to describe the unconscious and the relation of the conscious to the unconscious. She also draws upon metaphors of movement to represent the way the self intrudes into the unconscious rather than the other way around. This is a model of growth as 'retardation' according to Paul Ricoeur (1980) drawing upon the myth of Ulysses in which the temporal return of Ulysses to himself is supported by Ulysses' geographical return to his birthplace. Ricoeur cites an account of Ulysses as a 'trapped voyager' by Mircea Eliade who says:

> I think that the myth of Ulysses is very important for us. We will all be a little like Ulysses, for in searching, in hoping to arrive, and finally, without a doubt, in finding once again the homeland, the hearth, we find ourselves. But, as in the Labyrinth, in every questionable turn, one risks 'losing oneself'. If one succeeds in getting out of the labyrinth, in finding one's home again, then one becomes a new being. (1980: 11)

As with Jack, this movement in this quote is a shuttling to and fro rather than the uni-directional upward curve of the progress narrative (Stacey, 1997).

Deep selves

In a different view of how authentic transformation is achieved, Annette talks about how senior women managers who come onto her training courses are not properly transformed:

> They are not coming in and feeling confident. And they have done three or four assertiveness courses, but it hasn't, nothing has actually got to this point at which – they usually have done no role-play whatsoever – and it's just amazing. They don't call it assertiveness

> training, they call it personal development. It's the same stuff. But you know there are so many changes at a superficial level – it just hasn't got through.

For Annette, authentic change is not about suffering or bravery but the effectiveness of therapeutic technique in reaching and transforming an inner self. Like other personal development workers, Annette draws spatial metaphors to denote depth and interiority, specifically referring to an idea of the self as layered, in which the further into the interior self you go, the more meaningful the change will be. In contrast to Jude and Peter, for whom part of the inner self remains constant, in Annette's model, it is the inner self, which needs to be transformed.

Quick fixes

In this next quote, Jade Simon offers a model of transformation, which differs from the view of authentic change put forward so far. In this quote, she is discussing how she changed her mind about personal development having to be a lengthy process:

> People can't afford as much often, so they want, there is also the fact that people want quick fixes now and I resisted that. I didn't believe it for very many years, wouldn't believe it, because really, I told you I spent sort of 20 years training and 20 years getting myself together probably as well. So it didn't feel like you could have quick fixes, but I don't believe that any more, and I think there is an awful lot that we can do to help people and to give them something very immediate to try to change. That's very empowering for them, if they can change very quickly an aspect of their behaviour or feelings. And that means they can make a change in their life.

The quick fix has been seriously condemned by critics, who compare it to 'McDonaldised fast food' (See Ian Craib (1994, 1998); Kenneth Plummer (1995) and Simon Williams (2000, 2001) for what they see as the McDonaldised selves of therapeutic cultures. Their concerns are that speed of solution and standardisation of the solution lead to superficial or morally bankrupt changes to the self. In contrast, for Jade Simon, the quick fix and its speed is what capacitates clients, passing them the power to transform themselves. Clients, in this view, do not transform themselves through bravery or suffering, or through understanding themselves but through the recognition that they can act upon themselves to transform themselves.

The quick fix works with a model of self-transformation in which the core self remains constant but parts of it are patched up. The success of the patching up sets in motion further more radical transformations. Some things are seen as more complex to transform. Behaviours and feelings are seen as personal properties and closer to the self, therefore more amenable to speedier transformation. Changing feelings and changing life are viewed as matters of scale and time rather than requiring different approaches. The quick fix then is a similar model to the makeover in that it works with a similar model of speed, but in the quick fix the contrast, or distance, between the 'before' and 'after' states is not so big. In contrast to critics who see the quick fix as insubstantial and superficial, for Jade, it enables clients to tackle other more demanding changes. In this model, Jade's understanding of the self fits with humanist ideas in which the self is seen as both innate and a project to be achieved, both fixed and mutable, both essential and constructed (Cronin 2000a, 2000b; Lawler 2000).

Suzanne Madeley

With a similar perspective on low-key change, Suzanne discusses her own experience of being counselled:

> It just really appealed to me to be able to get a short fix. Something that helped now, quickly... I knew that I desperately needed to move forward and I felt that [counselling] was the way of moving forward. I trusted her to help me move forward, move on a bit. So I didn't just want to talk about it: I needed to just move on... I needed something really pragmatic.

For Suzanne, the duration and the lack of intensity in her counselling do not negate the authenticity of her transformation. This is because unlike other models above, she draws upon a model of transformation in which a small adjustment is seen to be progress. In Suzanne's model transformation is not like the makeover, but is an incrementalist project. Mobilising a popular model in which movement signifies progress, Suzanne sees a small first step as very significant because it starts the momentum of larger transformation.

Speedy change

With a similar positive view of speedy transformation, Andy Knight explains in this quote how he was influenced to take up the practice of

NLP. Explaining that it was due to a friend who had studied NLP working with his children, Andy continues:

> He actually came to my house to do some work on spelling strategies with my two youngest sons who are both dyslexic... My wife was very sceptical, sat there with kind of arms folded and 'go on then, do this'. And after an hour, he had got them spelling all the words they couldn't think of before, backwards, forwards. And it has remained with them ever since, and he passed on that technique to us.

Like Jade Simon's model of the quick fix, for Andy, the transformation comes instantly with an almost miraculous quality, and without the pain of Jack Routledge and Jude Britton's models. Although the speed of transformation is quick as in Jade Simon's model, the gap between 'before' and 'after' is larger, suggesting a 'makeover' model. In Andy's model, the transformation is not self-achieved but put into the client by the practitioner through technique. As in many makeovers on television, the expert passes on their technique.

In a similar vein, Jane Vincent presents a makeover model in her answer to my asking which clients growth groups work best for:

> My genuine belief is that it works for everybody for where they are in their lives. The most profound shifts are for those that have never had it, because it is the biggest shock, because the lights really go on, when you know nothing and you suddenly go into this world with all this stuff... As I say, the most profound shifts are the less you have done, the bigger the explosion, the less you have done in this work, in this field... I look at my mum and dad; they are very salt of the earth, very working-class people. They can't really remember the course very much but they know how to say, 'I love you'. And they will giggle about it and my mother, who is a very prissy, prim little lady learnt to say, 'fuck'.

Jane Vincent uses words like 'shock' and 'explosion' to suggest the intensity of the makeover transformation. Jane Vincent's version contrasts with Jade's quick fix model in that the transformation achieved is much more profound. It is more consistent with Andy's model of the makeover in its sudden transformation and the degree of difference between the self before and the self after. This is evidenced by Jane Vincent's representation of her mother moving from being a prudish non-curser to using the word 'fuck', popularly seen as the most extreme form of swearing. The swearing and the use of 'I love you' not only demonstrate that tranformation has taken place but also exemplify particular ideal selves. In Jane Vincent's account, the ideal transformed self is from an inhibited constrained self to a more spontaneous, emotionally expressive and therefore, liberated self.

Small changes

In marked contrast to the models of acute authentic transformation, Violette Turner offers a different version of transformation. In this excerpt, Violette has been discussing the role of the therapist in psychodrama who acts like the director of a play:

> Elaine: So as it is going along, you are interacting as the director, asking questions of the protagonist?
>
> Violette: Yeah, with the aim... with the aim of sort of the protagonist maybe shifting a little cog at the end of it, so that they come away with a slightly different perception.

Drawing upon a metaphor of the self as machine, Violette sees transformation as much lower key, but one in which small changes can set larger changes in motion. For Violette, successful transformation means that people start seeing things differently, rather than doing things differently. But this change in how they see things will lead to people behaving in different ways. This model is based on the idea that people's view of themselves or the world affects what they do and who they are. The self-to-be is not a renunciation of the self that is, but a re-angling of the self that is so that its actions will be improved as a result.

In a similar train, Dennis Fournier also stresses the importance of the client's perceptions:

> If people don't notice they've changed it's as if they haven't... It's as if the change itself doesn't matter. But the realisation of the change does... It's wonderful, fabulous. Each step they are aware of progressing every time. And it's speeded up the progress no end...Even profound issues. I'm not forcing them to change. I'm giving them the means to change. And the means to notice they've changed.

Unlike the makeover model, in which the gap before and after is dramatic, and therefore obvious, for Dennis, clients can change without realising it. This type of unconscious change is meaningless for Dennis because of the client's lack of agency in relation to the change. Echoing Giddens' (1991, 1992) discussion of how therapeutic cultures install agency into habits, Dennis' ability to install consciousness into the client means that they can change whatever they want to.

Self experiments

In line with the idea of incremental but authentic transformation, several personal development workers talked about the idea of experimentation as a form of transformation. In this next quote, Jade Simon explains here how she uses experimentation with her clients:

> I see that with my clients and I tell them that 'you know I can't tell you it's going to work, let's try it, if it works, fine, if it doesn't, I have got a hunch it might, let's try, let's see'.

This model of transformation is based on trial and error and pragmatism in which the practitioner is not presented as an expert. The preparedness to experiment in the client is seen as the start of the transformational process. The end result is what justifies the means.

In a similar vein, Jude Britton also discusses experimentation in answering my question about whether Gestalt works better in groups or with individuals. Jude Britton comes at experimentation from a different angle from Jade Simon:

> And a lot of creative experiments work a hell of a lot better if you've got a larger setting. Just simple things like, 'try saying what you said to me to someone who you are a bit scared of, someone you feel very safe with'. You can't do that if there's just the two of you. But in a group that is incredibly possible for somebody to be able to play with some possible change just like that and it's in a laboratory situation. There's so much at stake if you're the therapist and you ask me to do that. It might mean that I've got to confess that I am scared of you or not scared of you or just be stuck into the thing we are such buddies that I'm not actually going to take any risks and say anything. It's more limited.

In Jude Britton's model, the client can experiment with different changes without committing to any of them, by trying on different emotional relations with her peers. Different futures can be tried on. In the group, the frame of experimentation means that the meaning of different emotional relations, whilst 'true', is seen to be temporary. Jude's use of the word 'laboratory' underscores how this practice is seen to be abstracted from 'real life', and yet offer help with real life.

Summary

This section has shown a diverse range of models, process and forms of transformation used by the personal development workers interviewed. There is a variety and complexity here, which is not represented in critics' accounts, in which one model, the confession, the testimony or the makeover is seen to stand in for all models of transformation in therapeutic cultures. To show this diversity, I argue there is a typology of models in operation. The first of these models is the 'suffering model' in which the self is seen to be transformed through undergoing some trial or ordeal. The nature of the suffering and its meaning varies with different versions of this model. In Jane Vincent's version, the self remains constant throughout the process of suffering, but is enhanced through its ability to transcend its suffering. In Jack Routledge's model, suffering takes the form of degradation, and an internal struggle with itself. For him a transformed self is one which can reconcile itself with its inner hellish self whilst at the same time identify with an external idealised self. In this model, the self is seen as innate and constructed. For Peter Pope, it is potential suffering in the form of fear that the self transcends and is transformed through its bravery in the face of risk. In all of these models, the 'growth' of the self is not seen as programmed or 'genetic' but something which is 'earned' through a contest of some kind.

My research reveals a second model of transformation, that of 'the makeover'. This offers a fantasy that the gap between the 'self that is' and the 'self to be', seen to be of great distance, can be instantly closed. In the makeover, the client is not imagined as accomplishing these transformations through suffering or hard work. Instead the practitioner is seen to close the gap through their own expertise, use of technique or some magical or charismatic means. Jane Vincent has several versions of the makeover: in one model, the new self is seen as more authentic than the old self and this is represented by markers of authenticity such as emotional expressiveness, and spontaneity (Dyer, 1991). In another model, the new self is seen as an awakening of what was lying dormant inside the old self. In a third model, Jane Vincent sees the makeover as enhancing her current self, imbuing it with refined qualities. In Andy Knight's model of the makeover, it is imagined that techniques put into the self from an expert produce the new self rather than the new self being innate, as for Jane Vincent.

The third model is that of the 'quick fix' described by Jade Simon and Suzanne Madeley. In their model, some aspect of the self is improved or replaced so that the small transformation sets in motion larger transformations that are needed by the self to move closer to its ideal. The transformation in this model is seen as a slow, incremental cumulative project, which is more in line with critical and popular understandings of development. In Dennis Fournier's model of the quick fix as 'updating', the self is seen as quickly getting out of date rather than being false.

Jade Simon and Jude Britton also present the 'experiment' model of transformation. Through the experiment, changes are seen to be achieved through a series of trial and error whereby the client tries out different therapeutic techniques and practices of the self and evaluates their effects. The 'experiment' differs from the 'quick fix' in that in the former it is not clear which changes are best to make or which end-point is being aimed for. In all of these models, a core self is imagined which then adds to itself through trying on new experiences or behaviours. This typology suggests that there is not simply one version of the self being prescribed as the ideal self in therapeutic cultures for the personal development workers interviewed. This next section takes the notion of the ideal self further and examines the desired endpoints imagined by the personal development workers in comparison with critics of therapeutic cultures.

The shape of things to come

For many critics of therapeutic cultures including Giddens (1991, 1992) and Rose (1989, 1996a), the reflexive and autonomous selves are seen to be the ideal endpoints of therapeutic approaches. This section examines whether this was the case for the personal development workers interviewed. If they conceptualise other models, what forms do they take? What are the endpoints seen to be? Does the self in therapeutic cultures renounce or disconnect from its previous self? Or does it involve uncovering, revealing a true self buried under layers of socialisation?

Good selves

This section begins with an excerpt from Jane Vincent because she draws upon a model of the self which is representative of the humanist self. In this quote she is discussing how she was transformed when she attended her first growth group:

> I suppose what happens is you know, here goes the thirty-year-old housewife, well I wasn't a housewife because I was a business

> woman. But I had never really looked at myself. I had never really heard my own thoughts. I had never really given my thoughts and my beliefs and my values much airtime. And I sat in the room and I listened to a trainer offer a whole lot of philosophies and approaches to life and values. And a whole lot of it rang true for me and I thought 'My God. I am okay. I do have these things'... And here was somebody voicing all the love that is in me, all the decency in me so it was the recognition, the reassurance, the confirmation of that who I was, was OK, was amazing. It was a very, very powerful experience. So the point I am trying to make is take an ordinary person off the street and it happens for most people, it is as if all the valuable bits get, come alive and get recognised.

In this model of change, Jane Vincent's true self is uncovered through identification with and recognition by another. Rather than revealing herself through the talking cure, she does so through listening to the trainer. Jane also draws upon a model of the self resonant with Nolan's (1998) model – the emancipated self in which the true self is good and innocent. Many critics are scathing about these kinds of 'untroublesome selves': see for example, Ian Craib (1994, 1998) and Wendy Simonds (1992, 1996). This good self can only be animated through recognition by another. It then involves a retrospective claiming by the individual that they had been that person all the time.

In this next quote, Jane Vincent expands on her model of the self as accomplished through transformation in growth groups:

> I don't know of any other training, framework, situation that could give me such a fantastic mirror to see myself, to become more aware and conscious and to make huge shifts in my life because that is what happens. It is a huge transformation, you know you shift, you don't change from an apple to an orange but the apple might become more juicier.

Jane Vincent's model suggests that she is drawing upon an essentialist view of the self. Drawing upon the natural image of the apple and the mirror as truth-teller to show that she was always her self, Jane presents transformation as becoming even more herself, a better version of her self rather than something new. Development in this example is not a gradual unfolding of the self over time but the instant releasing of what lay inherent. This transformation happens because Jane is awakened to the reality of her true self which was already inside of her.

Dennis Fournier

Drawing upon a similar model of the ideal self, Dennis Fournier explains how NLP works in relation to a particular client:

> He's not become someone else. He's become ever more himself than he's ever been before. Which is the right way. The surface behaviour is what they're not happy with. But under the surface is good and wonderful. And reconnecting with that good and wonderful means that they can shed that old persona that old pattern and let the real self emerge.

In this model, as in Jane Vincent's, the ideal self is already inside. Reproducing a common view that inside selves are much better versions of our selves than the current self being experienced on the outside, Dennis sees transformation as a repair. Using an allusion to the shedding of skins, for Dennis this transformation can only take place if the redundant self on the surface is no longer performed.

Risky selves

In this next example, Jane Vincent continues to explain about her experiences on the growth group and the effects it had on her:

> It was a very beautiful experience and sometimes I wish I could have that sense again but of course it wouldn't be because it is an experience that can never, I have forgotten the language. I am not being very eloquent today but the language, I, it was a first time experience and it could not be repeated because it was full of surprise elements. And I had this incredible radiance and energy for a good three years and I did some crazy things. I wouldn't be sitting here today if I hadn't done that course. I would probably be miserable, married, living in Cape Town and I have had a crazy life since then. I have taken enormous risks with my life and gone up and down like a yo-yo because I take risks and because I learnt on that course the possibilities and I had enormous amount of acknowledgement.

The self which Jane Vincent presents here does not fit easily with Giddens' notion of the reflexive self or Rose's idea of the autonomous self, with their connotations of self-surveillance and responsibility. This contrast is underlined by her repetitions of 'crazy' and 'risks'. Jane draws upon on religious conversion language in this excerpt to highlight the charisma her transformation brings to her and others. Jane's version of the ideal self is wild, passionate, seeking out new experiences, and living life to the full, and as with Jack's earlier model of the self, this involves highs and lows. This version of the self is more transgressive and impulsive than the calculating, rational, self-scrutinising model in Giddens' reflexive self and Rose's enterprising autonomous self.

At ease with the self

This next quote comes from Violette Turner who offers a different model of the self from Jane. She begins by responding to my asking which therapies have worked the best for her:

> Violette: I get confused because I have done so many different therapies; there are so many different theories about.
>
> Elaine: How do you make your way through that?... Different things give you different messages, how do you?
>
> Violette: I think the messages are the same, aren't they? It's all to do with autonomy in the end. Trying to find your true self. The self that you are happy with, who you can be at ease with, and like.

In contrast to Jane Vincent's model of highs and lows, Violette's version of the true self is seen to be true because it is undemanding. This version resonates with what Hilary Radner suggests in relation to self-help books that 'heterosexual romance' has become 'not only the model of all relationships between partners but the model of the relationship of the self to its "self"' in that Violette's ideal self is like some popular descriptions of partners (1995: 51). Unlike Rose's enterprising self, Violette's ideal is completed and content, rather than self-challenging and continuously transforming.

Open selves

Richard Brown's model of transformation also stands in opposition to the ideal models suggested by Rose and other critics:

> Richard: I find it hard to envisage genuine personal development that is amenable to a formula, and it is formulaic essentially.
>
> Elaine: What makes you say that, that being formulaic would get in the way?

> Richard: I think what is at the heart of why I say it can't be formulaic is that I think personal development is a creative process not a discovery process. I think personal development means creating yourself not discovering yourself. You know people talk the language of going on a voyage of personal discovery and as I say, I don't think I believe that. I think the formulaic is limited to ways of discovering, not ways of creating... I do think personal development is an artistic process not a scientific process. And I don't know of any great works of art that have been created from a formula and I think personal development should be a work of art not a work of science.

Unlike Jane and Dennis, for Richard, there is not an inner core self which needs remembering, uncovering or transforming. Richard sees personal development as a form of self-making, which is open-ended in its process, open-ended in its result. The idea of the individual as artist invokes a kind of 'romantic humanism' – 'humanist' in that individuals are seen to be able to master their own destiny rather than following and revealing God or Nature's blueprint, and 'romantic' in that it is imagination and creativity rather than logic and rationality, which create the self. In drawing upon a conceptualisation of the self as an artist and artwork, Richard invokes the idea of 'individuality' and 'uniqueness' that Charles Taylor (1989, 1991) sees as obligations for the self to demonstrate in order to be seen as properly distinctive and personal. The endpoint of Richard's self is less clear and rational than in the case of Rose's autonomous self. In Richard's model, the achievement of a particular ideal self is less important than the artistic open-ended process that invokes self-hood in and of itself.

Growing selves

In a similar vein, Sally Thompson doesn't think ideal endpoints for the self help it to transform. She begins by explaining how the practitioner must not set up these endpoints for the client:

> You've got to... reach a point where you can shed your desire to have an end goal for the client other than help them become more aware... People change when they become fully themselves. They change anyway. So the process of growth is: we grow. We're human; we grow all the time as we interact with the environment. We make

choices and we grow. We only stop ourselves growing because we're not aware of what we're doing... I'm never going to change if I say 'Right. This is what I am going to change'. The minute you set up goals like that you're setting up patterns of resistance.

Sally's model implies a genetic version of the self and its development. For Sally, the self has its own organic sense of momentum and endpoint that can be thrown out of kilter with too much reflexivity. In this model, growth is seen as a form of behaviourist learning but one in which all experiences will result in progression and development. Rather than seeing the self as an unfolding or a revealing, the self is an ongoing project of evolution.

Summary

This section has shown how personal development workers have opposing understandings of the self. In Jane Vincent's models, the better self is innate but hidden and awaiting discovery through it being recognised that it is there. Transformation in this case is a process of becoming who you really are and takes place in an instant. For both Jane Vincent and Dennis Fournier, the self is not cumulative over time but extensive, in that the self becomes more of itself. In Sally's model, the self is like a seed that will grow into itself over time if allowed to interact with the environment, be exposed to stimulating events and not be tampered with by the practitioner. Change is intrinsic to the self. Echoing Lois McNay's (2000) model of identity as continuous and yet dynamic, the self is seen as innate and constructed. For Violette, the ideal self is not a perfect self, but one that you can get along with, and is not developed over time, but found. In Richard's model of transformation, the self is seen as 'a work of art', the endpoint for the self is open-ended, and the transformed self is imagined to be unique and original, rather than pre-existing (Taylor, 1991). For Taylor (1991), this is a dominant model of the self in contemporary times, and yet in these interviews, it is only drawn upon by Richard Brown. According to this understanding of the self, the refusal of an endpoint is important since a truly transformational self is seen as the forger of its own horizons. These various models of transformation and ideal selves throw up different ideas about time, and temporality, and in this next section, these issues will be addressed in more depth, by examining the personal development workers' understandings of the operation of the past, present and the future in relation to the self.

Times of change

Notions of temporality are seen by many social theorists of the self to be central to therapeutic understandings of the self. For example, in psychoanalytic therapies, the past is seen to 'haunt' (Grosz, 1999) or 'drag on' (Boyarin, 1995) the present. The origins and solutions to problems in the present are seen to lie in the past, in particular in childhood. Both remembering that past and forgetting the past are seen to be central to therapeutic processes (Hacking, 1995). Drawing upon self-help books to examine therapeutic understandings of temporality, Giddens (1991, 1992) argues that the concept of 'self-actualisation', the idea that we can realise our potential, implies the control of time. So for example, in Giddens' view, the self-help books suggest that the present can be slowed down and changed through us being continuously reflexive in the present moment, and living life to the full. They also promote the idea, he argues, that this allows the future to be moulded as individuals ask 'How can I use this moment to change?' In this model, he suggests, the future is 'thought of as resonant with possibilities, yet not open to the full play of contingency' (1991: 77). He refers to this as a 'colonisation of the future', an attempt to shape future selves and future lives through setting up a particular chain of causality located in the self, in which the future unfurls from particular actions in the present. For Giddens then, the main focus in the self-help books is the focus on the future rather than the past.

However, the past is seen by Giddens to be amenable to transformation in therapeutic cultures. The model of the past presented in self-help books Giddens argues, is one in which it is seen as full of resources but also waste. These need to be sorted through, and classified to distinguish the building blocks, which will provide the desired future from the dead ends and dead weight. The self can become trapped by the past and held in stasis, frozen in time. By being stuck in the past, the self is seen to be inauthentic because it is controlled by past situations imposed on it, and therefore, inhibited from opening itself up to the future, and its possibilities. To achieve the ideal of autonomy, the self has to break free of past feelings and events. Through being more conscious of time, the individual can shape their lives rather than being the subject of habit or 'prisoners of events' (1991: 72). This may involve the individual in breaking with the past, habits, established patterns and undertaking 'novel courses of action' (1991: 73) and 'retrieving the past – a process of going back, and recapturing half-remembered or repressed childhood experiences – but only in order to release it' (Giddens, 1992: 102). This controlling of time allows us to subject more of life to decisions rather than being the outcomes of habits.

There are other authors who have written about temporality and different therapeutic cultures. So for example, using the case study of the AA, Eve Kosofsky Sedgwick (1994) points to a model of temporality and reflexivity which contrasts with Giddens' notion of the colonisation of the future. Sedgwick argues that the technique in the AA of focusing on 'one day at a time... severs every moment of choice (and of course they are infinite) from both the identity-history and the intention-futurity that might be thought to constrain it' (1994: 134). This is part of a more general cultural trend, for Sedgwick, to find the ever-receding space of 'pure voluntarity' (1994: 134).

Given these different understandings of temporality by writers on therapeutic cultures, how do personal development workers conceptualise time in their understanding of their practices? How important is the past in their view in determining the self, and how should it be dealt with? Is the future colonised in ways that Giddens suggests, or is it seen to be foreshortened as in Sedgwick's view? What are the relations between forgetting and remembering for these personal development workers?

Past selves

I start with an example from Andy Knight because it takes the commonly-held view that our childhoods are important to the make-up of the self. In this quote, Andy is explaining what characterises NLP:

> Lots of it is finding early childhood traumas or things like that and then just trying to dispose of them.

In this model, childhood traumas are seen to be one of the constitutive events for the self. But for Andy, they are not to be understood but to be put to one side to lessen their effect. For Kevin Hetherington (2001), disposal is different from wasting in that disposal involves 'holding things in a state of absence', whereas wasting is a more final getting rid of things. Hetherington's conceptualisation of disposal helps us to see that Andy's model is about keeping these memories at bay rather than remembering or understanding, or even forgetting childhood traumas, as Ian Hacking (1995) suggests. They cannot be 'wasted' as they are constitutive of the current self, but they can be contained so that they do not disturb the order of the new self. The past is paused, so that a new future can begin.

In a different example of the past's operation on the present, Andy discusses a particular therapeutic technique in NLP:

> The woman who was a cripple [sic] had gone back to her birth on her time line and then back to her mother's, who's dead, time line. And discovered that her mother kind of wanted her to use crutches and sticks and what have you. So when she went back and put this right on her time-line, and came back, she decided she didn't need them. And just literally chucked them away and walked without them. So it is the power of the mind really.

The past is seen to have the key to the problem but unusually the past does not belong to the client as in many models of therapy and Giddens' model of time. As in Andy's previous example, it is not interpretations of the past that have the therapeutic impact, nor this time disposing of the past, but revisiting and changing the past. In this model, it is not only possible to revisit one's own past as if in a time-machine, but also those of other people, in this case the person's mother, who is dead. By visiting her mother's past, the client is able to understand her mother's responsibility in 'making' her disabled. The attribution of her disability to her mother means that it can be seen as chosen rather than determined but also means that the client herself is not blamed for the disability. In this model, what is usually seen as physical, i.e. disability, becomes a matter of the mind. In drawing upon an example reminiscent of biblical miracles, Andy's model underscores the power of the technique, and the need for our faith in believing that it took place.

In this next quote, Andy gives a more detailed account of how time operates in one of the techniques:

> A time-line is when you stand on your time-line and generally you can go through time or in time depending on whether your line goes this way, or forwards and backwards. And the initial exercise we did in that was to point to your past and point to your future. Now my past was here in front of me and fairly close, and my future wasn't particularly visible which meant I was carrying a lot of crap round in my head. And I did some work then with one of the assistants on the programme who actually turned the time-line around so

> that the past was where it belongs, behind me, and the future came into view, and was there [Andy points to where this is], which made a significant difference.

This technique rests on a concept in which the presentness of the past affects how accessible the future is. Time in Andy's account is spatialised both in terms of a notion of a linear trajectory from past to future, and in representing its relationship to Andy's experience of self and life. In this model the past should be sufficiently distant from the self and the present in order to reduce its effect. Its effect is less about the content of the past, and more about its hanging around in the present. In Andy's case, the past is not past enough, and this means that he has no future. This is not a model in which the past will always return, as in the psychoanalytic model, but involves the past becoming past enough so that it has no effect. This has some links with Giddens' ideas on the way the past is let go of in therapeutic cultures, but whereas Giddens argues that this allows for a colonisation of the future through choice and planning ahead, in Andy's model the future is already decided, and needs to be allowed to come into view.

Reconfiguring the present

In a different vein, Paul Patterson discusses the importance of reconfiguring the present instead of the past:

> NLP would aim to look at what is the process through which... experience has been created here and now. So it has a present time purpose. It is quite, a horrible word again, but 'empowering' in a sense that it puts forward that we can create and change the nature of our experience now. Our experience now is not necessarily determined by past events, which we remember.

Although writings on time problematise the presentness of the present, for Paul, the present can be made present by unhooking it from the past. Paul's model connects with Giddens' discussion above on the self-help book's recommendation that people develop a 'here and now' reflexivity. For Giddens, this enables the future to be made, rather than determined, whereas for Paul, it is the present itself that is transformed. Paul's model is a speeded up version of Sedgwick's idea of 'temporal fragmentation' in the AA, in which for Paul each moment is open to choice and intervention (Lury, 1998: 146).

In the next example, Paul Patterson expands on his understanding of choice:

> There is something about almost any experience you have that can be a personal development experience. It is a question of how it is approached and what level it is considered. So if I have these issues going on that I mentioned earlier – to do with legal issues – to what extent do I look at those as a nuisance and a problem interfering with my life and to what extent do I look at those through a frame saying 'Is this something for me to be learning about?' In what way is it reflecting back to me and other things I come across elsewhere in my life? Do I use a frame of reference that says 'Aha, this is the university giving me some feedback' or a frame of reference saying 'Is this life kicking me in the backside, or whatever else?'

In Paul's model, choice can be extended by the ways in which you interpret your context. In this model of therapeutic practice, it is not the technique or process used by an expert that can transform your self but how you read what is happening to you on an everyday basis. The meaning of events can be read in many ways. The way to read developmentally is to neutralise evaluative, emotional responses and to see what is happening as information about yourself and the way you operate. Transformation comes for Paul from the self recognising the choices of interpretation that are available at every moment. This transformation is achieved through the opening up of options produced through the different readings that he can create. By choosing interpretations which see events and the environment as having messages for him to learn from – life as a curriculum – Paul can re-create his experience in the present.

Choice

In this next example, Peter Pope gives an extensive discussion on choice, in response to my asking whether poorer people have choices:

> Obviously our choices are limited. But in a way, the less choices, or the less easy choices people have, the more they need to be aware of the choices... I have worked with people with mental health problems and if you have plenty of money, a comfortable life, and a reasonably comfortable routine, you don't actually have to be aware of choosing that much because things are all going fairly well. If you

> are in a position where you have very few choices and most of those are in some ways not good... then the need for choices is actually much greater. And I think one of the nastier things you can do to people like that is to tell them that they have no choice... So if someone is poor they will be making choices about, so some people will say, 'I am not going to be poor any more', so they start stealing, selling drugs and they are not poor. But they have other disadvantages, but they have made a choice. Some people, who are poor, are poor on their own, and there are communities where there are a lot of people out for themselves. And then you get other communities where people support each other. So there's never a problem if you are getting a job for someone to look after your kids, because there is always somebody else who would do that. So choices about how sociable people or non-sociable people are ...how much you're spending your time resenting what you don't have or finding out what the possibilities are.

What is central to Peter's model here is that the content of the choice is less important than the making of a choice. Making a choice to steal or sell drugs is better than not making a choice both in terms of ethics and outcomes. This is a model congruent with the view of Rose (1989, 1996a), and others, that choosing has become the defining characteristic of the contemporary self. For Peter, it is not simply a case of making rational or beneficial decisions, but being conscious of making a choice. This is a model in which choice defines the self more than poverty, so life is experienced differently because of existential decisions rather than lack of material resources. Making choices makes a difference to the future. In this model, however, choice is differentiated by wealth, with poorer people having fewer choices in life. With fewer choices, the impact of each choice on the self and its future is increased. In this model, choices can be made on a variety of aspects of the self and life: on how you feel, what kind of community you want, what kind of material circumstances you live in. In her discussion on addiction, Eve Kosofsky Sedgwick (1994) discusses how the extension of the powers of willpower has lead to the idea that we can micromanage absolutes, and Peter's model of choice epitomises that argument. His particular model is linked to long-standing debates on idealism and materialism, in which his model of choice comes firmly down on the idealist view, in that what we believe is more important than what we have or don't have in terms of resources. For many social theorists, it is now believed that by making a choice, we perform our duty to ourselves but also to wider society, and in Peter's example, poor people are most in need of undertaking this duty (Cronin, 2000a, 2000b; Rose, 1989, 1996a).

Possible selves

Moving away from discussions on choice and to specific techniques which involve the future, Violette Turner is explaining process in psychodrama, which involves 'tracking to the future and to the past':

> You can look at what you might be like in five years' time or ten years' time. What somebody else might be like and what you would like it to be like. And you can speak to yourself in the future and do all sorts of things. Also you can go into the past. And you can go into many scenes in the present which if you have got a relationship problem; you might see one relationship, and another relationship or even a third relationship, and then a holiday you had been on, or whatever. And it all progresses. And it all comes from the protagonist and we might say, 'Who is behind this?'

In Violette's model, the future is as amenable to exploration as the past and present. One form of the future is the self you will become if you stay as you are but project this into the future. This future self can also take the form of a possible or desired self. As with Andy, the possibility of looking at future selves is not limited to the self that belongs to the client themselves, but can also be done with other people's future selves. The future is not colonised in Violette's model as Giddens suggests, so much as sought out in order to illuminate the present. In this model, the present can also be opened out, like digital photography, to offer different perspectives with which to view oneself. The popular notion of the self as the accumulation of the past, and development as a uni-directional linear journey is complicated by Violette's conceptualisation here in that time can be reversed.

Future selves

In a related model of the future, Suzanne Madeley is explaining a technique she calls the 'future self', a process used in her coaching practice:

> You say to the client 'Relax and think of yourself in twenty years. Think about the self you're becoming'. The future self process is discovering the person you're becoming. And it involves a relaxation

> exercise and a visualisation where you take the client twenty years into the future. And you get them to notice what's around them. You know what kind of place their future self is living in. You get them to go to the door and say that the person you are becoming comes to the door and what are they like. I'm really abbreviating this. What are they saying to you? What do you want to ask them? Blah blah blah. What have they said to you... Once you've got your future self, you can reference it again... I had some profound insights from doing my future self-visualisation.
>
> Elaine: Is the future self an idealisation or what you will be if you carry on being as you are inevitably?
>
> Suzanne: It's not who you want to be. It's who you are becoming. You are talking to part of yourself when you're asking your future self questions. You're asking some wiser part of yourself unburdened from today's worries... a person who is in the future and has left those things.

In this model of the future self, Suzanne draws upon a kind of humanist model of the self as already 'inside' and in the possession of superior qualities. This is because the future is seen as an improvement on the past. The future self is innate, contained in the present self. In Suzanne's model, the future self's superiority comes from its time advantage, rather than its intrinsic qualities, meaning that it can see the past for what it is. This is a model of time in which the future is also imagined as giving a better vantage point on the present than being in the present because the true meaning of the present becomes clear in the future.

Summary

In conclusion, it can be seen that these models throw up some complexities in the way that temporality and the self are seen to interact. In Paul Patterson and Peter Pope's model of transformation, the act of choosing is imagined to perform the self in a way that multiplies the self into a series of micro-decisions. This model relies on a belief in idealism, in which the self is seen as the origin of all events. In Paul's model, it is imagined that the present is slowed down into a sequence of replete moments, which can be opened up for intervention, which then change the self. The frequency of potential transformations of the self is speeded up as each moment becomes available for transforming the self. Andy's focus is the future and in contrast to Giddens (1991,

1992), for him, the future is determined rather than open-ended or available for transformation. The future extends from the present but is different from the present and has an optimistic hue due its extension outwards from Andy's current state of improvement. In a different model, Andy describes the past as a determinant of the self and at the same time as unfixed and open to intervention, rather than being seen as complete, unchangeable, and closed. This version of temporality means that the truth of the past is discovered in the present rather than in the future when it is often assumed the past will be properly completed (Malpas, 1996). 'What has been in what I am now' is transformed into 'What I shall have been for what I want to become'. In all of these models the present is seen to be imperfect and the future full of possibilities and optimism.

Conclusion

This chapter has analysed the diverse ways in which personal development workers conceptualise transformation in their practices and the types of selves seen as legitimate outcomes of these transformations. My findings show that characterising transformation of the self in therapeutic cultures simply as 'self-discovery', 'self-realisation' or 'self-actualisation' (Rose, 1990, 1996a; Giddens, 1991, 1992) does not do justice to the variation in models of the self and transformation put forward by the personal development workers interviewed. Embedded within these phrases are certain assumptions about the self: whether it is seen as constructed or innate, and also about the temporality of transformation, in which the progressive narrative with its linear time, and sense of closure and resolution, is assumed. As a way of starting to open up the multiple ways in which the self and transformation are imagined in my material, I have suggested that there are several different models operating which are based on a number of different beliefs about the transformed self, its mode of transformation, the temporality of transformation and its desired endpoints.

In summary it can be seen that different models operating in these accounts rest on different assumptions about the size, depth and intensity of the self's transformation, the speed of the transformation, the locus of transformation, the degree to which the improved self is seen to be preexisting and the openness of the ideal self, and the perfection of the ideal self. For some personal development workers, transformation involves big changes between the new and old selves. In contrast for others, the changes are seen to be very small. The size of the change is not isomorphic with the intensity or profundity of the transformation, with some large changes involving very little depth or intensity, and smaller changes being seen as deep. In the makeover and quick fix, change is imagined to be very fast, explosive and abrupt and again, this did not match neatly onto transformation being seen as unprofound. For others, transformation is gradual, progressive and incremental over a period of time. For some personal development workers, transformation starts from within through facing oneself, or awakening oneself. In other models, transformation is achieved through trying out different behaviours or through personal development workers putting techniques into the self. In some models, it is imagined that the transformed self is pre-existing and innate, if underdeveloped or hidden, and in contrast, for other personal development workers, the transformed self is seen as new and a replacement for the old self. Finally, the nature of the transformed self varies considerably, with some believing that this self is open-ended and others being clear what the ideal endpoint is. For those who have an ideal endpoint for transformation, the self is imagined as becoming more perfect and wonderful than its previous incarnation, whereas for others, the ideal self is flawed, and experiences highs and lows.

Self-Development

The concepts of temporality in many of the personal development workers' accounts problematise the linear progressive trajectory that is usually seen to constitute the notion of development. A central metaphor in Western thinking, development has been seen as a cumulative process, in which what is given at any moment is the cumulative result of what has gone before (Nisbet, 1969). In this model of development, it is imagined to be a system of growth in which an individual, a nation or a species is 'moving toward some end that is presumably contained in the process from the start' (Nisbet, 1969: 3). One of the most influential models of the self and its development is that of the journey or *bildungsroman* as Rita Felski (1995, 2000) and Ken Plummer (1995) suggest. In this model, the self is seen to progress to an improved state over time due to its accumulation of past experiences. This is typically believed to arise because of increasing self-knowledge. In contrast, many of the personal development workers' understandings challenge this narrative of the self as an accumulation of its past experiences. The notion of 'This person I am today is who I have been years becoming' (Rosenwald and Ochberg, 1992: 9) is replaced by some of these models with the model of 'This is what I was but am no longer'.

In some cases this is extended into a series of 'This is what I was then, what I was before that, but am no longer'. The significance in the personal development workers' accounts of the quick fix and the makeover as models of transformations of the self suggests that these are replacing that of the life long journey. Not only do these models suggest a seriality to the transformation of the self that is repetitive and yet authentic and meaningful, they also present a self made up of ruptures and discontinuities. In so doing, they complicate Gidden's progressivist and linear concept of the self as project.

Therapeutic fantasies

So how can we understand the significance of the quick fix and the makeover in these accounts? Both of these offer fantasies of instant self-transformation. In so doing, they challenge Giddens' (1991, 1992) model of reflexivity and transformation. For Giddens, transformation is accomplished by the self through a rational, calculative means as it creates a story that has both continuity and futurity. For Giddens, reflexivity and autobiography are essentially modes of 'cognition' (Steedman, 2000: 26). What are missing from this model of reflexivity are other mental processes such as fantasy, daydreaming, imagination, and make-believe. Drawing upon this research, it may be possible to think of alternative ways in which the self is constructed which rely less upon cognitive models of self-awareness, and more on other ways of being reflexive.

My findings show that we need to extend Giddens' concept of reflexivity to include understandings of the role of 'fantasy' as a form of self-work. In this chapter I have shown that approaches such as the makeover and the quick fix enable people to imagine that they can transform themselves in radical ways very quickly. Personal development approaches, as Rose (1989, 1996a) suggests also offer fantasy selves, although some of these were different from Rose's notion of the enterprising self. Personal development also offers fantasy practices such as role-plays, timelines, and psychodrama, which enable people to imagine themselves in different ways, try on new selves, and new lives. Therapeutic cultures also offer fantasies of what the self can do to transform itself. These involve imagined activities, which run counter to dominant views of time and the power of the self. Examples of this include the ideas of autopoeisis, and also the possibilities of changing the past and the future. So why are these types of fantasies important at the moment? As cultural studies theorists such as Jackie Stacey (1997) note, fantasies offer imaginary solutions to real contradictions. In the context of personal development, personal development enables fantasies of profound self-transformation in an era in which self-transformation is incited in the workplace and society. And as several critics note, the ideal selves on offer in contemporary culture are impossible to achieve, and so fantasy practices are an essential part of how one can close the gap between what one is and what one could be, ought to be, or is really. In this context, therapeutic practices enable the self to imagine and create new selves. As Giddens points out, people are often unsure of what and who they should be, and therapeutic fantasies are one way in which they can imagine their transformed selves.

7
Getting in Touch with Their Feelings?

In the previous chapter I explored the multiple, and complex ways in which workers conceptualise transformation of the self in personal development practices. I argued that these very different models of transformation were re-conceptualising contemporary understandings of the self, and its relations with the self, as evidenced by the increasing replacement of the traditional model of transformation as a journey by concepts of the 'makeover' and the 'quick fix'. I concluded that many of these models draw upon complex temporalities that have moved away from uni-linear progressive models, which enable fantasies of the power of the self and its capacities for self-transformation. I argued that this is significant at a time when self-transformation has become a cultural imperative. In the workers' discussions on self-transformation, the significance of emotions is a constant theme, albeit conceptualised in different ways.

Therapeutic cultures and the emotionalisation of self and society

The aim of this chapter is to investigate this theme in more detail, by first providing an overview of current ideas on emotions in relation to therapeutic cultures, drawn from sociologists of therapeutic cultures such as Giddens (1991, 1992) and Nolan (1998). However, it also uses other academic writing on emotions taken from the sociology of emotion, anthropology, cultural studies, critical psychology and feminism, because of the relative lack of attention given to the analysis of emotion expressions and the way that emotion become essentialised. In their discussion of the work of psychologist Silvan Tomkins, Eve Kosofsky Sedgwick and Adam Frank (1995) argue that in many contemporary theories of emotion, 'affect is treated as a unitary category, with a unitary history and unitary politics' (1995: 17). As Jeff Hearn (1993) in his discussion on emotion in organisations notes, 'emotions are not just any one thing', what is of interest is how the concept of 'emotion' is used, invoked and understood (1993: 149).

Accordingly, I turn to the interviews to explore how personal development workers interviewed conceptualise the expression of emotions. I ask how personal development workers imagine emotions as best performed, given that there are many different forms in which emotions can be 'expressed'. This is particularly important, given a common assumption in academic literature and popular culture that the main form of expressing emotions in therapeutic cultures is verbal articulation. For example, Toby Miller and Alec McHoul (1998a) write that people go to therapeutic cultures to learn how to express their feelings; see also Ian Craib (1994) and Deborah Cameron (2000a) for similar views. I also explore the specific emotions which personal development workers see as the successful endpoint of their practices. For some critics, such as Ian Craib (1994) and Frank Furedi (2004), many therapeutic cultures focus on 'nice' emotions, rather than intense, messy or so-called negative emotions. This chapter examines whether this is the case for the personal development workers interviewed. It explores which emotions are seen as legitimate by these workers and why these might be emphasised, and others might be ignored. Finally, and significantly in the light of critics' worries about the increase in emotional expressivity in society, this chapter looks at the relationship between the control of emotions, therapeutic cultures and expressivity.

Emotionality at large

In recent years there has been a widespread turn to the emotions in academia. Much of this stems from the enormous interest in emotions in wider culture and society, often glossed as the 'emotionalisation of society'. See for example, Elspeth Probyn who writes of the 'massive return to the affective that we are now experiencing in theory and in real life' (2002: 1). Stephen Fineman defines this trend as 'a new emotionality at large' (2000b: 107). Ian Craib (1994) describes it in more pejorative terms: 'our culture is obsessed with emotions' (1994: 86). Frank Furedi writes that 'the language of emotionalism pervades popular culture, the world of politics, the workplace, schools and universities and everyday life' (2004: 1).

In essence, this emotionalisation is seen to be typified by a number of characteristics. For many theorists, such as James Nolan (1998) (See also Richard Sennett (1986); Frank Furedi (2004); Corinne Squire (2000), there is now an extensive privileging of emotion as a form of truth, knowledge and morality, and therefore seen as an important source for political, and personal judgement. Consequently, public figures present themselves and their ideas in the language of emotions. For many commentators, Princess Diana and Tony Blair are the exemplars of this. It is argued as a result that this means that emotional detachment and restraint are seen as pathological (Cameron, 2000a; Furedi, 2004).

Emotional expressivism

The second aspect of the emotionalisation of society is perceived to be an extension in the places and spaces in which emotions are now expressed and discussed, a result of the so-called informationalisation and de-ritualisation of emotions, bringing a growth in the range and intensity of emotions and emotional expressions and emotions legitimated in public (Wouters, 1986, 1989, 2002). So public spheres such as the workplace and politics are now seen to be 'emotionalised-up'. The workplace is now seen as a crucible place for emotion work, the commodification of emotions, the emotionalisation of relations between managers and employees, and the organisation and employees, the emotions of work, 'emotional engineering' and the 'emotionally intelligent' (Fineman, 1993, 2000a, 2000b, 2000c). In fact it is argued that politics and the state are largely preoccupied with the emotional presentation of politicians and the government of citizens' emotions (Cloud, 1998; Furedi, 2004; Nolan, 1998).

It is also suggested that emotion defines popular culture and the media, and is frequently the main topic on chat shows, soap operas, television interviews, and even the news. Finally, accompanying all of this, it is proposed that there is an increase in the outlets and means for invoking, expressing and amplifying emotions across all social spheres, resulting in the growth of 'emotional industries' such as extreme sports or counselling and an intensification in expert knowledges and technologies of emotion (Wouters, ibid; Williams, 2000, 2001; Mestrovic, 1997). Academic evaluations of these trends vary from the hostile: Dana Cloud (1998); Frank Furedi (2004); James Nolan (1998); Richard Sennett (1986); Simon Williams (2000, 2001); the pessimistic: Lauren Berlant (1997); Jean Bethke Elshtain (1997) to the ambivalent: Deborah Lupton (1998); and Corinne Squire; and the optimistic: Anthony Giddens (1991, 1992); Michel Maffesoli (1996).

Therapy as emotion work

The question of the role of therapeutic cultures in the emotionalising of society is central to critiques of therapeutic cultures. For many sociologists of therapeutic cultures, they are pivotal to the increase in the privileging of emotion, and the valorising of particular performances of emotion in public and private. For example, in an analysis of emotion in contemporary society, Simon Williams writes:

> ours is an age characterised not simply by the significance we invest in emotions (i.e. what we feel, how we feel, why we feel the way we do), but also by the way in which we seek advice for our 'emotional problems'. Today... we're given up the idea of 'cures' and replaced it instead by a growing number of therapies in which the emphasis is placed upon... lengthy conversations about the self in order to get us 'in touch' with our feelings through the emotional content of the therapeutic encounter. Seen in these terms, therapy is 'emotion work' par excellence. (2001: 148)

For the most part, critics see the influence of therapeutic approaches on how we understand, value, and perform emotions as very dangerous. There are a number of different arguments about why they perceive this to be the case. So for critics such as James Nolan (1998), the increasing authority accorded to emotion has lead to an emotionalisation of the state and citizenship, leading to the regulation of particular emotionalised performances in the legal system, the prison service, the welfare system and the education system. For Nolan, Furedi and others this is resulting in the increased colonisation and policing of the private self by the state.

Economy of emotions

Another major concern for critics is the hierarchy of emotions they see endorsed by therapeutic cultures. In this view, a therapeutic economy of emotions is being propagated, leading to the stigmatisation of certain versions of the self. For example, critics such as Frank Furedi (2004) argue that the feeling of 'happiness' is held up as the ideal emotion. He argues that 'strong' emotions such as rage, 'political' emotions such as anger, and emotions that tie us to other people, are all being pathologised by therapeutic cultures, leading to a de-politicisation and domestication of these emotions. Concomitant with this take on emotions, Furedi (2004) argues, is a model of the self as emotionally vulnerable, emotionally damaged and emotionally at risk. As a result of these strands, in his view, our emotions are problematised as we are seen as emotionally deficient, and in need of expertise to help us manage and control our emotional lives.

Feminised emotions

Furedi (2004) argues that all of this boils down to the valorisation of a new fragile, feeble, feminised emotional self and the denigration of the masculine, restrained, active self. For him the optimistic, active, self-seeking, self-fulfilment has been replaced by a conservative self focused on survival. David Wainwright and Michael Calnan (2002) also argue that there is a cultural privileging of this new feminised model of the self in current understandings of stress. In their view, this self is comprised of a vulnerable body and mind, and seen to be a victim, and leads to the stigmatisation of the masculine self and the pathologisation of human agency. For them, this development is partially attributed to what they see as a feminist critique of the heroic, active, self-controlled masculinity. They argue that the antidote to this limiting view of the self is the development of 'the mentally competent, emotionally resilient subject who has high expectations of human potential' (2002: 197). They argue that 'rather than actively engaging in the world and struggling to transform it, men and women are encouraged to retreat inside themselves, to lead more contemplative and expressive lives' (2002: 157). Ian Craib (1994, 1998) is also worried about what he sees as the over-appreciation of culturally feminine feelings. He writes that 'talking about feelings has changed from an irrelevant feminine pastime to a sign of social status' (1998: 114). (See Deborah Lupton (1998) for a more positive discussion on the feminisation of masculine emotionality).

Emoting

As well as the view that the wrong emotions are being emphasised in therapeutic cultures, critics are concerned about emotions being expressed in the wrong ways. One of these wrong ways is the expression of emotions in public. For Frank Furedi the increased emphasis on expressing emotions means that traditional British qualities of 'reserve, understatement and reticence' are swept aside (2004: 18). For Nolan there is a widespread imperative to express emotions 'without constraint or discrimination' (1998: 6).

Conformity

A related concern is around the increasing standardisation of these expressions and the resulting emotional conformity. For example, for theorists such as Ian Craib (1994, 1998), the expression of emotions has become too conventionalised by therapeutic thinking, with idiosyncratic expressions becoming 'McDonaldised', programmatic, domesticated and commodified. To illustrate his argument, like other critics, Craib (1994, 1998) argues that therapeutic cultures privilege verbal utterances as *the* quintessential therapeutic emotional expression. In his view this is eroding our experience and understanding of emotions. In a similar vein, Richard Sennett (1986) believes therapeutic cultures have impoverished our emotional expressions through making us lose sight of the difference between manifesting an emotion, and crafting an expression of an emotion, by privileging the former. For many critics then, therapeutic forms of expression are not expressive enough.

The main problem with these developments for many critics of therapeutic cultures is the progressive de-valuing of private and public spheres. In this view, the public is becoming more private, and the private is becoming more public, blurring boundaries and distinctions between these two spheres. Megan Boler (1999) uses the example of the valorisation of emotional intelligence in the workplace as evidence of a shift in the pedagogy of emotions. For her, it represents an overlapping of the private and public, as the family is no longer the only place where emotion is educated.

For social commentators such as Richard Sennett (1986) and Lauren Berlant (1997, 2000), the emotionalisation of the social is problematic because it has lead to a privileging of subjectivism, de-rationalising public life, and shrinking what counts as 'political' to the 'private'. In this view, the ideal model of relations between people is now one of intimacy, where intimacy refers to a sharing of what is imagined to be personal, private and emotional.

In contrast to the view that the emotionalisation of society is a uniformly pessimistic trend, some critics argue that it is more complex. So for Giddens (1991, 1992), life itself has become more emotional due to the effects of de-traditionalisation. Using the concept of ontological insecurity, Giddens argues that we feel more anger, fear, anxiety, love, guilt and especially shame in everyday life, due to changing social conditions. The good news is that for Giddens these can be alleviated through having more egalitarian emotional relations with each other, either as couples or friends, in the form of what he calls the 'pure relationship'. According to Giddens, these changes are optimistic and bring new forms of emotional democracy in the shape of openness, honesty and equality to our private and public lives. In contrast to Lauren Berlant (1997, 2000), the transformation of intimacy holds out new possibilities for our emotional life. The bad news is that the pure relationship can exacerbate our feelings of ontological insecurity because of the gendered ways of dealing with emotional life, with men 'emotionally lagging behind' women, due to conditions which mean that 'men are unable to construct a narrative of self that allows them to come to terms with an increasingly democratised and reordered sphere of personal life' (Giddens, 1992: 117). Overall, Giddens is much more upbeat in his assessment of changes in emotional life than most other sociologists of therapeutic cultures.

Emotions and self-formation

The argument on the expression of emotions in the public sphere can also be made more complicated by looking at different literatures outside of the sociology of therapeutic cultures. So for example, in his discussion of new social movements, Kevin Hetherington (1998) suggests that there is a long tradition of social theorists being critical of expressivism and emotion. He argues that influential critics such as Weber and Adorno and Horkheimer have seen expressivism and emotion as apolitical, irrational and potentially amoral. In contrast, for Hetherington, in social movements emotions can be the basis of identification and a source and focus for self-formation. According to Hetherington, new social movements offer expressive modes of identification through providing 'ways of expressing oneself through identifying with others ... based in the expressive world of feeling and emotion and forms of collective sentiment' (1998: 51). Unlike Nolan (1998), who is dismissive of emotions as a source of ethics, Hetherington sees emotions as an important part of the morality of new social movements.

Semiotics of emotions

It can also be argued that the means and forms of expression are relatively under-examined in the sociology of therapeutic cultures. So

Hetherington shows the importance of the body, and its symbolic meanings in performing expressivism in new social movements. Typically the body is stylised in new social movements in excessive ways to symbolise an identity which is 'marginal, different, other, unpresentable and in flux' (Hetherington, 1998: 153). In a similar vein, understandings of the body and its expressions in anthropological and historical literature on gesture problematise the conceptualisations of emotional expression in the sociology of therapeutic cultures. For example, ethnographic studies show that emotional expressions are ritualised, stylised and structured according to conventions involving their timing, sequence, location, form, duration and intensity (see for example, Clark, 1997; Wellenkamp, 1988). These studies show how emotional expressions have their own semiotics. In contrast to critics of therapeutic cultures, who to a large extent imagine emotional expressions as de-ritualised or simplistically conventionalised, these studies suggest that things may be more ethnographically complex. This raises questions about how personal development workers interviewed understand emotional expressions in personal development. How are they patterned? What specific forms do emotional expressions take? And what are they used to mean? To answer these questions in more depth, this chapter turns to the interviews.

Learning to say what you feel

I start this section with Jane Vincent because she draws upon a bodily expression of emotion, which illustrates the ritualised nature of emotions in personal development workers' understandings of personal development. In this section, Jane Vincent is discussing how people can find what she calls their 'diamond', or core self, in growth groups.

> Elaine: How do you know when people have found that core, that diamond?
>
> Jane: It is a particular process that is set up and it is a lot to do with energy as well... It is an actual process that is created so people are set up for it. They don't know what is going to happen and all they are told is that they are going to have an opportunity to get in touch with their self-esteem, their self-confidence and their self-worth, and the answer is not going to come from their head... And they are wound up. And they are sitting in a semi-circle with a flipchart. And they don't know what the hell it is about. And the energy builds. And people eventually, it just comes... And they get to that place where they put words on the board that they don't

> even think that they were going to put. And it is usually around 'I am loveable, I am loving, I am beautiful'. Mine was 'I am sexy'. And I couldn't say the words. That one doesn't come up so much these days. But the one underneath, that is 'I am loveable' does. And they come out, these words come out. And you will see that absolute energy change. Some people will burst into tears. Some people jump sky high. Some people burst into laughter, but there is an absolute typical cathartic stuff. There is an absolute physical change in the body. They might start shaking or whatever. And then they are rocked and they are carried and they are cuddled.

In Jane Vincent's model, particular expressions of emotions are imagined to provide evidence of the transformation of the self. In contrast to many critics' representation of emotional expressions as verbal articulation, Jane Vincent presents these in terms of the body. In her view, the expressions have a specific form: they are intense, demonstrated by a particular rhythm in which there is speed of both the 'take off' of the expressions and also their demise. This intensity is performed also through the physical manifestations of emotion on the body and quite extreme bodily movements. The emotional expressions are seen to be brought about by a particular therapeutic technology of emotion in which energy is imagined to build suspense leading to a moment of transformation evidenced by the bodily expressions. There are different models of energy in contemporary understandings of the self, but for Jane Vincent energy is 'inside' and symbolic of an old self being summoned up to be exorcised. Intense bodily expressions of emotion are often seen as the most impulsive, natural and uncontrollable of expressions, making them truthful signs of the emotions being subjectively experienced. This is reinforced by the speed and 'excess' of the emotional expressions symbolising involuntary spontaneity as opposed to deliberate, artificial poses. In using images of energy and the body, Jane Vincent is also able to show how the intellect is bypassed because energy is seen to be inside the body, and the body is seen to be a different interior and symbolic space from the head, where it is imagined the mind is situated. The more extreme the movement on the surface of the body, the more it is imagined that the intellect is not involved. In this understanding of the self, the intellect is seen as less embodied than emotions, and therefore more distant from the self. This is important for Jane Vincent because transformation of the self for her does not come from the intellect. This is further symbolised in the way these expressions are also bodily rather than verbal. However, verbal utterances do have a role to play in this model, but not as emotional expressions but as 'identification speech acts' in which certain idealised self-descriptions are seen to produce the self they describe.

Letting go

The range of emotions expressed is broad, suggested by the familiar idiom in which 'tears' and 'laughter' are juxtaposed. This range indicates that the nature of the feelings experienced in this therapeutic process is less significant than their expression. Jane Vincent also refers to the bodily expression of emotions as cathartic. There are many different understandings of catharsis, from the re-experiencing of past emotions through to it being seen as a purging of current emotions. In Jane Vincent's model, catharsis refers to the letting go of the old self rather than to the purging of past emotions.

For Jane Vincent, emotions are seen as both the means of transformation and their expression as a sign that transformation has taken place. In fact, in this model, the form of the expression is more significant than the specific emotion being expressed or experienced, and in which changes performed on and through the body signify changes in the self. The surface of the body is shown as conveying what is going on 'inside', which is that the 'old self' is being removed in preparation for the 'new self'. Emotional expressions are stylised through particular bodily performances, in this example, to show the narrative of the transformation, but this form of emotional expression, however, can be seen as *the* paradigmatic emotional act in therapeutic cultures, as the next section shows.

Crying

Taking forward the idea of the significance of the expression's form, this next section looks at the emotional expression of crying as it is the expression of emotion most discussed by the personal development workers interviewed. Not all therapeutic schools see crying as essential to therapeutic practice. For some schools, such as cognitive therapies, it is a meaningless side effect, whereas for Rogerian client-centred therapies, it can signify therapeutic breakthrough (Lutz, 1999). More generally, the conventions about the correct place and style of crying have undergone several changes in the past 300 years (Vincent-Buffault, 1991). Anne Vincent-Buffault notes that in the eighteenth century, both men and women were encouraged to cry in public as a sign of their refinement. As Vincent-Buffault argues, this did not mean that crying could be expressed in any way; there was an 'art of crying [which] had its nuances, its stakes and its limits' and a set of conventions on how to cry in public to denote their fine sensibilities (1991: 38). In the nineteenth century, new sets of conventions developed promoting a model of self-control for men in which they were to show self-mastery of their tears, as these had become associated with weakness, femininity and childhood. These studies examine the importance of understanding the production of tears rather than seeing them simply as 'natural', asocialised expressions of sadness.

Typologies of tears

Today there are many different views on the purpose and meaning of tears. As Tom Lutz (1999) writes, for some scientists crying is simply a form of chemical excretion for eliminating potentially harmful chemicals and for Darwin, tears were a way of cooling eyes overheated through emotion. But crying also has many symbolic meanings, which have accrued and changed over time. Today, crying is often seen as the most sincere and authentic of emotional expressions, signifying 'a surplus of feeling over thinking' (Lutz, 1999). It is also seen in cultural representations as a characteristically feminine behaviour, in spite of the association of crying with many men throughout history in their roles as monks, epic warriors, saints, and as mentioned above, noblemen (Lutz, 1999). As part of their symbolism, there were different typologies of tears. For example, medieval monks used to characterise different types of tears, which included moist ones which washed away sins, salty ones which restrained the flesh from sin, warm tears to stop unfaithfulness and pure tears of people cleansed of their sins (Lutz, 1999). As well as leading to different types of tears, crying can take on many different physical forms, from weeping to sobbing to the moistening of the eyes (Harper and Porter, 1996). So how does crying figure in the accounts of the personal development workers interviewed? What does it seem to symbolise? How is it conceptualised in relation to their practices? What kinds of tears are seen to be important in therapeutic cultures?

Bottling up feelings

I start with a quote from Andy Knight because he gives an extended discussion of crying. In this quote, Andy is describing a particular NLP exercise, which proved to be an epiphany for him:

> And I had a lot of bottled feelings. So I had feelings come out during some of the work we did for, yeah, one example was a girl I was

> going out with kind of vaguely. At the time I had never expressed any true feelings to her. And this came out 20, 25 years on, and most feelings were still there and came out of one of the exercises. And I thought 'Shit. I should have done something about that at the time'. So now I am much more able to share feelings and to say what I want because what was behind that at the time was a fear of rejection. There is a kind of situation in which you have nine chances [that] she will say yes to it and have a relationship, and one that she won't. Therefore you miss the nine nice opportunities in life for the sake of the one, that okay she may say no, so what, you know, you have not lost anything in actual fact...I mean I kind of sat around and cried my eyes out for half an hour because suddenly this thing that had been there for 30 years had gone... And the thing I learned: I didn't express feelings particularly. I carried them around and bottled them up.

As in Jane Vincent's example, Andy demonstrates that he is transformed through the emotional expression of crying. But in Andy's example, the target of his transformation is his inability to express his emotions. In some contexts, crying would be seen to be an embarrassing expression of emotions, but not in this context. Crying is performative in that in expressing his emotions, Andy is seen to have transformed into someone who does now express his feelings. The form of Andy's crying is also significant. In particular, the duration of his crying has symbolic meaning. In contrast to the concentrated eruptions of emotional expressions performed on the body in Jane Vincent's model, Andy describes a more prolonged, and yet equally forceful, expression of emotion, manifested largely through the eyes and face. The eyes and the face are seen to be the most public parts of our body, and yet they also have access to and reveal our depths.

In a discussion on romanticism, Colin Campbell (1989) points out you need to convince people you are crying enough. In this context, an hour's worth of crying is seen as appropriate, and intelligible because of the length of time – thirty years – that Andy has been suffering. It is also appropriate given the nature of his suffering, which involves loss, sadness and unexpressed love, all feelings that are seen to linger for life. The emphasis on love and suffering means that as a man he does not have to represent his crying as shameful, as might be the case for other public situations, given the association between crying and femininity. The duration and intensity are isomorphic with the way his memory is from a long time ago, and difficult to access. Crying also symbolises the externalisation of the 'inside', with the move from past to present being mirrored by the move from outside to inside. As with Jane Vincent, the body is being used to make visible these invisible movements. In particular, tears have a special relationship to the past, and his crying shows that the past which is invisible to the naked eye, is being engaged with.

Crying can be the expression of a number of feelings: suffering, pain, pride, grief, frustration, awe, pity, joy (Lutz, 1999: 46). Andy does not specify the feelings he felt although we can tell from his crying that he is indeed overcome with emotion. It is the most emotional of emotional expressions in which the body is seen to take over from cognition, and emotions can no longer be expressed in words. Crying comes to represent being feelingful in Andy's model, and therefore symbolises his ability to express emotions. Crying also represents closure – for Andy, not being able to express emotions comes to an end.

Stored emotions

Andy also draws upon a popular understanding of emotions as 'stored' inside of us, and which can be accessed years later, given the right conditions. The emotions Andy expressed through the personal development exercises were the original feelings he had at the time thirty years ago. They have been stored for so long because they were not expressed at the time, and because they were part of his true self, which he suppressed. Implicit in this is the idea that parts of the self that are the true self need to be expressed. In drawing upon a notion of unexpressed past emotions as the true self put on hold, Andy can claim that his new expressive identity is his true self, started up again through the liminality of crying.

True selves

In this example then, the reliving of past emotions reconnects the present self with a former true self. Being true to one's true self involves asking for what one wants. Andy experiences two types of emotion in relation to this past experience: those that inhibit his true self, and those that express his true self. In his example, the emotion of fear of rejection stops him asking for what he wants. So in this example, Andy is not suggesting that all emotions should be expressed. Fear of rejection needs to be suppressed through rational cost benefit thinking in order that his true desires can be expressed. Expressing feelings of love is characterised by 'ambivalence and anxiety' (Lupton, 1998) as people can reveal too much of their feelings which may not be reciprocated. This can represent a risk to oneself. Andy is seen to have over-controlled the expression of his feelings. This has now all been put right as symbolised through Andy's crying.

In tears

In this next quote, Violette Turner, like Andy, takes crying as a sign of transformation but she has a different angle on it from Andy. In this quote, Violette is answering my question about what drew her to psychodrama:

> Well actually I had had personal growth before. I had been to a psychologist so it wasn't as though it was new. I think because I spent the whole time in tears I think. The whole weekend in tears and it was the first time I had been anywhere and spent the whole time in tears and still functioned.

As for Andy, tears, and the duration of the tears are significant. In Violette's case, the expression has a much longer duration than Andy and Jane Vincent discuss, but is less an outcome of a specific event or technology. For Violette her tears symbolise that the approach was effective as they represent a special connection with the inner self. Reproducing a popular model of crying as a threat to our sense of self-possession, Violette does not see crying on its own as bringing therapeutic benefit. She sees the intellect as integral. Given the associations of crying with femininity, and lack of emotional control with women, perhaps it is not surprising that Violette, describes herself as in control (Lutz, 1990).

Purifying

In this next quote, Paul Patterson presents crying as therapeutic but not integral to his approach. In this excerpt, he is explaining why he was drawn to NLP as a practice:

> I think what I have liked in NLP is when emotions are part of the holistic part of the process, catharsis is allowed but... as a means to an end. For example, I remember [in] the Master practitioner training there being a time-line exercise whereby I walked through some

> experiences in my life from before the time of my conception through to the future. And repeatedly walked through these. And clearly in sensory terms, could feel quite profound differences as I walked along this line just in terms of changes in my body state. It was very, very marked. And doing this repeatedly. And at some point, I can't remember exactly where, I went into tears for a good ten or fifteen minutes and it felt wonderfully cleansing. It felt a very spontaneous part of doing that process that would have been very inappropriate for someone to come along and say 'Oh dear Paul is in tears; let's put him into a more resourceful state'. That would have been more than crass but at the same time it wasn't a necessary part of the process. It wasn't that the process couldn't work unless I went into that kind of catharsis. So it was there and it was fine and helpful and for me, cleansing but it wasn't sought out, it wasn't something that ought to happen.

Unlike for Jane Vincent and Andy, the expression of crying for Paul is not the main signifier of transformation. Neither is it the main aim of transformation. Although Paul draws upon a common trope of tears as purifying (Lutz, 1999; Grosz, 1994), he does not see this purification as central to the therapeutic benefit of this practice. The duration of Paul's crying is less than Andy's but it is still significant for Paul. As with Andy, it symbolises a visit to the past but as part of a technology of time in which events in his life are experienced as 'private bubbles'. So unlike Andy and Violette's expressions, which are very public, Paul presents his crying as something he steps into, expressing them almost silently. This is because they are not like a lightning bolt full of meaning but one event amongst many. His tears represent one memory enacted upon his body alongside of other memories and so these tears do not constitute the main event. Although not a central part of the therapeutic practice, Paul does see the expression of tears as a delicate process of the self, in which a particular course has to be run rather than stopped. The idea that people in tears are in a fragile and potentially dangerous state is a popular model in some therapeutic cultures. Some models of catharsis see the expression of past emotions as purifying in that emotions are viewed as working on the self in the present in unhelpful ways, and purifying gets rid of those past emotions. Although Paul's model is related to past emotions, Paul's approach does not involve interpreting these past emotions. The body's symptoms are not those of repressed traumas that need decoding.

Secrets

In these models, the body is used to symbolise a connection with the inside, and in the case of tears, to the past. In his analysis of crying, Tom Lutz (1999) cites the work of Mark Taylor, who sees tears as rips or ruptures, i.e. tears which symbolise a radical break between one state and another. Taylor also sees a connection between the words 'secret' and 'secretion', a secret being an outside, which is inside, and a secretion, is an inside that is outside. But this understanding does not encompass all the personal development workers' representations of crying in these interviews. For Violette and Paul, there is no secret that is revealed. And for Andy, it is less a secret than a forgotten memory.

For these workers, the quality of the tears is not significant as in Lutz' typology of religious tears in medieval times, nor is the volume of tears, as might be indicated by verbs such as shedding or flowing, or the noise of crying such as sobs or wailing. Instead, what is most important is the duration of the crying. Crying indicates a particular kind of therapeutic event, in which remembering and the passing of time are key, symbolised by the duration of the crying which is seen to be isomorphic to the depth, significance and pastness of the memory. In this model, the stopping of crying symbolises some kind of closure, whether that be as in Andy's case, the end of the influence of a particular memory in constituting the self; and in Paul's case, indicating the end of one memory before moving on to a different memory.

Drawing upon metaphors of exteriorisation and interiority, the personal development workers draw a parallel between the movement of the tears coming out of the body, and the past self being released. The body is seen to contain the inner self and its past, and bodily emotional expressions are used to symbolise the transformation of both, so as the body changes with crying, so the self is seen to be changing. Crying in personal development is best understood as liminal spaces, which symbolise particular relations to the self, its past and transformation rather than simply a spontaneous expression of emotions, which has universal meaning. Therapeutic tears then represent particular forms and meanings of crying and in contrast to crying being seen as us at our most inarticulate, or emotionally incontinent, it can be seen from these accounts that crying forms communicate more than we sometimes imagine.

Happy, shiny people?

In these examples so far, I have argued that the personal development workers view the form of expression and a general state of emotionality itself as more significant than particular specific feelings. However the personal development workers interviewed do discuss particular specific feelings, especially as hallmarks of successful therapeutic transformation. One of the main criticisms aimed at therapeutic cultures by critics such as Craib (1994, 1998) is that therapeutic cultures promise clients that they will feel happier as result of their involvement. In Craib's view, many current forms of psychotherapy make unrealistic promises, deny negative experience and produce 'an easy, "optimistic" and... rather glib view of life' (1994: 158). In so doing, they encourage us to avoid acknowledging our own disappointments with our selves and our life, unlike Craib argues psychoanalysis would do. 'The public face of psychotherapy and counselling', he observes, 'is a comforting and understanding face, providing help and support, easing pain, sorting out difficulties and problems, resolving conflicts' (1994: 6). Part of this lack of stoicism, for Stjepan Mestrovic (1997) results from the way therapeutic cultures concentrate on orderly, pleasant, pleasurable and predictable emotions. Therapeutic cultures themselves have become 'pseudotherapy' by being too gentle and nice, he stresses, instead of being 'authentic' which means 'rough' and not nice (1997: 127).

We are being encouraged, according to Nolan (1998), to be less 'stoical' towards negative emotions. 'In pre-modern moral orders,' he observes, 'pain, suffering, and injury were viewed as part of life. They were understood to contribute toward the refining process that helped the individual to surrender self and grow in virtuous character' (1998: 15). In contrast, for Frank Furedi (2004) there is far too much concentration on people's suffering and pain. Given these models, which emotions do the personal development workers see as most significant?

Love

In this first excerpt, which critics might see as characteristic of the problems they discuss, Jane Vincent provides an example of the expression of love as evidence of successful transformation. In this example, she recounts her experience of attending a growth group:

> It was the first time in my life that I ever hugged my parents, that I told my mother I loved her. That is what is profound for me. I had

> never told my mother I loved her. I didn't think I had heard my mother say she loved me. It didn't exist in our family. Today, all these years later we all say 'I love you'. Basically it opened up my ability to communicate. It has opened up my channels and it has opened up the channels in my family and I think that is the most precious situation to have. To have our family working on another level. The sort of level we all aim for is to have open, warm, loving relationships. And they all had shutters in front of them before we did the training.

In Jane Vincent's model, the main evidence of transformation is not bodily but a verbal articulation. Although some theorists are concerned about the increase in the expressions of emotions in public, Jane Vincent is concerned with what is understood by people to be the private domain. Unlike earlier examples, in this model the evidence of transformation is performed outside of the therapeutic encounter in everyday family life. Jane Vincent's model of expressing love represents the kind of cliché through therapy that some critics argue is attenuating our emotional experience, and yet for Jane Vincent, it symbolises a profound transformation. As Lauren Berlant writes, 'Banality can also mark the expression of deeply felt emotion as in the case of "I love you"' (2001b: 134).

This expression is a speech act performative of more emotional family relations. In mobilising this speech act repeatedly, the family make themselves a loving family. In so doing they perform a particular idealised version of the family seen to be valorised in today's society as discussed by Giddens (1991, 1992). In this model, the expression of loving has to take particular forms, which are seen to denote sharing, openness and communication, all part of a version of the family based on emotional ties rather than duty or responsibility. As such the family is seen to be the site for the production of the self, in particular during early childhood. As Lynn Jamieson suggests:

> Ideas of being a 'good' parent and of 'natural affection' have changed in the course of this century. A contemporary child faced with ...undemonstrative parents might come to feel they lacked the love and care they needed, possibly with profound consequences for their sense of self and approach to subsequent relationships. (1998: 10)

The lack of love performed according to particular norms is seen to have a 'damaging' effect on children, and this is believed then to manifest itself in adulthood. In some therapeutic models, it is seen as never too late to undo the 'damage' that may have been done by lack of expressed love by parents. Love is seen to have healing properties and so the expression of love by Jane Vincent's family means that they are not only acting as a well-adjusted family should, but also repairing any damage that may have been done by their not expressing love earlier. In drawing upon analogies of depth and openness as good, and concealment as bad, Jane Vincent is suggesting that the private sphere can be too private, and in mobilising the speech act of 'I love you', she is not simply reporting a feeling but reproducing a particular set of values on privacy and publicity.

Pain

In this next excerpt, Sally Thompson discusses emotions that are usually seen as less positive than love. Sally is discussing her own experience as a client on a Gestalt workshop:

> It was an incredibly painful experience. It was brilliant in lots of ways. And very painful in other ways. But I did become clearer about what I find painful... I felt incredibly raw coming away from it. I found it very hard to encounter people in the ordinary world like taxi drivers...

For Sally, the intense feeling of emotional pain provides a form of transcendence, taking her away from the everyday and mundane. It also symbolises her true commitment to self-transformation. Culturally, pain is seen as a particularly transformatory emotion, as Lauren Berlant (2001a, 2001b) suggests, because it is viewed as both the true core of personhood and as a special form of knowledge about the self. These views come about from pain's supposed self-evidence, objectivity and sharpness. For Frank Furedi (2004), the suffered, pained self leads to a passivity of the self, whereas for Sally it brings a new sensibility and connection to the self.

Sally and I continue our discussion:

> Elaine: What is fantastic about it? You said you felt painful and raw afterwards.
>
> Sally: It's about being able to connect with people on a level which is significantly lower than 'How are you?' 'Fine. How are you?'

> Getting to who are you as a person and who am I as a person in interaction with you: what's it really all about? Not just in conversation but in movement. In all sorts of ways of expressing. People who are showing their pain. During psychoanalytic work, being with people who are exposing such vulnerability. It felt really privileged to be with people who would do that and enabled me to do the level I was capable of at the time. That there could be human expression at that kind of depth. That intensity of fulfilment that I hadn't got anywhere else.
>
> Elaine: What do you mean when you say working at depth?
>
> Sally: When people feel enabled to let go of their mantle, of their role, or whatever façade they put up and you start interacting with the vulnerable person underneath.

In Sally's model, the expression of pain between people is seen to constitute a special form of intimacy. The expression of pain is seen to reveal a depth and privacy about a person, which is more real and meaningful than what happens on the surface. Sally's focus is on the expression of pain rather than the content of pain, because it is deemed to be more risky than the expression of other emotions, because pain is seen as more private, and therefore, less mediated by public convention (Berlant, 2000). Revealing the private is seen as risky because it is more the true self than social conventions are, and if it is rejected in any way, then it is the true self that has been rejected. The rarity of its outings makes it more precious, as frequency makes something more trivial and public.

Being human

In a related example, Annette Dobson talks about vulnerability in relation to assertiveness training. In this quote, Annette is responding to my asking how her model of assertiveness is different from other models:

> Power has become – the meaning of power in an assertiveness sense now is almost synonymous, I think, with confidence. Assertive means being confident. It means being prepared, articulate. It's easy: aggression is a no-no and the passive is a no-no. But this sense of assertiveness has become quite, quite stuck with this idea of confidence, and being prepared, and being articulate, and knowing

> what to do, a sense of sureness, of self-containess... I just don't think that's assertiveness. You can be assertive and confident and prepared. But you can also be assertive when you are inarticulate, and you are confused, when you're vulnerable. Because what that model does, it allows no room for being human, right? And so it's a nonsense. It's nothing to do with being assertive. It's to do with something else. That's not even the right meaning of confidence to me. It's almost a denial of anxiety. So there's no room for roundness, there's no room for confusion, there's no room for making mistakes. There's no room for vulnerability of any kind. There's no room for emotion. There's no room for truthful. There's no room for anything, other than conforming to a convention of power, that is getting it right, and that's for me, that's never been what assertiveness is about.

Annette contrasts her idea of assertiveness with popular models she sees as based on normative masculinity. In her version of assertiveness, people can become more human by being more feminine. Drawing upon a spatial metaphor, she shows how this feminine self is a more complete version of the self. As we have seen, many critics believe that therapeutic practices encourage the expression of emotion, expanding the space for emotion, but Annette suggests here that most models of assertiveness training do not allow enough expression of emotions.

In this next quote from Annette, she discusses a range of so-called negative emotions in relation to her model of assertiveness. In this excerpt, Annette is describing her own model of assertiveness in contrast with other models.

> What I have always devoted everything to for twenty years is trying to get women to redefine their own power. But in order to do that, which involves really learning about self-love, and learning about your own beauty. And learning about often loneliness. It's learning how to stand alone. But it means, I think it means, acknowledging a huge amount of grief at what they have lost. And most women I've met aren't willing to face that, because it is very painful.

In Annette's view, the successful endpoints of assertiveness training are pain, loss and grief not happiness. In so doing, Annette's model moves away from Ian Craib's (1994, 1998) view that therapeutic cultures are comforting. At the same time, she also reconfigures the emotional progression narrative of transformation seen to typify therapeutic cultures, in which people move from being sad to being happy, from being alone to being with others. This model is also opposite to Sally's take on mutual vulnerability, which is seen to show the interconnectedness between people. For Annette, women's oppression can only be addressed by their becoming independent of other people. Although her model may seem to reproduce the view of Frank Furedi (2004) that an emasculated model of the self is being promulgated by therapeutic cultures, in Annette's model the feminised self is powerful, has agency and is more complete than his proposal that therapeutic cultures promote the diminished passive self.

Summary

These examples suggest that it is difficult to sum up the emotional self of therapeutic cultures in any one formula. However, with their emphasis on pain and vulnerability, the conceptualisation of feelings reproduced by the workers interviewed are more aligned to understandings of the contemporary emotional self, as in pain discussed by Lauren Berlant (2000, 2001a) and being vulnerable, as proposed by Frank Furedi (2004). For Berlant, the centrality of pain as the sign of the true self is dangerous because it takes one aspect of subjective experience as the truth of living, and assumes that pain can be assuaged by the mutual disclosure of pain. For Furedi (2004), the problem with these models of the suffering self is that they reproduce a notion of selfhood as passive, limited and diminished. In contrast to Berlant, the pain that Sally and Annette describe is not something that can be consoled or made better and contrary to Furedi, for them pain, suffering and vulnerability are seen as empowering and active rather than diminishing and inert. This is not to say that there are no problems with the politics of pain, particularly when comparisons and equivalences between different forms of suffering are drawn and when empathy is seen as the main mode of political action. Nevertheless, Sally's and Annette's models can be seen as allusions to the ordinary suffering and alienating effects of transformations in the workplace and wider society that is part of everyday life, and the intimate spaces of personal development where these subjective disappointments and hurt can be examined and understood.

Letting it all hang out?

As discussed earlier, the debates on our increased expression of emotions in public are complex. For some critics, like Ian Craib (1994,

1998), although therapeutic cultures claim to be anti the repression of emotion, they encourage a stance towards the expression of feeling which involves a 'control over feeling'. He writes, 'doubtless historically, elements of regulation have always been there, but now it has become public and organised, perhaps primarily through the growth of psychotherapy, and counselling' (1994: 165). Therapeutic cultures, he argues, encourage the 'dream of emotional management, in the sense of expecting a stable and ordered emotional life, and if that does not occur, the assumption is that something is wrong' (ibid: 104). In his view, this leads to us believing that 'we really could control ourselves and our lives' (1994: 107). For Arlie R. Hochschild (1994) this sense of control has been intensified for women in the suggestion, promoted by self-help books, that women should now act coolly in relation to others. This represents, she argues, an over-control in personal relations in which women ape men, and relationships are subject to distrust and caution. Catherine Lutz (1990) suggests that because women are seen as more emotional, with its associations of disorder, they have to draw upon metaphors of being in control of their emotions. For other critics, there is not enough control of our emotions and we are not being detached or rational enough (Sennett, 1986; Nolan, 1998).

Emotional control

In a discussion on hedonism and consumption, Colin Campbell (1989) argues that we should distinguish between the regulation of emotions and emotional control. For him, the regulation of emotions refers to the cultural conventions on *when* and *how* we should *express* wanted emotions, and *suppress* unwanted emotions. This form of control, in his view, is mainly focused on suppressing the subjective feeling component of emotion, and more often, the behavioural expression of that subjective feeling. The other form of control, what Campbell refers to as emotional control, describes the ability that people have today to decide on the type and intensity of the emotions that they want to feel. So how do these ideas compare to the conceptualisation of emotional control in the personal development workers' interviews? Do they see us needing to express our emotions more or control our emotion more? How do the personal development workers conceptualise the control of emotions? What is it that they seek specifically to control and why? Does control of emotions mean that they amplify them or suppress them?

Deep love

To begin the exploration of these questions, this section turns to a quote from Jade Simon as she discusses the issue of control in relation to the emotion of the therapist; a theme not discussed much in the sociology of therapeutic cultures:

> In actual fact you can get to a position where you really do love the other person and you really care very deeply about them, and I do, very quickly. I was doing a workshop for counsellors recently and once again I was very aware of how I had moved on and I don't think the workshop went down very well ... There is no way they were really buying a lot of what I was saying or buying me really... I was talking about how it's very important for me to feel I can have a handle on my ability to love and control that emotion because I want to be able to use it. I want to be able to love my clients very deeply, but still be in control and a lot of them found that really, really difficult. They said that was wrong, that they didn't love. And you shouldn't get that involved emotionally with a client.

For Jade Simon, the control of emotion is a beneficial therapeutic technique. Seeing love as a therapeutic technique, Jade draws upon a model of love as transformational and reparative. Her use of the concept of love is different from popular understandings of love in that genuine love is often seen as something that is beyond instrumentality and control. For Jade, love can be controlled and authentic and useful. Mobilising an analogy of depth, love is a technique that reaches 'deeper' inside of the client so that they can be transformed. In parallel to what some might see as a commodification of love, Jade frames her description of the group's response to her using a metaphor of buying. In this model of emotional control, Jade is stopping the two-way traffic of love, externalising her love towards her clients but not letting any effects internalise in her self. Drawing upon a model of emotional control as intensifying, directing and monitoring the feelings of love as in Campbell's model, she presents her self as someone who can control powerful emotions, a person with higher emotional competence. This model of authentic, beneficial intensification and management of love complicates Craib's understanding of emotional control as de-authenticating.

Too warm

In a similar vein, in this next quote Violette Turner suggests that the control of emotions is important. In response to my asking whether there are some people for whom psychodrama might not be appropriate, Violette replies:

> You can say to somebody 'I think you are too warmed up. I think it's best that you don't work today'. Whatever the words are. You don't have to work with people and they don't have to work with... Because they can hold it, they can hold it in the rest of their life. There is nothing that is actually totally urgent that somebody has to do something at that moment. Because we all juggle things, don't we? And that is the thing to remember. That people are actually living their lives. It might be coming out as great distress but that is because they are given permission to get into the feelings that they have been squashing down all the time. And they are very good at squashing it down so on the whole people are not incapable of controlling themselves.

In contrast to some theorists' views that therapeutic cultures provide refuges from society for the liberal expression of emotions, Violette presents the therapeutic space as regulated. Drawing upon a common cultural pressure metaphor to describe the type of control a person has over their emotion, psychodrama is seen to act as a safety valve to release feelings (Coward, 1989; Lupton, 1998). In this view of emotion, intense feelings can be seen as a danger and in need of controlled release.

Portraying a particular view of interiority, Violette sees feelings as something that are collected, hoarded inside of us and suppressed throughout life and then expressed in a controlled environment. This enables her to present emotions as subject to our control as we can pick and choose when to express them. In contrast to Craib, Violette suggests a continuum of control, in which psychodrama allows for more expression of feelings than other places and times in people's lives, but in which there is still a need for the regulation of emotion. Violette's model draws upon a commonly held belief that there are certain places where the control of certain emotions is more important. So there is a popular view that emotions should be controlled in the workplace, although theories on emotions in the workplace show how the expression of certain emotions is encouraged by different social groups (Fineman, 1993, 2000a). For Violette then, the therapeutic space is not a place for the expression of emotion without restraint or the simple, controlled de-control of emotions, but a space with its own inhibitions on certain productions of emotion.

Not just in the head

Similarly, Annette has a positive view of emotional control. In this excerpt, Annette is responding to my asking why she thinks some forms of assertiveness training are not effective:

> You really can't teach assertiveness as a lecture. You can give someone interesting ideas but because you see, because assertiveness is about changing behaviour and it therefore has to involve emotion. It has to involve your heart because you can't do it in your head alone, and that's why you have to have the role-play, because if you don't have the role-play, it stays at head level. Only when you do it in your own role-play, when you actually physically manage the anxiety of whatever it is you're trying, or you find hard to do. It's only then that you have the possibility of behavioural change. You can't do it in your head – ever.

In contrast to critics' understandings of contemporary expressivism, for Annette Dobson, real transformation for women comes from controlling not expressing emotion. In Annette's model, the therapeutic technology of role-play enables women to mobilise and intervene in their emotion, by initiating anxiety through the imagination, experiencing it to a small degree and then inhibiting its manifestation. The role-play is central for Annette because it accesses the deep self. It enables the behaviours performed on the body's surface to act as a lightning rod through to the 'other side' of the body, where it encases the deep self. For Annette, assertiveness comes from the body and not the mind. As with Jane Vincent, Annette sees intellect as unreal and distant from the self, reinforced by her metaphor of head and heart, which draws upon a cultural model of the heart as close to the self. The heart is a metaphor with a long history symbolising a whole range of aspects to do with the self including the innermost self, the secret self, the open self, the centre of the self and as the seat or container of emotions (Erickson, 1997; Jager, 2000; Schafer, 1976).

In Annette's model, control of anxiety is not simply the repression of the feeling or the suppression of its expression but a stimulation of emotion followed quickly by its suppression through the body. In this way, for Annette, control of the self is not repressive but expressive.

Summary

For the personal development workers, therapeutic cultures are not simply about the unconstrained expression of emotions. This applies to the personal development workers and the clients. In the examples cited above, personal development workers are not simply reproducing a model of the romantic humanist self, whose emotions are imagined to lie deep within, awaiting release in the liberal conditions of the therapeutic space. Furthermore, these examples complicate critics such as Craib and Furedi's understandings of emotional control. So all three personal development workers understand control in analogic terms, seeing emotions as things whose intensity and form can be varied, rather than in the somewhat digital terms of Craib. Both Annette and Jade Simon's models of control of emotion fit with Campbell's understanding of the experience of emotion as something that can be varied purposively. In Jade's case the control of love is not seen to be an inauthentic experience for herself or her client, as might be suggested by Craib, but as something that brings relief to her client and pleasure to her self. In Annette's example, the control of emotions is seen to be expressive of the self, problematising the opposition of control and expressivity in critical accounts of emotional expression in therapeutic cultures.

Conclusion

The specificities of emotions and emotional expressions that emerged in my research open up the category of emotions in therapeutic cultures. Many critics have assumed that emotional expressions in therapeutic cultures are simply manifestations of emotions, drawing upon a model of emotions and their transparent communicability that is very similar to the understanding of emotions that they ascribe to therapeutic cultures. So for example, Sennett (1986) suggests that emotional expressions should be more formalised and conventionalised, and yet my material here shows that this is the case. Rather than being simple manifestations of emotions, emotional expressions are symbolic and meaningful in ways largely under-explored by critics of therapeutic culture. My data shows that the significance of emotions for personal development workers goes beyond the 'cliché' of 'getting in touch with feelings', often used to characterise the operation of emotion in therapeutic cultures by critics. Emotional expressivism has also been seen as one of the main characteristics of the cultural intermediary occupations but little empirical work has been done to examine what kinds of emotional expressivism are drawn upon (Featherstone, 1991).

In contrast to most critics, my material shows that workers in personal development are concerned with the form and mode of emotional expression as much as the 'content' of the expressions. The 'how' of expression has symbolic meaning for the personal development workers over and above the 'what' of expression. This is one of the aspects of the operation of emotion in therapeutic cultures that has been under-analysed and under-theorised by critics of therapeutic cultures and by sociologists of emotion.

Verbal articulation

As I argued earlier, critics mainly focus on the verbal articulation of emotions as the pre-eminent medium of emotional expression as if it characterises all modes of emotional expressions. In this research, the verbal articulation of emotions has some significance for some personal development workers interviewed but they clearly relate it to particular situations or emotions, rather than seeing it exemplifying a generalised emotional expressivity in the way that critics suggest. In these interviews, verbal articulations of emotions were mobilised as what I call 'evidential' expressions, expressions believed to demonstrate the performance of a successfully transformed self, specifically an emotional self. 'Evidential' expressions were seen as best performed in public so that the new self and its emotionality could be given recognition. In spite of critics' concerns about the formulaic nature of expressive forms in therapeutic cultures, for Jane Vincent the conventionalised verbal form of this expression does not lessen its intensity. In fact it is precisely its idiomatic form that marks it as the most axiomatic expression of love (Gratton, 2000). In drawing upon this concept of love, Jane Vincent is reproducing a set of values, and an identity based on those values in which the family is seen as a source of community and relationality but also as a potential well of dysfunction if the right emotions are not shared. In mobilising this quintessential emotional expression, Jane Vincent is producing herself as a desirable self who is seen to be open, authentic and emotionally expressive rather than closed and alienated.

Non-verbal expression

My material suggests that the principal expressions of emotions for the personal development workers were non-verbal rather than verbal. These were performed on and through the body in contrast to critics' representations of emotional expressions that focus on verbal articulation of emotions (Nolan, 1998). Unlike verbal articulations of emotions, these expressions were seen as spontaneous and uncontrolled. Some of these were produced through the face and eyes, as in crying, and laughter, and others brought about through the use of the rest of the body, arms and legs. The expressions most referred to in the interviews were characterised by intensity, and an emotional, almost melodramatic excessiveness that would be seen as inappropriate in other social spheres. Intensity was represented by the rapid onset of the expression, the duration of the expression, and the scope and amplitude of body movements that suggested a forcefulness, concentration and quantity to the feelings being felt. The kinetic intensity of the expressions is important because it symbolises the transformation of the self.

Transforming emotions

The non-verbal emotional expression referred to most consistently, and seen as the most quintessential expression of emotions by the personal development workers, was crying, a kind of 'therapeutic close up', and yet it is an expression unexamined in the critical literature on therapeutic cultures. Crying was seen to be expressive of an externalisation of the past self rather than simply being an expression of a particular emotion. Its form in the personal development workers' accounts mirrored the transformation of the self so the progression of the self from past to new self is paralleled in the movement of emotion from inside to outside. The movement from inside to outside needs to be of some distance, indicating a depth to the emotions and the self. Weaker expressions would indicate emotions that are less close to the self, and would signal a lacking of conviction by the client, and a less pronounced form of self-transformation. These expressions of emotions are what I would call 'transmutative' emotional expressions, embodied expressions that were seen to symbolise the experiencing of self-transformation as it was happening.

Intense bodily expressions were seen as most legitimate because they symbolised the relegation of intellect as a means of self-transformation. They symbolised successful transformation as they were seen to have a reality that the intellect was seen not to have. The body is used to symbolise self-transformation, in which a changed body is seen as symbolising a changed self, and a changed relationship between self and body. In these accounts the intensity and physicality of the bodily emotional expressions are seen to enable a visibility and legibility demonstrating the self and the body have transformed. This comes from a set of assumptions that emotions are honest, pure, uncultured parts of the self, not superficial or artificial bits of the self. The significance of this emotional mode is less its feeling content and more its bodily performance.

Emotionality

My research also shows that although the emotional expressions had nuanced, complex forms, they were not always linked by the personal development workers to specific nuanced feelings. Instead, these expressions, which I term 'emotionalist expressions' were imagined as conveying a state of emotionality, a readiness to be affected by emotions, rather than manifesting particular singular emotions. Imagined in this way, emotionality was not seen as an excess of emotions or expressivity, or evidencing an indiscriminate approach to emotions (Campbell, 1997) or a lack of control as might be viewed by critics. Emotionality represents the ability to be unrepressed, free and easy, impulsive, natural and therefore more vital and engaged with the world. In contrast, for the workers interviewed 'emotionalist expressions' enable the person to be seen as being emotionally fluent rather than just having a feeling. As we have seen, many critics of therapeutic cultures use the category of 'emotion' in such a way that it appears to be a unified concept like 'emotionality' but this does not capture the way that 'emotionality' was seen to work in therapeutic cultures by the workers.

At the same time that personal development workers referred to 'emotionality' as a generalised state, some workers did also discuss some specific feelings. Whilst Jade Simon and Jane Vincent referred to love and happiness, more personal development workers such as Annette, Paul and Sally mentioned fear, pain, anxiety, grief and vulnerability, culturally coded as feminine. This focus by the workers on more so-called negative feelings challenges Craib's view that so-called positive emotions are privileged in post-psychoanalytic therapies in the process of therapy and also as successful endpoints of therapy. These feelings were seen to constitute the true self more than others as they were viewed as more private and more risky to express. Indeed, they were seen less as expressed, in terms of being externalised, and more as revealed as the loosening of self-control is released. In Sally and Violette's models, the mutual revelation of pain and vulnerability was seen to provide a transcendent and transformational bond between people. Pain and vulnerability are seen to contain more of the real self than other emotions, and because people's real selves are imagined to be rarely on show, the sharing of them is seen to be a privileged form of identification.

Empathetic relations

In contrast to the dominant model of trauma and reparation in Berlant's (2000) discussion, Sally and Violette do not conceptualise pain and vulnerability as feelings to be relieved, but more as a universal condition, in which these feelings do not have a brisk onset or offset, but are imagined to be constant. Pain and vulnerability, at the same time as being universal, are seen as unique in that what has given you pain varies with childhood history and relationships. The mutual revelation of these emotions is seen to develop empathetic relations in which compassion and sympathy are imagined to be therapeutic as much as the revelations themselves. The model of the self is not innocent as Nolan suggested but more traumatised, and emotions in this model are not seen as seen as energising and vital (Morawski, 1997) but more as signs of sensitivity.

Rather than seeing themselves as passive victims as Furedi (2004) might suggest, this mode of emotion enables personal development workers to produce a sense of their selves as complex, delicate, refined through their suffering and decent and caring in terms of their empathy. These types of emotions endow personal development workers with a sense of moral worth in which they are seen as having more depth than might be seen with more positive and 'superficial' emotions like happiness. Rather than reinforcing individualistic, solipsist states, for Sally and Violette, the sharing of mutual suffering builds connections.

In Annette's model, the feelings of grief, loneliness and pain also represent the endpoint of successful transformation, but for her, they symbolise the lack of relationality and community that comes with being assertive. Being assertive in this model brings with it certain advantages but also means loss. Grief, loneliness and pain represent a certain kind of worldly wisdom, but unlike Sally and Violette's models, a solitary experience of emotions. For Annette, the model of the self is not the sensitive suffering self of Violette or Sally but the self as honest and authentic. In summary, in contrast to how critics characterise so-called negative feelings in therapeutic cultures, in these models negative feelings are not disapproved of or suppressed, but on the contrary are encouraged because of what they are seen to symbolise.

Emotives

So how does my analysis suggest we might understand emotional expressions in a different way from what is largely presented in the sociology of therapeutic cultures? One way is to build on the influential feminist Judith Butler's (1990) notion of speech acts and gender because it provides a very different way of understanding expression. Speech acts are understood as performatives, i.e. utterances which are also actions, bringing into being what they claim simply to name. For Butler, gender is also performative, produced from stylised acts of the body and voice, not expressed through these gendered acts. If we were to understand emotion expressions as 'emotion acts', this would result in us seeing emotional expressions as ritualised and contextualised behaviours, which work performatively to enact the emotions and the emotional selves they are said to reveal. In relation to personal development, emotion acts would be seen as stylised performances, which 'mime' dominant conventions on emotions but inflected by the therapeutic context. This means that emotion acts are both artificial and yet real, creating particular material changes to the body and the self in ways which fit with the way that some personal development workers present crying as liminal spaces. A recent poetry book is entitled *Doing Things with Tears* and the term 'emotion acts' draws our attention to the things that emotional expressions do, to the effects they create.

In her discussion of gender, Butler writes that gender performatives produce the effects of interiority, depth and surface in relation to the body. Similarly, it could be argued that emotion acts in personal development enact different kinds of emotional interiorities and surfaces. So for example, Sally's model of emotion presents a version of interior selves as experiencing the feeling of pain, in which the depths of the self can be 'revealed' to others deliberately through enacting particular expressions, in verbal utterances and bodily performances. In contrast, in one of Jane Vincent's models of emotional expressions, the depths of the self cannot be purposefully revealed, but spontaneously show themselves on the surface of the body through its movement. For Andy, crying brings the interior self to the exterior of the body, with its depths revealed by the duration of the crying.

Building on the personal development workers' interviews, I want to argue that emotion acts in personal development produce different types of emotional selves. They perform the self as being authentic and truthful as in one of Jane Vincent's models. For Sally and Violette, they produce a self that is suffering, sensitive and empathetic. In another of Jane Vincent's models, emotions create an emotional self that is presented as a warm, vital and well-rounded self in opposition to an alienated or disengaged cold self. For Annette, emotion acts produce a self of worldly wisdom. These different modes highlight the diverse and contradictory models of emotions on which the personal development workers draw, some of which have a long history and have not simply arisen out of therapeutic thinking. My research suggests that any discussion of the emotionalisation of social spheres needs to take account of the specificities, and meanings of emotion acts in their context. Furthermore, much of contemporary work on the self has explored how identities are created from commodities, lifestyles, and bodies but this chapter builds on the work of Hetherington (1998) to suggest that the self is also produced through emotion acts. This has been under-analysed in much of the sociological literature on therapeutic cultures.

8
Worked Up Selves

Introduction

At the beginning of this book I argued that insufficient empirical work had been done within the sociology of therapeutic cultures. This is particularly so I suggested regarding personal development workers. Throughout I maintained this relative lack of empirical work, and this lack of focus on therapeutic workers has had the effect of homogenising the multiplicity of therapeutic cultures, including personal development. I argued that much of the literature in the sociology of therapeutic cultures whilst addressing questions about the proliferation of therapeutic cultures, largely neglects the particular contextual uses of therapeutic approaches, and meanings of therapeutic cultures for different practitioners, including personal development workers. I maintained that this is rather surprising given the concerns about the rise of therapeutic experts in the private and public spheres and their supposed power and influence. It is also problematic because this growing literature is extremely critical of therapeutic cultures, personal development workers and users.

I suggested that this critique is based on largely singular understandings of the practices in therapeutic cultures, meaning that when critics arrive at their evaluations of the politics of therapeutic cultures, these are founded on undifferentiated models of the therapeutic. My aim in this book has been to surface particularities in relation to the field of personal development by exploring personal development workers' understandings of their approaches and the significance of their versions of the self, transformation and emotion in personal development. Bringing these threads together in this chapter, I shall consider the more general conclusions of my research, then turn to the broader questions and wider implications arising from the book, and finish by raising further issues for future research on personal development and therapeutic cultures. Before moving on to my more general conclusions, I shall offer a brief summary of the main themes and ideas from earlier chapters to remind readers of their essential components.

Sociology of therapeutic cultures

Chapter 2 offered a brief overview of the history of therapeutic thinking and practices in wider culture and the workplace. Its purpose was to draw attention to the varied origins of personal development, the diversity of models of the self and its contents and the range of different prescribed interventions in the self in the workplace.

Chapters 3 and 4 provided a wide ranging review of current literatures on therapeutic cultures from an array of disciplines. Chapter 3 focused on the work of influential sociologists who provide a more macro theoretical take on the rise of therapeutic thinking. Each theorist offers a different set of conceptual resources with which to interrogate the proliferation of personal development, and arrive at contrasting stands on the effects and politics of the propagation of therapeutic practices, ideas and ideologies.

Chapter 4 outlined less well known theorists, many of whom are feminists and who provide textual analyses and more empirical studies on the reception of therapeutic cultures. This literature suggested that self-help book readers are more ambivalent in their response to therapeutic ideas. It is likely, of course, that these readers are operating in a different context and relation to therapeutic ideas than Nolan puts forward in his idea on the therapeutic state. Motivated by a feminist project, several authors identified how much self-help literature reproduces and at the same time, domesticates feminist tenets. There are, however in this literature, two main areas in therapeutic cultures that have remained relatively unexamined: personal development workers' understandings of therapeutic cultures and the field of personal development, particularly in relation to its interface with the workplace. I suggested that this is an important omission because, as many critics note, the workplace is a significant site in the proliferation, and production of therapeutic cultures.

Expertise and power

Starting to address this relative gap, and supporting my general claim that the ideas that underpin personal development are diverse, Chapters 5, 6 and 7 contain detailed close readings of the most significant themes that emerged from my interviews with personal development workers.

Chapter 5 argued that many critics of therapeutic cultures underestimate the complex ways in which personal development workers construct the power dynamic between them and their clients. My material showed that this issue of power is also of great concern for the personal development workers and understood on very different terms to the leading critics. I suggested that the context in which personal development workers operate and the particular nature of their client-practitioner mobility meant that there is a specificity to the models of power mobilised by the personal development workers which does not feature in critical accounts of therapeutic cultures. This can be seen to muddle the supposed clear distinction in power relations. For many critics, asymmetrical power relations in favour of the personal development workers are created because of the supposed authority of expert knowledge upon which they draw. I argued that personal development workers define their 'expertise' on different terms than expert knowledge, using more 'non-professional' types of expertise including knowledge through experience and their own charisma. In fact in Annette Dobson's case, there was an explicit refusal of expert knowledge.

These moves meant that there was a split between those personal development workers who saw themselves as 'special' in relation to their clients, either through them being 'sorted out' people, or having charismatic powers, and those who imagined themselves as being similar to their clients in not being fully sorted out.

In spite of these differences amongst the personal development workers' models, I proposed that the theme of equality was of great significance to all of the personal development workers. I argued that their equality was seen to be achieved through what I called 'charismatic exchange'. I concluded the chapter by suggesting that the anthropological concept of the 'gift' could be used to help elucidate the different models of power and relations mobilised by the personal development workers, enabling us to see a two-way transfer between personal development workers and clients. Drawing together the analogy of the gift with the concept of charisma, I argued that charisma itself operates as a type of gift in which the personal development workers exchange their exceptional qualities through a number of mechanisms such as conversion and techniques. In return, the clients offer their loyalty, faith, emotional commitment and transformation. I concluded that 'charismatic exchange' was based on different conceptualisations of charisma from being a role model of someone sorted out, to being a free spirit, or having the power to have profound or wide-ranging effects on people, having personality, charm, magical powers, and fame. It also operated in different relations with clients from conversion, traumatisation, identification, love, admiration, awe, transformation at a distance, harmony and commitment. Although charisma took on different forms, they were all derived from the personal development workers having 'been there', having lived an ordinary life which they then improved upon, or survived, in special ways. This set of ideas builds on Bourdieu's idea of the cultural intermediary. Bourdieu writes that cultural intermediaries 'sell themselves as models and guarantors of the value of their products...and is sincerely "sold" on the value of what he [sic] sells' (1984: 365).

Changing the self

Chapter 6 moved on to consider how personal development workers saw clients being transformed through their approaches. In particular, I argued that rather than one model of the self such as the entrepreneurial self underpinning all of these diverse conceptualisations as some critics argue, understandings of the self varied quite considerably, as did the ways to transform them.

As a result, I proposed a typology of models of transformation to capture the diversity of these understandings of self-transformation. This typology included the suffering model of transformation, the makeover, the quick fix, the experiment, the work of art and the genetic growth models. From this analysis, we can understand that a commonplace assumption of 'development as a journey' is being replaced by very different models. In particular, I suggested that the lifelong search for an ideal self is being replaced by the idea of the makeover, the quick fix.

These have their own versions of temporality. They can be seen as recasting relations between the 'old' and 'new' self, and relations between our selves and our past, present and future, and the relationship between the self and self-knowledge. As a consequence, this means that the phrases 'self-discovery', 'self-realisation' and 'self actualisation' cannot be used as synonyms in analyses of personal development, as is often the case in the critical literature on therapeutic cultures.

In addition, personal development workers' accounts of transformation suggest that personal development offers fantasy practices such as role-play, timelines and psychodrama. They also provide fantasies about the self and its effects, how personal development workers and clients can effect transformations in the self, and in their contexts, pasts and futures.

These fantasy operations offer spaces and practices which enable people to find ways to try on different selves and lives. These offer resources and comfort in response to the imperative to transform our selves in the workplace and in wider contemporary culture and what Blackman and Walkerdine call the impossible fiction of the self in neoliberalism.

Emoting

In all of their discussions, personal development workers return to the significance of emotion. Chapter 7 argued that there is a commonsense model of emotion operating in much of the sociology of therapeutic cultures in which emotion is seen to be a unified category, presumed to operate in predictable, even superficial ways. Drawing upon my data, we can see that the category of emotion has a multiplicity of significations, which do different kinds of work in the personal development workers' accounts.

There was a specificity to the particular types of emotional expressions described by the practitioners, which has been under-analysed in the literature on therapeutic cultures. From my material I categorised several different forms of expression: 'evidential' emotional expressions, 'transmutative' emotional expressions, 'emotionalist' expressions, and 'self-control' expressions.

Through their descriptions of these expressions, personal development workers reproduced a similar unitary category of feeling of 'emotionality' as the critics do, but for them 'emotionality' symbolised a 'good' state of vitality and sensitivity to self and others, rather than an excessive approach to emotions.

In contrast to understanding the expression of emotions as simply revealing what is already existent, as is the case in much of the critical literature, one way to understand emotional expressivity in personal development is in terms of performativity. Drawing upon Judith Butler's notion (1990) of gender and performative acts, emotional expressions could be understood not as speech acts but as 'emotion acts'. This enabled key aspects of emotional expressions in the personal development workers' accounts to be brought to the fore: the stylised form of these expressions, their semiotics and the self-work that they do. These different expressivist modes create different kinds of selves, bodies, and ideas about its depth and interiority, the political implications of which need more examination. Making reference to how social scientists have suggested that identities are created from commodities, I build on Kevin Hetherington's work (1998) to show selves are also produced through different emotional modes and performances.

The selves of therapeutic cultures

Having discussed the specific arguments drawn from my analysis of the practitioner interviews, I now turn to more general arguments from the book as a whole. The first of these revolves around understandings of the 'self' in therapeutic cultures. My initial intention in the analysis of my data was to focus on the model of the 'entrepreneurial self' as put forward by Rose (1989, 1996a), because he suggests that this go-getting, self-managing self is the quintessential model of the self in therapeutic cultures, and of the workplace. It seemed as if this might provide a useful analytic framework for understanding personal development workers' accounts. But this proved problematic. In each of the three ethnographic chapters, the diversity of the selves presented by the personal development workers interviewed was striking.

What emerged as more meaningful is understanding that there are competing versions of the self in personal development. Some of these are idiosyncratic and sometimes contradictory, and cannot be boiled down into one over-arching model of the self. However, many critics propose such over-arching models, although interestingly, these are often quite different: Giddens (1991, 1992) suggests the 'reflexive self', Furedi (2004) the 'diminished self', and Nolan (1998) the 'emotivist self'. It can be argued from my material that the selves conceptualised by the personal development workers interviewed do not overlap with any one of these models. So for example, as I detailed in Chapter 5, the ideal assertive self represented by Annette Dobson is a flawed self. For her, the assertive self is not the achievement-focused entrepreneurial self of Rose (1989, 1996a). Unlike the entrepreneurial self, Annette suggests the assertive self makes mistakes, is vulnerable, and likely to fail. But as I discussed in Chapter 7, although there appear to be similarities between the emotions defining Annette's assertive self, and Furedi's (2004) passive suffering victim, they are in fact, very different selves. As I argued, for Annette, the suffering of the assertive self is understood in political terms as the result of women's oppression in society, and gendered expectations of being successful and influential. For Annette, this self is understood as active, independent and powerful in that she is able to deal with this oppression. The downside is that in transforming in this way, she loses the basis of her connection with other women.

There are some overlaps in the personal development workers' accounts with parts of Giddens' 'reflexive self'. Thus, Paul and Peter draw upon the importance of 'choice' in defining a 'good' self, although their understandings of 'choice' fracture Giddens' sense of the self as a project, as choosing may be needed moment by moment. Similarly, Jade Simon's model of the self as an experimenter, grafting new bits on to its self through trial and error, does not fit with Giddens' calculative coherent reflexive self, which plots and plans its future, making itself into a project, pulling itself together through a coherent narrative. Instead, the self is seen by Jade as shaped by circumstance and the performance of mini-experiments to meet or deal with those circumstances.

The transformation of the self, albeit variously defined, was also seen to be significant by all the personal development workers. For all the personal development workers, transformation of the self by the self was imagined as something that was desirable and possible to do. Again what emerged from my material is that transformation of the self was conceptualised in very different terms: thus, transformation was imagined as re-adjustment, repair, revealing, unfolding, evolution, mutation, and makeover. Sometimes it was imagined as entailing difficulty or suffering, but in many of the accounts it was seen as relatively easy, painless and quick.

In contrast to the critics, these easier and speedier transformations were seen as being equally profound or helpful for clients. To transform the self in these quicker ways, the self is seen as accessible and transformable by the self. Although emotion is claimed as a source of depth and complexity in some versions of personal development in my research, generally the self in personal development is seen as relatively uncomplex and unmysterious. Consequently, the interiority of the self is being re-cast so that traditional markers of interiority in therapeutic cultures such as trauma and memory are seen as less significant in personal development than perhaps in other therapeutic cultures (Berlant, 2000, 2001a; Stanley, 2000; Seltzer, 1998).

A hermeneutics of the self has been replaced in many of these models as knowledge of the self, its past is seen as less important as 'know yourself' has become transform 'yourself' – I change therefore I am. As I argue, this should not mean that we see these versions of the self as less 'authentic' or meaningful for the personal development workers. For example, the transformations undertaken by Jade Simon's 'experimenting' self were not presented as leading to a problem of throw-away selves as critics suggest, but as events which could liberate, materially, spiritually and psychologically, even if temporarily.

The significance of this diversity in understandings of the self and its transformation cannot be underestimated. Thus it can be argued that therapeutic cultures are more confusing, messy and contradictory than critics suggest when they reduce the complexity down into one example which is supposed to stand for all models. The fact that critics come up with very different models of the self, for example, Rose's enterprising self compared with Furedi's diminished self, highlights some of the contradictions and variety in therapeutic cultures. At the most general level, this diversity could be characterised as evidence that personal development workers and other participants in therapeutic cultures are producing their own models and understandings of the self. This means that there is no one ideal self, or therapeutic self, or one version of the good life in these accounts. As cultural intermediaries, they are drawing upon different cultural resources, some of which support workplace ideals, neoliberal ideals and at other times, do not.

Expert systems?

When I began this research I had expected to understand the personal development workers' models through Rose's (1989, 1996a) concept of 'psy' expertise. For him, therapeutic expertise is based on psychology's supposed special competence in interpersonal relations and an associated body of techniques and procedures based on this knowledge (1996a: 11). In his view, psychology's claims to know the truth about the self have provided a rational form of authority for a number of professional groups across a number of social spheres.

However, the personal development workers interviewed did not conceptualise their authority in these terms. This leads to my second general claim, which is that this research suggests that the way critics such as Rose define therapeutic relations in terms of expertise is unsatisfactory and that we need different models of expertise and authority to understand the way that personal development workers present their knowledge in personal development.

The personal development workers interviewed did not define their authority in terms of scientific or professional psychological knowledge. Bondi and Fewell (2003) show how voluntary counsellors conceptualise their authority in terms of relationship skills rather than formal 'psy' expertise, and for the personal development personal development workers interviewed, their authority was derived from their own real, grounded experience of life. Of course, the concept of experience as an unmediated possession of the self has been problematised by feminists. (See for example Joan Scott 1992).

In contrast to Rose, the truth of their claims was not seen to come from the truth of psychology, but from the fact that they have 'been there too'. Within this, personal development workers' understanding of their relation to experience varied, with some seeing themselves as getting the better of life, whilst others seeing themselves still struggling with life. Although there is this variation, all of them see their experience resulting in a knowledge of what 'real' living is like, and how it can be made easier to cope with. These encounters with 'real life' gave the personal development workers charisma, albeit in different forms.

For many of the personal development workers, their charisma was enhanced by their refusal of expertise, and their lack of promoting their charisma. For these personal development workers, their authority derived from their charisma, and their ability to perform charisma through their carrying out special rituals, converting people, and their ability to transform others. Writers on charisma have noted that people who are understood to be charismatic are imagined to have an important relation for what are central values in society, what is at the heart of life, and for these personal development workers, the heart of things is everyday emotional life (Bryman, 1992). In drawing their expertise from 'real life', the personal development workers' position themselves as part of the 'everyday', and ordinary, using their own, and their client's 'commonsense' and experience rather than abstract ideas.

Rather than being like experts, they present themselves in terms closer to Giddens' (1994) sense of 'guardians', i.e. sages and wise men [sic], who can decipher universal truths from long-standing tradition and its artefacts, like sacred texts. But unlike Giddens' notion of guardians, these personal development workers are less interested in tradition as a form of knowledge, and universal truths embedded in tradition. They align themselves more with knowledge about the everyday, and situational, temporary 'truths'. Distancing themselves from the depersonalised knowledge of experts and guardians (Giddens, 1991), the personal development workers imagine themselves more like 'guides', people who have been there, and know some of the way, even if they too find the route difficult, but whose knowledge of the everyday paradoxically gives them charisma, because they have survived the everyday.

This is not the same as Weber's notion of the routinisation of charisma in which charisma gets replaced by the everyday in charismatic relations. Instead, it suggests contact with 'everyday experience' brings a form of charisma to the personal development workers, in a way which 'distant', abstract knowledge does not. At the most general level this approach to expertise could be characterised as the result of a particular form of reflexivity, a self-consciousness that personal development workers have about the general critiques of their practices in academia and popular culture. Their downgrading of expertise, their reliance on experiences and their espousal to equality are a response to critiques of their power and their knowledge base. I would argue that these conceptualisations of knowledge challenge Rose's assumption that therapeutic cultures are based predominantly on 'psy' expertise, and that different professions from social workers to managers will draw upon 'psy' expertise in the same way. Personal development workers do draw upon 'psy' expertise but not in any programmatic, coherent way. For personal development personal development workers, their lack of professional status and personal development credentials means that they use charisma as a form of authority to intensify their relations with their clients, and equality as a response to academic and popular critiques about their power and expertise.

Emotionocracy?

My third general argument is that many of the critical literatures are misleading in their understanding of emotions in therapeutic cultures. This is significant because many critics base their political dismissal of therapeutic cultures on their understandings of the operation of emotion in therapeutic cultures. Emotion has been seen by critics as what is most problematic about therapeutic cultures. For critics like Craib, Furedi and Nolan, therapeutic cultures are impoverishing our experience and understanding of emotions, our individual and collective lives. One important aspect of this for Craib and Furedi is the hierarchy of emotions in therapeutic cultures, in which they argue domesticated emotions are over-valued. This research shows that some of their critiques are evidenced in the personal development workers' accounts in some respects, so for example, seeing pain as a transcendent feeling; but overall, I conclude that the personal development workers' conceptualisations of emotion are much more complex than the critics suggest.

I would argue that although some of what the critics say is true, for example, an emphasis on 'feminine' emotions, there is more going on here. Some critics seem to underestimate that people need spaces to understand or get on with their emotional lives. For the personal development workers interviewed, examining and transforming emotional life in personal development is not meaningless, formulaic or superficial as some critics suggest. For them personal development offers intimate spaces where certain issues, problems, questions about living can be discussed and listened to. Some of it may be consoling as Cloud (1998) suggests, but it also represents a deep emotional engagement with the world, and is not simply privatising or individualising disengagement from the world (Gauntlett, 2002a, 2002b). In these personal development workers' accounts, personal development involves the provision of emotional resources for coping with a world in which emotions and the self are becoming more complex at home and at work, particularly given the increasing emphasis on emotional labour, emotion work, self-labour and self-work.

Personal development has developed its own private spaces where the difficulties of, and contradictions in, affective encounters and intimacy practices at home, and increasingly at work, can be discussed and transformed. These spaces can provide strategies for dealing with the changing formations of the public and private, what Sennett calls the pathologies of neoliberalism and the new cultures of intimacy. They offer opportunities for introspection, reflection and fantasy and moments for creativity and play with the self.

As can be seen from the personal development workers' accounts, they are aware of the complexities of life and do not regard personal development as always resolving problems, and if they do, it is seen as only temporary. Personal development then represents a particular kind of emotional public and intimate space, with its own emotional semiotics, which is not necessarily the same as other emotional spaces such as daytime chat shows or religious confessions. I would argue that this conclusion shows us that we need to understand emotionalisation in more detail, acknowledging the very different ways in which emotions may be mobilised in cultural practices. I would add that we should not see therapeutic cultures as the large-scale normative programming of emotions as some critics suggest. As I argued earlier, personal development workers do not just take ideas on without question or changing them. Some critics such as Craib and Furedi assume that they know which emotions and emotional expressions are best for people and yet this material shows that personal development workers of personal development do not have such a clear prescriptive agenda as these critics do.

Cultural intermediaries

One of the interesting themes in my material is the diversity of ideas drawn upon by the personal development workers, influenced by behaviourism, psychoanalysis, cognitive therapy, NLP, role plays, Romanticism, New Age, feminism, Protestantism, aphorism, clichés, stories, myths, their own experiences and personal resources, books they have read etc. There is no one overarching framework or theory that appears to guide their thinking. As cultural intermediaries, they are mediating many different cultural forms and types of knowledge.

One way to understand them is the postmodern knowledge worker par exemplar. Postmodernism has, of course, been subject to much debate. The word has been used to describe a contemporary epoch, an aesthetic style, and an epistemological stance in which traditional notions of knowledge are viewed with scepticism and suspicion. With this latter mode comes a radical critique of modernist knowledge ideas such as progress, and other 'metanarratives' such as Marxism. For postmodern thinkers such as the postmodern philosopher, Jean Francois Lyotard (1984), the critique of metanarratives on the basis of the problems of truth and representation means that we are left with 'petit recits', little local stories. In similar vein, feminist philosopher, Jane Flax (1990) argues that fragments are a good form of knowledge for contemporary life. For her, fragments represent non-unified and non-progressive bits of knowledge that we can use to make sense with. Flax's idea of the fragment might be present in the notion of a story.

In line with this idea of petit recits and fragments, one of the quintessential forms of postmodern knowledge is the collage. The collage acts as a metaphor for the multiple and contradictory sources, and fragments of knowledge that can be drawn upon, temporarily and sceptically. The collage also highlights the lack of foundation underpinning or coherence inherent in the sources.

Bricolage

The activity of putting together a jumble of fragments has been called 'bricolage'. So artists, shoppers, academics have all been understood as doing 'bricolage', or being bricoleurs. Bricolage is an everyday French word, referring to the handy-person's way of 'making do' with whatever materials and tools are at hand to get a job done. The bricoleur has been defined by the anthropologist, Claude Levi-Strauss as follows:

> The 'bricoleur' is adept at performing a large number of diverse tasks; but, unlike the engineer, he does not subordinate each of them to the availability of raw materials and tools conceived and procured for the purpose of the project. His universe of instruments is closed and the rules of his game are always to make do with 'whatever is at hand', that is to say with a set of tools and materials which is always finite and is also heterogeneous, because what it contains bears no relation to the current project, or indeed to any particular project, but is the contingent result of all the occasions there have been to renew or enrich the stock or to maintain it with the remains of previous constructions of destructions. (Levi-Strauss, 1966: 17)

Thus, bricolage is opportunistic, tactical, creative and original. Yiannis Gabriel (2002) and Bill Martin (1998) both suggest that managers can be thought of as bricoleurs in the way they take a bit of this and a bit of that and see how it works in practice. The term, then, gets at the makeshift and improvisatory in practice, emphasising the spontaneous rather than the planned (Gabriel, 2002). It also highlights the significance of utility which guides the use of particular materials or tools as opposed to being dictated by some overarching theory. This is something which Lyotard sees as the characteristic of postmodern knowledge. So for Lyotard, contemporary knowledge is valorised if it is of 'use' rather than it being seen as 'true' (Stacey, 1997).

> Bricolage doesn't worry about the coherence of the words or ideas it uses. For example, you are a bricoleur if you talk about penis envy or the oedipus complex and you don't know anything about psychoanalysis; you use the terms without having to acknowledge that the whole system of thought that produced these terms and ideas, i.e. Freudian psychoanalysis, is valid and 'true'. In fact, you don't care if psychoanalysis is true or not (since, at heart, you don't really believe in 'truth' as an absolute, but only as something that emerges from a coherent system, as a kind of illusion) as long as the terms and ideas are useful to you. (Klages, 1997, cited in Gabriel, 2002: 145)

Brioleurs 'lift' ideas out of different contexts and discourses, to make use of them situationally with little concern for their original formulations, or systems of thought that produced these ideas (Gabriel, 2002). As well as lifting materials, bricoleurs adapt, combine and re-combine ideas and tools (Gabriel, 2002).

Middle class bricoleurs

In a similar vein, Bill Martin (1998) argues that new middle class occupations such as managers have to put together experience 'toolkits'. These toolkits are forms of bricolage taken from formal education, training, education and individual opportunities and experiences. Experiences can be from work, life, family. As he puts it, life becomes a form of investment for the CV. This toolkit of the self, assembled through eclectic experiences and resources becomes the sign of individuality and individuation: 'a unique personal knowledge bundle offering new forms of socially useful knowledge' (1998: 671). The uniqueness becomes a key feature in the labour market. Again, for Martin knowledge resources are not based on accuracy but utility. The de-traditionalised self has no unfolding teleological life story – you have to keep your options open (ibid). As a result, commitment to knowledge has to be provisional – worklife is unpredictable and complex. In his view, the person becomes the toolkit they have assembled to sell to the labour market as they see their bricolage as consciously authored rather than just as bits and pieces (ibid: 672). This toolkit needs to emphasise one's particular unique personality package.

Therapeutic bricoleurs and toolkits

These ideas of bricolage and toolkits can help us understand the combination of knowledges and experiences that personal development workers discuss in my material. As intermediaries, they relay between different realms – private and public, formal knowledge and aphorisms, their own experiences, habits, and motivations, femininity and masculinity – to produce themselves as experts in using eclecticism and improvisation as work. In particular, skills associated with femininity such as the expression of emotions, intimacy and relationship skills are deemed to be important resources which professionals and managers need to be able to perform, regardless of gender (Kerfoot, 1999; Adkins, 2002a, 2002b). Therapeutic bricolage as described by the personal development workers interviewed involves more feminised performances of the self such as crying, being vulnerable, listening, empathy, sharing intimate information and being easily transformed.

These ideas also enable us to see that as cultural intermediaries, personal development workers are part of the toolkit production, they help disseminate resources – therapeutic bricolage – for clients to produce their own self-toolkits. Therapeutic bricolage allows these middle class workers to claim expertise without displaying loyalty to any one overarching theory, which would make one a hostage to fate or the sell-by date of one's knowledge (Martin, 1998).

Therapeutic bricolage has come to the fore because it mediates between the fragmenting realm of sexual and family relations and the domain of workplace relations. In this way, it arbitrates the contradictions of capitalism and postmodernity.

This idea of bricolage then might act as a 'middle range' sociological theory to elucidate what the practitioners interviewed describe in their practices: heterogeneity, improvisation and utility. In understanding personal development workers more as 'bricoleurs' than 'engineers of the soul' (Rose, 1989), we can destabilise a certain growing received wisdom on therapeutic cultures. For example, it underlines that there is no one central, dominant technique, such as the confession, being mobilised in therapeutic cultures as might be imputed from Rose's work. Seeing personal development workers as bricoleurs also confirms Giddens' understanding of our simultaneous turn to expertise while at the same time we see all forms of contemporary expertise as temporary and contingent.

There are dangers with the concept of bricolage. In focusing on the makeshift and anything at hand, it can seem like anything goes. And this is not the case. Although the sources of therapeutic cultures are varied, some resources are better than others. There is some kind of institutional isomorphism in operation.

It can also conceal the expertise in operation in deciding which sources to use. Several commentators on the self in contemporary society, such as Beverley Skeggs (2004) and Lisa Adkins (2002a, 2002b), argue that there are particular resources which are seen as legitimate and productive in making the self, and especially producing a self with value. One privileged site for producing a self of value is the workplace. Seen as a significant site of reflexivity and de-traditionalisation, individuality and personalisation are central to the production of a self of value, as several authors have noted (Adkins, 2002a, 2002b; Featherstone, 1991). With the growing aestheticisation and feminisation of the self at work, there is capital to be derived from the self's claims to charisma, personality and difference. In particular, Skeggs suggests that resources such as time, knowledge and access to resources are needed to make the self. Not all workers have access to these resources. In some work contexts, the resources are dictated and imposed. Thus, bricolage for the self can be seen as a middle class pursuit. In this view, the bricoleur is like a cultural omnivore (Skeggs, 2004), ransacking cultural resources for the self from different sources. The middle class omnivore seeks resources from all walks of life, their home, work and leisure life to produce a value accumulating idiosyncratic self (Skeggs, 2004; Martin, 1998). Like management consultants, personal development workers can be understood in some ways as exemplary neoliberal subjects. They are 'self-employed, sorted, entrepreneurial, feminine and masculine, networking, working on themselves, flexible, unique but not deviant' (Furusten, 2003: 230). But my material shows that these workers represent themselves as temporarily sorted as failure provides resources for them as much as success.

> Therapeutic practices concentrate on emotions such as vulnerability, pain and passivity because of the kinds of psychology and subjectivity being produced in neoliberalism and flexible capitalism that place unrealistic demands on men and women to be both emotional and detached, authentic and synthetic, intimate and autonomous. (Blackman, 1999)

Concluding reflections

In summary, what has repeatedly emerged from my material is the diversity of understandings of the self, transformation and emotion. This variety shows that we need to modify the 'received wisdom' on therapeutic cultures emerging from influential critical accounts. Focusing on personal development which stands at the interface between 'traditional therapies', management training and the workplace, what this research suggests is that this cross-over brings its own specificities, raising questions about the way that therapeutic cultures are seen as monolithic and transcontextual, having universal effects across social spheres.

In line with critics' views, my research demonstrates that certain therapeutic ways of making sense of experiences and producing the self are proliferating and extending into different social spheres but that these take on different shapes from the ones presented by many critics. Therapeutic cultures are transformed by, and transform local ways of thinking about the self, its experiences and its relations with others, which result in diverse understandings of the self in personal development. This research tells us how meta-criticisms can be inadequate for our evaluation of therapeutic cultures and personal development. The personal development workers interviewed for this research are not all saying the same thing. This is important because it shows that personal development is not simply a normative programme but is messy, contradictory, and confusing.

Perhaps therapeutic cultures are not like a huge monolithic assembly line, churning out standardised selves or frameworks, as critics seem to suggest. Personal development workers are doing their own things, being selective about what they take on board, drawing upon other sources of information about the self and life, and responding in different ways, some of which will be a response to the larger critique of therapeutic cultures in academia and popular culture. This is not to say that the politics of this work does not need questioning and researching.

Politics of the example

The main aim of this book was to begin to address a relative absence in studies of therapeutic cultures in the area of empirical work on personal development workers in the area of personal development. In particular, I wanted to examine to what extent personal development workers' accounts fitted with current understandings of the self and its transformation in the sociology of therapeutic cultures. Using a close textual analysis of interviews with personal development workers, I have shown that there is a 'politics of the example' at play in critical accounts. Much of the sociological literature on therapeutic culture provides analyses at the level of social institutions and these inevitably gloss detail in therapeutic cultures. One school of thought or therapeutic idea is used to represent all others, which has the effect of creating a monolithic understanding of therapeutic cultures, concealing significant specificities and their implications. Details are important because they have meanings for personal development workers, which are currently under-theorised as I have said.

Furthermore, therapeutic cultures are seen by many critics as having important political implications for society, and these political evaluations are based on their homogenising representations of therapeutic cultures. My main aim was to show that personal development had its own specificity and significance and my research has demonstrated that personal development workers draw upon complex models and forms in their understanding of what they do, and what they think of what they do, which challenge many of the assumptions in the sociology of therapeutic cultures.

Although I have used the concept of 'therapeutic cultures' in this book, my research raises questions about how useful a term it is to convey the significance and meanings of these different cultural practices. Therapeutic cultures has been a useful umbrella term for discussing personal development, but as I argue in my critique of the homogenising effects of the work of some sociologists on therapeutic cultures, it also smoothes over some important differences between therapeutic cultures for example, voluntary counselling and personal development in the workplace. As more empirical work is undertaken on different subcultures in therapeutic cultures, then we can understand where there is common ground and where there are fundamental differences.

Future research

Taking forward this idea of empirical work, my general arguments have raised questions for future research. I have argued that therapeutic cultures are not monolithic or homogeneous, and that they offer important emotional spaces. Future research could extend the arguments put forward here by examining how clients themselves experience personal development or other therapeutic cultures. This research has focused on personal development workers because their views are under-represented in the sociology of therapeutic cultures. Their conceptualisations could be put in dialogue with those of clients. Like the personal development workers, it is unlikely that clients passively accept ideas and practices, so how do they mobilise therapeutic ideas in the understanding and production of their selves and their emotions. What kind of transformations do they want from therapeutic cultures and how do they imagine themselves to be changed as a result of their participation in therapeutic cultures? Do they see differences between diverse approaches and what do they make of their relations with their personal development workers? Do they go to therapeutic personal development workers to get help with emotional issues? And if not, how do they understand their participation? Answers to these questions can help us to evaluate more carefully how worked up we should get about the significance of therapeutic practices in how people work up their selves.

Further work needs to be done on the gendered, classed and racialised aspects of personal development work and resources, particularly in the workplace (Swan, Stead and Elliott, 2009). Who has access to these resources and how they do they operate as cultural capital in the workplace? What kinds of ideas about gender, class and race do these reproduce and how do they reinforce or challenge disadvantage and oppression?

Mediation

Finally, this book has tried to open up discussions about the politics of therapeutic cultures and personal development as they have felt somewhat over-determined in the denunciative school of literature. I have tried to show that personal development provides important workplace resources and constraints and conditionalities (Garsten and Jacobsson, 2004: 282). The personal development workers mediate a number of different cultures, knowledges, experiences. They offer training in emotional and therapeutic capital. They mediate the demands on men and women to be both emotional and detached, authentic and worked on intimate and autonomous. As cultural intermediaries, personal development workers also mediate the tensions, difficulties, complexities, failures, disappointments with work, neoliberalism and individualism (Blackman, 1999). These can be problematic resources, to be sure, in that they can be depoliticising and over-individualised, but they can also be helpful. Of course, therapeutic cultures may represent a cultural safety valve, dissipating and consoling any potential radical rebellion. We need to do more work on the politics. This will require more nuanced, ethnographic work. But as mentioned earlier, we need to start understanding personal development and therapeutic cultures, as Romero (1997) writes, as perhaps radical in some ways and reactionary in others: oppositional but not liberating, conservative but not outright colonising or rationalising.

Bibliography

Abercrombie, Nicholas, Hill, S. and Turner, Barry (1986) *Sovereign Individuals of Capitalism*. London: Allen and Unwin.

Ackers, Peter and Preston, Diane (1997) 'Born Again? The Ethics and Efficacy of the Experience in Contemporary Management Development', in *Journal of Management Studies*, Vol 34, No 5: 676–701.

Adkins, Lisa (1995) *Gendered Work: Sexuality, Family and the Labour Market*. Milton Keynes: Open University Press.

Adkins, Lisa (2002a) *Revisions: Gender and Sexuality in Late Modernity*. Buckingham: Open University Press.

Adkins, Lisa (2002b) 'Reflexivity and the Politics of Qualitative Research', in Tim May (ed.) *Qualitative Research in Action*. London: Sage.

Adkins, Lisa and Lury, Celia (1999) 'The Labour of Identity: Performing Identities, Performing Economies', in *Economy and Society*, Vol 28, No 4: 598–614.

Allwood, Robin (1996) 'I Have Depression, Don't I? Discourses of Help and Self-Help Books', in Erica Burman et al. *Psychology Discourse Practice*. London: Taylor and Francis.

Alvesson, Mats and Wilmott, Hugh (2004) 'Identity Regulation as Organizational Control: Producing the Appropriate Individual', in Mary Jo Hatch and Majkin Schultz (eds) *Organisational Identity: A Reader*. London: Sage.

Anderson, Harlene and Goolishian, Harold (1992) 'The Client is the Expert: a Not-Knowing Approach to Therapy', in Sheila McNamee and Kenneth J. Gergen (eds) *Therapy as Social Construction*. London: Sage.

Ang, Ien (1991) *Desperately Seeking the Audience*. London: Routledge.

Anthony, Peter (1994). *Managing Culture*. Milton Keynes: Open University.

Antze, Paul (1996) 'Telling Stories, Making Selves: Memory and Identity in Multiple Personality Disorder', in Paul Antze and Michael Lambek (eds) *Tense Past: Cultural Essays in Trauma and Memory*. London: Routledge.

Antze, Paul and Lambek, Michael (eds) (1996) *Tense Past: Cultural Essays in Trauma and Memory*. London: Routledge.

Armstrong, Nancy (1987) 'The Rise of the Domestic Woman', in Nancy Armstrong and Leonard Tennenhouse (eds) *The Ideology of Conduct: Essays in Literature and Society*. London: Methuen.

Armstrong, Nancy and Tennenhouse, Leonard (1992) *The Imaginary Puritan: Literature, Intellectual Labour, and the Origins of Personal Life*. Berkeley: University of California Press.

Arnaud, Gilles (2003) 'A Coach or a Couch? A Lacanian Perspective on Executive Coaching and Consulting', *Human Relations*, 56, 1131–1154.

Aull Davies, Charlotte (1999) *Reflexive Ethnography: A Guide to Researching Selves and Others*. London: Routledge.

Axtell Ray, Carol (1986) 'Corporate Culture: The Last Frontier of Control?', in *Journal of Management Studies*, Vol 23, No 3: 287–297.

Babock, Marguerite and McKay, Christine (1995) *Challenging Co-dependency: Feminist Critiques*. Toronto: University of Toronto Press.
Back, Kurt W. (1987) *Beyond Words: The Story of Sensitivity Training and the Encounter Movement*. New Brunswick: Transaction.
Baistow, Karen (2001) 'Behavioural Approaches and the Cultivation of Competence', in Geoff C. Bunn, A.D. Lovie and Graham D. Richards (eds) *Psychology in Britain: Historical Essays and Personal Reflections*. Leicester: BPS Books.
Bakhurst, David and Sypnowich, Christine (eds) (1995) *The Social Self*. London: Sage.
Banta, Martha (1993) *Taylored Lives: Narrative Productions in the Age of Taylor, Veblen and Ford*. London: University of Chicago Press.
Baritz, Loren (1974) *The Servants of Power: A History of the Use of Social Science in American Industry*. Westport, Connecticut: Greenwood Press.
Battaglia, Debbora (ed.) (1995) *Rhetorics of Self-Making*. London: University of California Press.
Baumeister, Roy M. (1987) 'How the Self Became a Problem: A Psychological Review of Historical Research', in *Journal of Personality and Social Psychology*, Vol 52, No 1: 163–176.
Baumeister, Roy (ed.) (1999) *The Self in Social Psychology*. Hove: Psychology Press.
Beck, Ulrich (1992) *Risk Society: Towards a New Modernity*. London: Sage.
Beck, Ulrich (1994) 'The Reinvention of Politics: Towards a Theory of Reflexive Modernisation', in Ulrich Beck, Anthony Giddens, and Scott Lash (eds) *Reflexive Modernisation: Politics, Tradition and Aesthetics in the Modern Social Order*. Cambridge: Polity Press.
Beck, Ulrich, Giddens, Anthony and Lash, Scott (eds) (1994) *Reflexive Modernisation: Politics, Tradition, and Aesthetics in the Modern Social Order*. Cambridge: Polity Press.
Bell, Daniel (1979) *The Cultural Contradictions of Capitalism*. London: Heinemann.
Bell, Emma and Taylor, Scott (2003) 'The Elevation of Work: Pastoral Power and the New Age Ethic', in *Organization*, 10 (2): 329–349.
Bell, Emma and Taylor, Scott (2004) '"From Outward Bound to Inward Bound": The Prophetic Voices and Discursive Practices of Spiritual Management Development', in *Human Relations*, 57 (4): 439–466.
Bellah, Robert N., Madsen, Richard, Sullivan, William M., Swindler, Ann and Tipton, Stephen (1985) *Habits of the Heart*. Berkeley: University of California Press.
Bendelow, Gillian and Williams, Simon (1998) *Emotions in Social Life: Critical Themes and Contemporary Issues*. London: Routledge.
Berger, Peter, Berger, Brigitte and Kellner, Hansfried (1974) *The Homeless Mind*. Harmondsworth: Penguin.
Berking, Helmuth (1999) *Sociology of Giving*. London: Sage.
Berlant, Lauren (1997) *The Queen of America Goes to Washington City: Essays on Sex and Citizenship*. Durham: Duke University Press.
Berlant, Lauren (2000) *Intimacy*. Chicago: The University of Chicago Press.
Berlant, Lauren (2001a) 'Trauma and Ineloquence', in *Cultural Values*, Vol 5, No 1: 41–58.
Berlant, Lauren (2001b) 'The Subject of True Feelings: Pain, Privacy and Politics', in Elisabeth Bronfen and Misha Kavka (eds) *Feminist Consequences: Theory for the New Century*. Chichester: Columbia University Press.

Berlant, Lauren and Warner, Michael (2000) 'Sex in Public', in Lauren Berlant *Intimacy*. Chicago: The University of Chicago Press.

Berne, Eric (1996) *Games People Play*. Reissue edition. New York: Ballantine Books.

Blackman, Lisa (1999) 'An *Extra*ordinary Life: The Legacy of an Ambivalence', in *New Formations*, Diana and Democracy Special Issue, Vol 36: 111–124.

Blackman, Lisa (2000) 'Ethics, Embodiment and the Voice-Hearing Experience', in *Theory, Culture and Society*, Vol 17, No 5: 55–74.

Blackman, Lisa (2001) *Hearing Voices: Embodiment and Experience*. London: Free Association Books.

Blackman, Lisa and Walkerdine, Valerie (2001) *Mass Hysteria: Critical Psychology and Media Studies*. Basingstoke: Palgrave.

Boddy, Janice (1988) 'Spirits and Selves in Northern Sudan: The Cultural Therapeutics of Possession and Trance', in *American Ethnologist*, Vol 15, No 1: 4–27.

Boler, Megan (1999) *Feeling Power: Emotions and Education*. London: Routledge.

Bondi, Liz (2003) 'A Situated Practice for Re (situating) Selves: Trainee Counsellors and the Promise of Counselling', in *Environment and Planning A*, Vol 35: 853–870.

Bondi, Liz and Fewell, Judith (2003) 'Unlocking the Cage Door: the Spatiality of Counselling', in *Social and Cultural Geography* (forthcoming).

Bonner, Francis and du Gay, Paul (1992) 'Representing the Enterprising Self', in *Theory, Culture and Society*, Vol 9, No 2, May: 67–92.

Bourdieu, Pierre (1984) *Distinction: A Social Critique of the Judgment of Taste*. London: Routledge.

Boyarin, Jonathan (1995) 'Self-Exposure as Theory: The Double Mark of the Male Jew', in Debbora Battaglia (ed.) *Rhetorics of Self-Making*. California: University of California Press.

Brammel, Dana and Friend, Ronald (1981) 'Hawthorne, the Myth of the Docile Worker and Class Bias in Psychology', in *American Psychologist*, Vol 36, No 8: 867–878.

Bremmer, Jan and Roodenburg, Herman (eds) (1993) *A Cultural History of Gesture*. Cambridge: Polity.

Brewis, Jo (1996) 'The "Making" of the "Competent" Manager: Competency Development, Personal Effectiveness and Foucault', in *Management Learning*, Vol 27, No 1: 65–86.

Brickell, Chris (2000) 'Heroes and Invaders: Gay and Lesbian Pride Parades and the Public/Private Distinction in New Zealand Media Accounts', in *Gender, Place and Culture*. Vol 7, No 2: 163–178.

Brinthaupt, Thomas M. and Lipka, Richard P. (eds) (1994) *Changing the Self: Philosophies, Techniques and Experiences*. Albany: State University of New York Press.

Briskin, Alan (1998) *The Stirring of the Soul in the Workplace*. San Francisco: Berrett-Koehler.

Brooks, Peter (1994) 'Melodrama, Body and Revolution', in Jacky Bratton, Jim Cook and Christine Gledhill (eds) *Melodrama: Stage, Picture, Screen*. London: BFI.

Brown, Gillian (1990) *Domestic Individualism: Imagining Self in the Nineteenth Century*. Oxford: University of California Press.

Brown, May Ellen (1996) 'Desperately Seeking Strategies: Reading in the Postmodern', in Debra Grodin and Thomas R. Lindlof (eds) *Constructing the Self in a Mediated World*. London: Sage.

Brown, Steven (1999) 'Stress as Regimen: Discourse Analysis and Self-Help Literature', in C. Willig (ed.) *Applied Discourse Analysis: Social and Psychological Interventions*. Milton Keynes: Open University Press.
Brown, Wendy (1995) *States of Injury: Power and Freedom in Late Modernity*. Princeton: Princeton University Press.
Bruce, Steven (2000) 'The New Age and Secularisation', in Steven Sutcliffe and Marion Bowman (eds) *Beyond New Age*. Edinburgh: Edinburgh University Press.
Brunsdon, Charlotte (2000) *The Feminist, the Housewife, and the Soap Opera*. Oxford: Oxford University Press.
Bruzelius, Margaret (2001) 'The Tower of Babble', in Shelley I. Salamensky (ed.) *Talk, Talk, Talk: The Cultural Life of Everyday Conversation*. London: Routledge.
Bryman, Alan (1992) *Charisma and Leadership in Organisations*. London: Sage.
Budd, Susan (1994) 'Transference Revisited', in Susan Budd and Ursula Sharma (eds) *The Healing Bond*. London: Routledge.
Budd, Susan and Ursula Sharma (eds) (1994) *The Healing Bond: The Patient – Practitioner Relationship and Therapeutic Responsibility*. London: Routledge.
Burfoot, Jean (1983) 'The Fun-Seeking Movement in California', in Eileen Barker (ed.) *Of Gods and Men*. Macon: Mercer University Press.
Burkitt, Ian (1994) *Social Selves: Theories of the Social Formation of Personality*. London: Sage.
Burkitt, Ian (1994) 'The Shifting Concept of the Self', in *History of the Human Sciences*, Vol 7, No 2: 7–28.
Burnham, C. John (1988) *Paths into American Culture: Psychology, Medicine and Morals*. Philadelphia: Temple University Press.
Butler, Judith (1990) *Gender Trouble*. London: Routledge.
Butler, Judith (1995) 'Contingent Foundations', in Seyla Benhabib, Judith Butler, Drucilla Cornell and Nancy Fraser, *Feminist Contentions: A Philosophical Exchange*. London: Routledge.
Cameron, Deborah (1995) *Verbal Hygiene*. London: Routledge.
Cameron, Deborah (2000a) *Good to Talk*. London: Sage.
Cameron, Deborah (2000b) 'A Self Off the Shelf – Consuming Women's Empowerment', in Maggie Andrews and Mary M. Talbot (eds) *All the World and Her Husband: Women in Twentieth-Century Consumer Culture*. London: Cassell.
Campbell, Colin (1989) *The Romantic Ethic and the Spirit of Modern Consumerism*. Oxford: Blackwell.
Campbell, Colin (1996) 'Detraditionalisation, Character, and the Limits to Agency', in Paul Heelas, Scott Lash and Paul Morris (eds) *Detraditionalization*. Oxford: Blackwell.
Campbell, Sue (1997) *Interpreting the Personal: Expression and the Formation of Feelings*. Ithaca: Cornell University Press.
Cancian, Francesca M. (1987) *Love in America: Gender and Self-development*. Cambridge: University of Cambridge Press.
Cancian, Francesca M. and Gordon, Steven L. (1988) 'Changing Emotion Norms in Marriage: Love and Anger in U.S. Women's Magazines Since 1900', in *Gender and Society*, Vol 2, No 3: 308–342.
Caputo, John (1993) 'On Not Knowing Who We Are: Madness, Hermeneutics and the Night of Truth', in John Caputo and Mark Yount (eds) *Foucault and the Critique of Institutions*. Pennsylvania: Penn State Press.

Carbaugh, Donal (1988) *Talking American: Cultural Discourses on Donahue*. Norwood: Ablex.

Carter, A. (2003) *Executive Coaching: Inspiring Performance at Work*. Brighton: IES.

Casey, Catherine (1995) *Work, Self and Society: After Industrialism*. London: Routledge.

Casey, Catherine (2002a) *Critical Analysis of Organisations: Theory, Practice, Revitalisation*. London: Sage.

Casey, Catherine (2002b) '"New Age" Religion and Identity at Work', in Mike Dent and Stephen Whitehead (eds) *Managing Professional Identities: Knowledge, Performativity and the 'New' Professional*. London: Routledge.

Chappell, Clive, Rhodes Carl, Solomon Nicky, Tennant, Mark and Yates, Lyn (2003) *Reconstructing the Lifelong Learner: Pedagogy and Identity in Individual, Organisational and Social Change*. London: RoutledgeFalmer.

Child, John (1969) *British Management Thought: A Critical Analysis*. London: George Allen and Unwin.

Chriss, James J. (ed.) (1999) *Counselling and the Therapeutic State*. New York: de Gruyter.

Clark, Candace (1997) *Misery and Company: Sympathy in Everyday Life*. Chicago: University of Chicago Press.

Clarke, Timothy (1995) *Managing Consultants*. Buckingham: Open University Press.

Clarke, Timothy and Fincham, Robin (2002) *Critical Consulting: New Perspectives on the Management Advice Industry*. Oxford: Blackwell.

Clecak, Peter (1983) *American Quest for the Ideal Self: Dissent and Fulfilment in the 60s and 70s*. Oxford: Oxford University Press.

Cloud, Dana (1998) *Control and Consolation in American Culture and Politics: Rhetoric of Therapy*. London: Sage.

Coffey, Amanda (2002) 'Ethnography and Self: Reflections and Representations', in Tim May (ed.) *Qualitative Research in Action*. London: Sage.

Cohen, Stanley (1985) *Visions of Social Control*. Cambridge: Polity Press.

Cohn, Carol (1987) 'Sex and Death in the Rational World of Defense Intellectuals', in *Signs*, Vol 12, No 4: 687–718.

Costea, Bogdan, Crump, Norman and Amiridis, Kostas (2007) 'Managerialism and "Infinite Human Resourcefulness": A Commentary on the "Therapeutic Habitus", "Derecognition of Finitude" and the Modern Sense of Self', in *Journal of Cultural Research*, 11 (3): 245–264.

Costea, Bogdan, Crump, Norman and Amiridis, Kostas (2008) 'Managerialism, the Therapeutic Habitus and the Self in Contemporary Organizing', in *Human Relations*, Vol 61, (5): 661–685.

Coward, Ros (1989) *The Whole Truth*. London: Faber and Faber.

Craib, Ian (1994) *The Importance of Disappointment*. London: Routledge.

Craib, Ian (1998) *Experiencing Identity*. London: Sage.

Craib, Ian (2001) *Psychoanalysis: A Critical Introduction*. Cambridge: Polity Press.

Crawford, Mary (1995) *Talking Difference: On Gender and Language*. London: Sage.

Crisp, Jane (2000) 'Fashioning Gendered Identities', in Jane Crisp, Kay Ferres and Gillian Swanson, *Deciphering Culture: Ordinary Curiosities and Subjective Narratives*. London: Routledge.

Cronin, Anne (1997) 'Adventures in 3D: Consumerism, Potential and Dimensionality', Work in Progress paper presented at the 'Transformations' conference, Institute of Women's Studies, Lancaster University, UK, 17–19 July 1997.

Cronin, Anne (2000a) *Advertising and Consumer Citizenship: Gender, Images and Rights*. London and New York: Routledge.

Cronin, Anne (2000b) 'Consumerism and "Compulsory Individuality": Women, Will and Potential', in Sara Ahmed, Jane Kilby, Celia Lury, Maureen McNeil and Beverley Skeggs (eds) *Transformations: Thinking Through Feminism*. London: Routledge.

Cruikshank, Barbara (1993) 'Revolutions Within: Self-government and Self-esteem', in *Economy and Society*, Vol 22, No 3, August.

Cruikshank, Barbara (1999) *The Will To Empower: Democratic Citizens and Other Subjects*. London: Cornell University Press.

Csordas, Thomas J. (1997) *The Sacred Self: A Cultural Phenomenology of Charismatic Healing*. Berkeley: University of California Press.

Cummins, Anne-Marie and Hoggett, Paul (1995) 'Counselling in the Enterprise Cultures', in *British Journal of Guidance and Counselling*, October, Vol 23, No 3: 301–312.

Cushman, Philip (1990) 'Why the Self is Empty: Towards a Historically Situated Psychology', *American Psychology*, May, Vol 45, No 5: 599–611.

Cushman, Philip (1995) *Constructing the Self, Constructing America*. New York: Addison-Wesley.

Davidson, Joyce (2002) 'All in the Mind: Women, Agoraphobia and the Subject of Self-Help', in Liz Bondi, Hannah Avis, Ruth Bankey, Amanda Bingley, Joyce Davidson, Rosaleen Duffy, Victoria Ingrid Einagel, Anja-Maaike Green, Lynda Johnston, Susan Lilley, Carina Listerborn, Mona Marshy, Shonagh McEwan, Niamh O'Connor, Gillian Rose, Bella Vivat and Nichola Wood (eds) *Subjectivities, Knowledges, and Feminist Geographies: The Subject and Ethics of Social Research*. Oxford: Rowman and Littlefield.

Davis, John (1992) *Exchange*. Buckingham: Open University Press.

Denzin, K. Norman (1998) 'In Search of the Inner Child: Co-dependency and Gender in Cyberspace Community', in Gillian Bendelow and Simon J. Williams (eds) *Emotions in Social Life: Critical Themes and Issues*. London: Routledge.

de Swaan, Abram (1990) *The Management of Normality: Critical Essays in Health and Welfare*. London: Routledge.

Dickson, Anne (1982) *A Woman in Your Own Right: Assertiveness and You*. London: Quartet Books.

Dineen, Tania (1999) *Manufacturing Victims: What the Psychology Industry is Doing to People*. London: Constable and Company.

Diprose, Rosalyn (1994) *The Bodies of Women: Ethics, Embodiment and Sexual Difference*. London: Routledge.

Dittmar, Helga (1992) *The Social Psychology of Material Possessions: To Have or To Be*. Hemel Hempstead: Harvester Wheatsheaf.

Donzelot, Jacques (1991) 'Pleasure in Work', in Graham Burchell, Colin Gordon and Peter Miller (eds) *The Foucault Effect: Studies in Governmentality*. Hemel Hempstead: Harvester Wheatsheaf.

Douglas, Mary (1994) 'The Construction of the Physician: A Cultural Approach to Medical Fashions', in Susan Budd and Ursula Sharma (eds) *The Healing Bond*. London: Routledge.

Driessen, Henk (1993) 'Gestured Masculinity in Rural Andalusia', in Jan Bremmer and Herman Roodenburg (eds) *A Cultural History of Gesture*. Cambridge: Polity.
Drury, Nevill (1989) *Elements of Human Potential*. Dorset: Element Books.
Dubrofsky, Rachel (2007) 'Therapeutics of the Self: Surveillance in the Service of the Therapeutic', in *Television and New Media*, Vol 8, No 4: 263–284.
du Gay, Paul (1996) *Consumption and Identity at Work*. London: Sage.
du Gay, Paul and Salaman, Graeme (1992) 'The Cult(ure) of "The Customer"', in *Journal of Management Studies*, Vol 29, No 5: 615–633.
Dyer, Richard (1991) 'A Star is Born and the Construction of Authenticity', in Christine Gledhill (ed.) *Stardom: Industry of Desire*. London: Routledge.
Ecclestone, Katherine and Hayes, Dennis (2009) *The Dangerous Rise of Therapeutic Education*. Abingdon, Oxon: Routledge.
Edwards, Richard (2003) 'Ordering Subjects: Actor Networks and Intellectual Technologies in Lifelong Learning', in *Studies in the Education of Adults*, Spring 2003, Vol 35, No 1: 45–58.
Ehrenhaus, Peter (1993) 'Cultural Narratives and the Therapeutic Motif: The Political Containment of Vietnam Veterans', in Dennis Mumby (ed.) *Narrative and Social Control: Critical Perspectives*. London: Sage.
Ehrenreich, Barbara and English, Deidre (1978) *For Her Own Good: 150 Years of Expert's Advice to Women*. New York: Anchor Books.
Elias, Norbert (1991) 'On Human Beings and their Emotions: A Process-Sociological Essay', in Mike Featherstone, Mike Hepworth and Bryan S. Turner (eds) *The Body, Social Process and Cultural Theory*. London: Sage.
Elias, Norbert (1994) *The Civilising Process*. Oxford: Blackwell.
Elkins, James (2001) *Pictures and Tears: A History of People Who Have Cried in Front of Paintings*. New York: Routledge.
Elshtain, Jean Bethke (1997) 'The Displacement of Politics', in Jeff Weintraub and Krishnan Kumar (eds) *Public and Private in Thought and Practice*. Chicago: University of Chicago Press.
Ely, Margot, Vinz, Ruth, Downing, Maryann and Anzul, Margaret (1997) *On Writing Qualitative Research: Living by Words*. London: Falmer Press.
Erickson, Robert A. (1997) *The Language of the Heart 1600–1750*. Philadelphia: University of Philadelphia Press.
Ernst, Sheila and Goodison, Lucy (1981) *In Our Own Hands: A Book of Self-Help Therapy*. London: The Womens Press.
Fairclough, Norman (1989) *Language and Power*. Harlow: Longman.
Fairclough, Norman (1992) *Discourse and Social Change*. Cambridge: Polity Press.
Featherstone, Mike (1991) *Consumer Culture and Postmodernism*. London: Sage.
Felski, Rita (1989) *Beyond Feminist Aesthetics: Feminist Literature and Social Change*. Cambridge, Mass: Harvard University Press.
Felski, Rita (1995) *The Gender of Modernity*. Cambridge, Mass: Harvard University Press.
Felski, Rita (2000) *Doing Time*. New York: New York University Press.
Felski, Rita (2003) *Literature after Feminism*. Chicago: University of Chicago Press.
Feltham, Colin (1995) *What is Counselling?* London: Sage.
Feltham, Colin (ed.) (1997) *Which Psychotherapy?* London: Sage.
Feltham, Colin (ed.) (1999) *Understanding the Counselling Relationship*. London: Sage.

Ferrara, Kathleen Warden (1994) *Therapeutic Ways with Words*. New York: Oxford University Press.
Fielden, Sandra (2004) 'Literature Review: Coaching Effectiveness', report by Centre for Diversity and Work Psychology, Manchester School of Management, UMIST.
Fineman, Stephen (ed.) (1993) *Emotion in Organisations*. London: Sage.
Fineman, Stephen (2000a) 'Emotional Arenas Revisited', in Stephen Fineman (ed.) *Emotion in Organisations*. 2nd edition. London: Sage.
Fineman, Stephen (2000b) 'Commodifying the Emotionally Intelligent', in Stephen Fineman (ed.). *Emotion in Organisations*. 2nd edition. London: Sage.
Fineman, Stephen (2000c) 'Concluding Reflections', in Stephen Fineman (ed.) *Emotion in Organisations*. 2nd edition. London: Sage.
Fineman, Stephen (2003) *Understanding Emotion at Work*. London: Sage.
Finkelstein, Joanne (1991) *The Fashioned Self*. Cambridge: Polity Press.
Finnegan, Ruth (1997) 'Storying the Self: Personal Narratives and Identity', in Hugh Mackay (ed.) *Consumption and Everyday Life*. London: Sage.
Flax, Jane (1990) *Thinking Fragments: Psychoanalysis, Feminism and Postmodernism in the Contemporary West*. Berkeley: University of California Press.
Foote, Catherine E. and Frank, Arthur W. (1999) 'Foucault and Therapy: The Disciplining of Grief', in Adrienne S. Chambon, Allan Irving and Laura Epstein (eds) *Reading Foucault for Social Work*. New York: Columbia University Press.
Forrester, John (1992) 'In the Beginning Was Repetition: On Inversions and Reversals in Psychoanalytic Time', in *Time and Society*. London: Sage.
Foucault, Michel (1984) 'On Genealogy of Ethics', in Paul Rabinow (ed.) *Foucault Reader*. New York: Pantheon.
Fournier, Valerie (2002a) 'Amateurism, Quackery and Professional Conduct: The Constitution of "Proper" Aromatherapy Practice', in Mike Dent and Stephen Whitehead (eds) *Managing Professional Identities: Knowledge, Performativity and the 'New' Professional*. London: Routledge.
Fournier, Valerie (2002b) 'Fleshing out Gender: Crafting Gender Identity on Women's Bodies', in *Body and Society*, Vol 8, No 2: 55–77.
Fournier, Valerie and Grey, Chris (1999) 'Too Much, Too Little, Too Often: A Critique of du Gay's Analysis of Enterprise', *Organisation*, Vol 6, No 1: 107–128.
Fox, J. Nicholas (1993) *Postmodernism, Sociology and Health*. Buckingham: Open University Press.
Franklin, Sarah (1997) *Embodied Progress: A Cultural Account of Assisted Conception*. London: Routledge.
Fraser, Mariam (1999) *Identity without Selfhood: Simone de Beauvoir and Bisexuality*. Cambridge: Cambridge University Press.
Fraser, Nancy (1995) 'Politics, Culture, and the Public Sphere: Toward a Postmodern Conception', in Linda Nicholson and Steven Seidman (eds) *Social Postmodernism: Beyond Identity Politics*. Cambridge: Cambridge University Press.
Freeman, Mark (1993) *Rewriting the Self: History, Memory, Narrative*. London: Routledge.
Freund, Peter E.S. (1990) 'The Expressive Body: A Common Ground for the Sociology of Emotions and Health and Illness', in *Sociology of Health and Illness*, Vol 12, No 4: 452–477.
Fricker, Miranda (1991) 'Reasons and Emotions', in *Radical Philosophy*, No 57: 14–19.

Frijhoff, Willen (1993) 'The Kiss – Sacred and Profane: Reflections on a Cross-Cultural Confrontation', in Jan Bremmer and Herman Roodenburg (eds) *A Cultural History of Gesture*. Cambridge: Polity.

Furedi, Frank (2002) 'The Silent Ascendancy of Therapeutic Culture in Britain', in *Society*, March/April: 16–24.

Furedi, Frank (2004) *Therapy Culture: Cultivating Vulnerability in an Uncertain Age*. London: Routledge.

Furusten, Staffan (2003) God managementkonsultation – reglerad expertis eller improviserat artisteri? [Good management consultancy – regulated expertise or improvising artists?] Lund: Studentlitteratur.

Gabriel, Yiannis (2002) 'Essai: On Paragrammatic Uses of Organisational Theory – A Provocation', in *Organisation Studies*, 23/1: 133–151.

Garsten, Christina and Grey, Christopher (1997) 'How to Become Oneself: Discourses of Subjectivity', in *Post-Bureaucratic Organisations in Organisation*, Vol 4 (2): 211–228.

Garsten, Christina and Jacobsson, Kerstin (2004) *Learning to be Employable*. London: Palgrave.

Gauntlett, David (2002a) 'Self-Help Books and the Pursuit of a Happy Identity', extended version of material from *Media, Gender and Identity: An Introduction*. London: Routledge, posted at http://www.theoryhead.com/gender.

Gauntlett, David (2002b) *Media, Gender and Identity: An Introduction*. London: Routledge.

Gee, Paul James, Hull, Glynda and Lankshear, Colin (1996) *The New Work Order: Behind the Language of the New Capitalism*. St. Leonards, NSW: Australia: Allen and Unwin.

Gergen, Kenneth J. (1991) *The Saturated Self: Dilemmas of Identity in Contemporary Life*. London: Basic Books.

Gergen, Kenneth J. (1995) 'Metaphor and Monophony in the 20th-Century Psychology of Emotions', in *History of the Human Sciences*, Vol 8, No 2: 1–23.

Gerson, Kathleen and Horowitz, Ruth (2002) 'Observation and Interviewing: Options and Choices in Qualitative Research', in Tim May (ed.) *Qualitative Research in Action*. London: Sage.

Gervasio, A.H. and Crawford, M. (1989) 'Social Evaluations of Assertiveness: A Critique and Speech Act Reformulation', in *Psychology of Women Quarterly Press*, 13: 1–25.

Giddens, Anthony (1991) 'Modernity and Self-Identity: Self and Society', in *The Late Modern Age*. Cambridge: Polity Press.

Giddens, Anthony (1992) *The Transformation of Intimacy: Sexuality, Love and Eroticism in Modern Societies*. Cambridge: Polity Press.

Giddens, Anthony (1994) 'Living in a Post Traditional Society', in Ulrich Beck, Anthony Giddens, Scott Lash (eds) *Reflexive Modernization: Politics, Tradition and Aesthetics in the Modern Social Order*. Cambridge: Polity Press.

Giddens, Anthony and Pierson, Christopher (1998) *Conversations with Anthony Giddens: Making Sense of Modernity*. Cambridge: Polity Press.

Gill, Rosalind (2000) 'Discourse Analysis', in Martin W. Bauer and George Gaskell (eds) *Qualitative Researching with Text, Image and Sound*. London: Sage.

Gillespie, Richard (1988) 'The Hawthorne Experiments and the Politics of Experimentation', in Jill G. Morawski (ed.) *The Rise of Psychological Experimentation in American Psychology*. New Haven: Yale University Press.

Ginsburg, Faye (1989) *Contested Lives: The Abortion Debate in American Community*. London: University of California Press.
Glucksmann, Miriam (1994) 'The Work of Knowledge and the Knowledge of Work', in Mary Maynard and Jane Purvis (eds) *Researching Women's Lives from a Feminist Perspective*. London: Taylor and Francis.
Godbout, Jacques T. and Caille, Alain (1998) *The World of the Gift*. Montreal and Kingston: McGill-Queen's University Press.
Godelier, Maurice (1996) *The Enigma of the Gift*. Cambridge: Polity Press.
Gordon, Colin (1991) 'Governmental Rationality: An Introduction', in Graham Burchell, Colin Gordon and Peter Miller (eds) *The Foucault Effect: Studies in Governmentality*. Hemel Hempstead: Harvester Wheatsheaf.
Gratton, Johnnie (2000) *Expressivism: The Vicissitudes of a Theory in the Writing of Proust and Barthes*. Oxford: Legenda.
Gray, Ann (1992) *Video Playtime: The Gendering of a Leisure Technology*. London: Routledge.
Gray, Ann (2003a) *Research Practice for Cultural Studies*. London: Sage.
Gray, Ann (2003b) 'Enterprising Femininity: New Modes of Work and Subjectivity', in *European Journal of Cultural Studies*, 6 (4): 489–506.
Greenberg, Gary (1994) *The Self on the Shelf: Recovery Books and the Good Life*. Albany: State of New York Press.
Greenspan, Miriam (1993) *A New Approach to Women and Therapy*. 2nd edition. Blue Ridge Summit: TAB.
Grey, Chris (1994) 'Career as a Project of the Self and Labour Process Discipline', in *Sociology*, Vol 28, No 2: 479–497.
Grimshaw, Jean (1986) *Philosophy and Feminist Thinking*. Hemel Hempstead: Harvester Wheatsheaf.
Grodin, Debra and Lindlof Thomas R. (eds) (1996) *Constructing the Self in a Mediated World*. London: Sage.
Grosz, Elizabeth (1994) *Volatile Bodies: Toward a Corporeal Feminism*. Bloomington: Indiana University Press.
Grosz, Elizabeth (1999) 'Thinking the New: Of Futures Yet Unthought', in Elizabeth Grosz (ed.) *Becomings: Explorations in Time, Memory and Futures*. New York: Cornell University Press.
Gumbrium, Jaber F. and Holstein, James A. (1997) *The New Language of Qualitative Method*. New York: Oxford University Press.
Hacking, Ian (1986) 'Making up People', in Thomas Heller, Morton Sosna and David E. Wellbery (eds) *'Reconstructing Individualism: Autonomy, Individuality and the Self' in Western Thought*. Stanford: Stanford University Press.
Hacking, Ian (1995) *Rewriting the Soul: Multiple Personality and the Sciences of Memory*. Princeton, NJ: Princeton University Press.
Hacking, Ian (2002) *Historical Ontology*. Cambridge, Massachusetts: Harvard University Press.
Hall, Stuart and du Gay, Paul (eds) (1996) *Questions of Cultural Identity*. London: Sage.
Hallam, Elizabeth (2002) 'The Eye and the Hand: Memory, Identity and Clairvoyants' Narratives in England', in Jan Campbell and Janet Harbord (eds) *Temporalities, Autobiography and Everyday Life*. Manchester: Manchester University Press.
Hancock, Phillip, and Tyler, Melissa J. (2001) *Work, Postmodernism and Organisation: A Critical Introduction*. London: Sage.

Harding, Sandra (1987) 'Convicted by the Holy Spirit: The Rhetoric of Fundamentalist Conversion', in *American Ethnologist*, Vol 14, No 2: 167–181.

Harper, Sue and Porter, Vincent (1996) 'Moved to Tears: Weeping in the Cinema in Postwar Britain', in *Screen*, Vol 37, No 2: 152–173.

Harre, Rom (ed.) (1988) *The Social Construction of Emotion*. Oxford: Blackwell.

Harre, Rom and Gillet, Grant (1994) *The Discursive Mind*. London: Sage.

Harre, Rom and Stearns, Peter (eds) (1995) *Discursive Psychology in Practice*. London: Sage.

Hartley, J. and Hinksman, B. (2003) *Leadership Development: A Systematic Review of the Literature: A Report for the NHS Leadership Centre*. London.

Hatcher, Caroline (1999) '"Practices of the Heart": Constituting the Identities of Managers', paper presented at the First International Critical Management Studies Conference, UMIST, Manchester.

Hatcher, Caroline (2003) 'Refashioning a Passionate Manager: Gender at Work', in *Gender, Work and Organization*. Vol 10, No 4: 391–412.

Hayward, Rhodri (2001) '"Our Friends Electric": Mechanical Models of Mind' in Postwar Britain', in Geoff C. Bunn, A.D. Lovie and Graham D. Richards (eds) *Psychology in Britain: Historical Essays and Personal Reflections*. Leicester: BPS Books.

Hearn, Jeff (1993) 'Emotive Subjects: Organisational Men, Organisational Masculinities and the (De)construction', in Stephen Fineman (ed.) *Emotion in Organisations*. London: Sage.

Hedges, Ellie and Beckford, James A. (2000) 'Holism, Healing and the New Age', in Steven Sutcliffe and Marion Bowman (eds) *Beyond New Age*. Edinburgh: Edinburgh University Press.

Heelas, Paul (1990) 'The Sacralisation of the Self and New Age Capitalism', in Nicholas Abercrombie and Alan Warde (eds) *Social Change in Contemporary Britain*. Cambridge: Polity Press.

Heelas, Paul (1991) 'Cults for Capitalism – Self Religions, Magic and the Empowerment of Business', in *BSA Sociology of Religion Group*. London: Chameleon Press.

Heelas, Paul (1996) *The New Age Movement*. Oxford: Blackwell.

Heelas, Paul (2000) 'Expressive Spirituality and Humanistic Expressivism: Source of Significance beyond Church and Chapel', in Steven Sutcliffe and Marion Bowman (eds) *Beyond New Age*. Edinburgh: Edinburgh University Press.

Heelas, Paul (2002) 'Work Ethics, Soft Capitalism and the Turn to Life', in Paul Du Gay and Michael Pryke (eds) *Cultural Economy: An Introduction*. London: Sage.

Heelas, Paul (2008) *Spiritualities of Life: New Age Romanticism and Consumptive Capitalism*. Oxford: Blackwell.

Heelas, Paul, Lash, Scott and Morris, Paul (eds) (1996) *Detraditionalization*. Oxford: Blackwell.

Heller, Thomas, Sosna, Morton and Wellbery, David E. (eds) (1986) *'Reconstructing Individualism: Autonomy, Individuality and the Self', in Western Thought*. Stanford: Stanford University Press.

Henriques, Julian, Hollway, Wendy, Urwin, Cathy, Venn, Couze and Walkerdine, Valerie (1984) *Changing the Subject: Psychology, Social Regulation and Subjectivity*. London: Methuen.

Hepworth, Mike (1998) 'Ageing and the Emotions', in Gillian Bendelow and Simon J. Williams (eds) *Emotions in Social Life: Critical Themes and Contemporary Issues*. London: Routledge.

Herman, Ellen (1995) *The Romance of American Psychology: Political Culture in the Age of Experts*. California: University of California Press.
Hertz, Roseanna (ed.) (1997) *Reflexivity and Voice*. Thousand Oaks: Sage.
Hetherington, Kevin (1998) *Expressions of Identity*. London: Sage.
Hetherington, Kevin (2001) 'Consumption and Disposal'. Published by the Department of Sociology, Lancaster University at: http://www.comp.lancs.ac.uk/sociology/soc063kh.html.
Hewitt, John P. (1998) *The Myth of Self-Esteem: Finding Happiness and Solving Problems in America*. New York: St Martins Press.
Hinshelwood, Robert D. (1997) *Therapy or Coercion: Does Psychoanalysis Differ from Brainwashing*. London: Karnac Books.
Hobson, Andy (2003) *Mentoring and Coaching for New Leaders*. London: National College for School Leadership, Nottingham.
Hochschild, Arlie R. (1994) 'The Commercial Spirit of Intimate Life and the Abduction of Feminism Theory', *Culture and Society*, Vol 11, No 2: 124–142.
Hochschild, Arlie R. (1998) 'The Sociology of Emotion as a Way of Seeing', in Gillian Bendelow and Simon J. Williams (eds) *Emotions in Social Life: Critical Themes and Contemporary Issues*. London: Routledge.
Holliday, Adrian (2001) *Doing and Writing Qualitative Research*. London: Sage.
Hollway, Wendy (1989) *Subjectivity and Method in Psychology: Gender, Meaning and Science*. London: Sage.
Hollway, Wendy (1991) *Work Psychology and Organizational Behaviour: Managing the Individual at Work*. London: Sage.
Hollway, Wendy (1996) 'Masters and Men in the Transition from Factory Hands to Sentimental Workers', in David L. Collinson and Jeff Hearn (eds) *Men as Managers, Managers as Men: Critical Perspectives on Men, Masculinities and Managements*. London: Sage.
Hollway, Wendy and Jefferson, Tony (2000) *Doing Qualitative Research Differently: Free Association, Narrative and the Interview Method*. London: Sage.
Honneth, Axel (2004) 'Organized Self-Realization: Some Paradoxes of Individualization', in *European Journal of Social Theory*, 7 (4): 463–478.
hooks, bell (1993) *Sisters of the Yam: Black Women and Self-recovery*. London: Turnaround.
Hopfl, Heather and Linstead, Steve (1993) 'Passion and Performance: Suffering and the Carrying of Organisational Roles', in Stephen Fineman (ed.) (1993) *Emotion in Organisations*. London: Sage.
Howard, Alex (1996) *Challenges to Counselling and Psychotherapy*. London: Macmillan.
Hughes, Christina (2002) *Women's Contemporary Lives: Within and Beyond the Mirror*. London: Routledge.
Hyde, Lewis (1999) *The Gift: Imagination and the Erotic Life of Property*. London: Vintage.
Jackson, Brad (2001) *Management Gurus and Management Fashions*. London: Routledge.
Jackson, Cath (1989) '12 Steps to Heaven', in *Trouble and Strife*, Winter.
Jager, Eric (2000) *The Book of the Heart*. Chicago: University of Chicago Press.
Jamieson, Lynn (1998) *Intimacy: Personal Relationships in Modern Society*. Cambridge: Polity Press.

Jary, David (2002) 'Aspects of the "Audit Society": Issues Arising from the Colonisations of Professional Academic Identities by a "Portable Management Tool"', in Mike Dent and Stephen Whitehead (eds) *Managing Professional Identities: Knowledge, Performativity and the 'New' Professional*. London: Routledge.

Joo, B. (2005) 'Executive Coaching: A Conceptual Framework from an Integrative Review of Practice and Research', in *Human Resource Development Review*, Vol 4, No 4: 462–488.

Jossel, Ruthellen and Lieblich, Amia (1993) *The Narrative Study of Lives*. London: Sage.

Kaminer, Wendy (1992) *I'm Dysfunctional, You're Dysfunctional: The Recovery Movement and Other Self-Help Fashions*. Reading: Addison-Wesley.

Keat, Russell (1991) 'Introduction: Starship Britain or Universal Enterprise', in Russell Keat and Nicholas Abercrombie (eds) *Enterprise Culture*. London: Routledge.

Keat, Russell and Abercrombie, Nicholas (eds) (1991) *Enterprise Culture*. London: Routledge.

Kellner, Hansfried and Heuberger, Frank W. (eds) (1994) *Hidden Technocrats: The New Class and New Capitalism*. London: Transaction Publishers.

Kellner, Hansfried and Berger, Peter L. (1994) 'Life-style Engineering: Some Theoretical Reflections', in Hansfried Kellner and Frank W. Heuberger (eds) *Hidden Technocrats: The New Class and New Capitalism*. London: Transaction Publishers.

Kelly, Liz, Burton, Sheila and Regan, Linda (1994) 'Researching Women's Lives or Studying Women's Oppression – Reflections on What Constitutes Feminist Research', in Mary Maynard and Jane Purvis (eds) *Researching Women's Lives From a Feminist Perspective*. London: Taylor and Francis.

Kendall, Tim and Crossley, Nick (1996) 'Governing Love: On the Tactical Control of Counter Transference in the Psychoanalytic Community', in *Economy and Society*, Vol 25, No 2: 178–194.

Kenny, Michael G. (1996) 'Trauma, Time, Illness and Culture: An Anthropological Approach to Traumatic Memory', in Paul Antze and Michael Lambek (eds) *Tense Past: Cultural Essays in Trauma and Memory*. London: Routledge.

Kerby, Anthony (1991) *Narrative and the Self*. Bloomington, Indianapolis: Indiana University Press.

Kerfoot, Deborah (1999) 'The Organisation of Intimacy: Managerialism, Masculinity and the Masculine Subject', in Stephen Whitehead and Roy Moodley (eds) *Transforming Managers: Gendering Change in the Public Sector*. London: UCL Press.

Kirschner, Suzanne R. (1996) *The Religious and Romantic Origins of Psychoanalysis: Individuation and Integration in Post-Freudian Theory*. Cambridge: Cambridge University Press.

Kitzinger, Celia and Perkins, Rachel (1993) *Changing Our Minds: Lesbian Feminism and Psychology*. London: Onlywomen Press.

Kovach, John A. (1999) 'The Concept of a "Healthy Person": A Sociological Contribution toward a Truly Revolutionary Psychotherapy', in James J. Chriss (ed.) *Counselling and the Therapeutic State*. New York: de Gruyter.

Kravetz, Diane (1980) 'Consciousness-Raising and Self-Help', in Annette M. Brodsky and Rachel T. Hare-Mustin (eds) *Women and Psychotherapy*. New York: The Guildford Press.

Lamb, Sharon (1996) *The Trouble with Blame: Victims, Perpetrators and Responsibility*. Cambridge, Mass.: Harvard University Press.

Lambek, Michael (1996) 'The Past Imperfect: Remembering as Cultural Practice', in Paul Antze and Michael Lambek (eds) *Tense Past: Cultural Essays in Trauma and Memory*. London: Routledge.

Larson, Scarfatti Magali (1984) 'The Production of Expertise and the Constitution of Expert Power', in Thomas L. Haskell (ed.) *The Authority of Experts: Studies in History and Theory*. Bloomington: Indiana University Press.

Lasch, Christopher (1980) *The Culture of Narcissism*. London: Abacus.

Lasch, Christopher (1985) *The Minimal Self: Psychic Survival in Troubled Times*. London: Picador.

Lasch, Christopher (1995) *Haven in a Heartless World: The Family Besieged*. London: W.G. Norton.

Lasch-Quinn, Elisabeth (2002) *Race Experts: How Racial Etiquette, Sensitivity Training, and New Age Therapy Hijacked the Civil Rights Movement*. Oxford: Rowman and Littlefield.

Lash, Scott (1994) 'Reflexivity and its Doubles: Structure, Aesthetics, Community', in Ulrich Beck, Anthony Giddens and Scott Lash (eds) *Reflexive Modernisation: Politics, Tradition and Aesthetics in the Modern Social Order*. Cambridge: Polity Press.

Lawler, Steph (2000*) Mothering the Self: Mothers, Daughters, Subjects*. London: Routledge.

Lears, Jackson T.J. (1983) 'From Salvation to Self-Realization: Advertising and the Therapeutic Roots of the Consumer Culture 1880–1930', in Richard Wightman Fox and T.J. Jackson Lears *The Culture of Consumption: Critical Essays in American History 1880–1980*. New York: Pantheon Books.

Leary, David E. (1994) (ed.) *Metaphors in the History of Psychology*. Cambridge: Cambridge University Press.

Lee, J.H. (2004–08–14) 'Explaining the Hybridity of Peripheral "Wellness" Practices', Paper presented at the annual meeting of the American Sociological Association, Hilton San Francisco & Renaissance Parc 55 Hotel, San Francisco, CA, Online <**PDF**> 2009–03–04 from http://www.allacademic.com/meta/p109200_index.html

Legge, Karen (1995) *HRM: Rhetoric and Realities*. Basingstoke: Macmillan.

Leibowitz, Flo (1996) 'Apt Feelings, or Why Women's Films Aren't Trivial', in David Bordwell and Noel Caroll (eds*) Post-Theory: Reconstructing Film Studies*. Madison: University of Wisconsin Press.

Leidner, Robin (1993) *Fast Food, Fast Talk*. Berkeley: University of California Press.

Letherby, Gayle (2003) *Feminist Research in Theory and Practice*. Buckingham: Open University Press.

Levi-Strauss, Claude (1966) *The Savage Mind*. Chicago: Chicago University Press.

Leys, Ruth (1996) 'Traumatic Cures: Shell Shock, Janet, and the Question of Memory', in Paul Antze and Michael Lambek (eds) *Tense Past: Cultural Essays in Trauma and Memory*. London: Routledge.

Lichterman, Paul (1992) 'Self-Help Reading as a Thin Culture Media', in *Culture and Society*, Vol 14: 421–447.

Lilley, Susan (2002) 'Talking with the Magician's Apprentice: Fleshing Out GIS Users', in Liz Bondi et al. (eds) *Subjectivities, Knowledges, and Feminist*

Geographies: The Subject and Ethics of Social Research. Oxford: Rowman and Littlefield.
Lindholm, Charles (1992) 'Charisma, Crowd Psychology and Altered States of Consciousness', in *Culture, Medicine and Psychiatry*, Vol 16: 287–310.
Lindholm, Charles (2001) *Culture and Identity: The History, Theory, and Practice of Psychological Anthropology*. London: McGraw-Hill.
Lofland, John and Skonovd, Norman (1983) 'Patterns of Conversion', in Eileen Barker (ed.) *Of Gods and Men*. Macon: Mercer University Press.
Lubin, David M. (1997) 'Modern Psychological Selfhood in the Art of Thomas Eakins', in Joel Pfister and Nancy Schnog (eds) *Inventing the Psychological: Towards a Cultural History of Emotional Life in America*. New Haven: Yale University Press.
Luhrmann, T.M. (1989) *Persuasions of the Witch's Craft: Ritual Magic in Contemporary England*. Cambridge, Mass: Harvard University Press.
Luhrmann, T.M. (2001) *Of Two Minds: An Anthropologist Looks at American Psychiatry*. New York: Vintage Books.
Lupton, Deborah (1998) *The Emotional Self*. London: Sage.
Lury, Celia (1996) *Consumer Culture*. London: Routledge.
Lury, Celia (1998) *Prosthetic Culture: Photography, Memory and Identity*. London: Routledge.
Lutz, Catherine (1990) 'Engendered Emotion: Gender, Power and the Rhetoric of Emotional Control in American Discourse', in Catherine A. Lutz and Lila Abu-Lughod (eds) *Language and the Politics of Emotion*. Cambridge: Cambridge University Press.
Lutz, Tom (1999) *Crying: The Natural and Cultural History of Tears*. New York: Norton.
Lyon, Margot L. (1995) 'Missing Emotion: The Limitations of Cultural Constructionism in the Study of Emotion', in *Cultural Anthropology*, 10 (2): 244–263.
Lyotard, Jean-Francois (1984) *The Postmodern Condition: A Report on Knowledge*. Manchester: Manchester University Press.
Mac an Ghaill, Mairtin (1999) '"New" Cultures of Training: Emerging Male (Hetero)Sexual Identities', in *British Educational Research Journal*, Vol 25, No 4: 427–443.
MacIntyre, Alasdair (1985) *After Virtue: A Study in Moral Theory*. 2nd edition. London: Duckworth.
McCleod, John (1996) 'The Humanistic Paradigm', in Ray Woolfe and Windy Dryden (eds) *Handbook of Counselling Psychology*. London: Sage.
McCleod, John (1997) *Narrative and Psychotherapy*. London: Sage.
McDonald, Kevin (1999) *Struggles for Subjectivity: Identity, Action and Youth Experience*. Cambridge: Cambridge University Press.
McDowell, Linda (1997) *Capital Culture: Gender at Work in the City*. Oxford: Blackwell.
McFadden, Cyra (1978) *The Serial: A Year in the Life of Marin County*. New York: Signet.
McGee, Micki (2005) *Self-Help, Inc.: Makeover Culture in American Life*. New York: Oxford University Press.
McLellan, Betty (1995) *Beyond Psychoppression: A Feminist Alternative Therapy*. North Melbourne: Spinifex Press.

McNamee, Sheila and Gergen, Kenneth J. (1992) *Therapy in Social Construction*. London: Sage.
McNay, Lois (2000) *Gender and Agency: Reconfiguring the Subject and Social Theory*. Cambridge: Polity Press.
McRobbie, Angela (1994) *Postmodernism and Popular Culture*. London: Routledge.
McRobbie, Angela (2002) 'From Holloway to Hollywood: Happiness at Work in the New Cultural Economy?', in du Gay, P. and Pryke, M. (eds) *Cultural Economy*. London: Sage.
McWilliam, Erica (2002) 'Against Professional Development', in *Educational Philosophy and Theory*, 34 (3): 289–299.
McWilliam, Erica and Hatcher, Caroline (2004) 'Emotional Literacy as a Pedagogical Product', in *Continuum: Journal of Media and Cultural Studies*, 18 (2): 179–190.
Maffesoli, Michel (1996) *Time of Tribes: The Decline of Individualism in Mass Society*. London: Sage.
Malpas, Simon (1996) 'History Balancing the Scales: Time and the Trauma in Psychoanalysis', in *Time and Society*, Vol 5, No 3: 301–317.
Markus, Hazel and Nurius, Paula (1986) 'Possible Selves', in *American Psychologist*, Vol 41, No 9: 954–969.
Martin, Bernice (1981) *A Sociology of Contemporary Cultural Change*. Oxford: Blackwell.
Martin, Bill (1998) 'Knowledge, Identity and the Middle Class: from Collective to Individualised Class Formation?', in *The Sociological Review*: 653–686.
Martin, Emily (1994) *Flexible Bodies: Tracking Immunity in American Culture*. Boston: Beacon Press.
Martin, Emily (1997) 'Managing Americans: Policy and Changes in the Meanings of Work and the Self', in C. Shore and S. Wright (eds) *Anthropology of Policy*. London: Routledge.
Martin, Emily (2002) 'Flexible Survivors', in *Anthropology Newsletter*, 40 (6): 5–7.
Martin, Joanne (2001) *Organizational Culture: Mapping the Terrain*. Thousand Oaks: Sage.
Mason, Jennifer (2002) 'Qualitative Interviewing: Asking, Listening and Interpreting', in Tim May (ed.) *Qualitative Research in Action*. London: Sage.
Mauss, Marcel (1990) *The Gift: The Form and Reason for Exchange in Archaic Societies*. London: Routledge.
Mauthner, Natasha and Doucet, Andrea (1998) 'Reflections on a Voice-centred Relational Method: Analysing Material and Domestic Voices', in Jane Ribbens and Rosalind Edwards (eds) *Feminist Dilemmas in Qualitative Research: Public Knowledge and Private Lives*. London: Sage.
Maynard, Mary (1994) 'Methods, Practice and Epistemology: The Debates about Feminism and Research', in Mary Maynard and Jane Purvis (eds) *Researching Women's Lives from a Feminist Perspective*. London: Taylor and Francis.
Maynard, Mary and Purvis, Jane (eds) (1994) *Researching Women's Lives from a Feminist Perspective*. London: Taylor and Francis.
Melchior-Bonnet, Sabine (2001) *The Mirror: A History*. London: Routledge.
Mestrovic, Stjepan G. (1997) *Post Emotional Society*. London: Sage.
Meyers, Diana Tietjens (ed.) (1999) *Feminists Rethink the Self*. Abingdon: Westview.
Michael, Mike (1996) *Constructing Identities*. London: Sage.

Miers, Margaret (1999) 'Nurses in the Labour Market: Exploring and Explaining Nurses' Work', in Geoff Wilkinson and Margaret Miers (eds) *Power and Nursing Practice*. Basingstoke: Macmillan Press.

Miller, Hillis J. (1995) 'Narrative', in Frank Lentricchia and Thomas McLaughlin (eds) *Critical Terms for Literary Study*. Chicago: University of Chicago Press.

Miller, Peter and Rose, Nikolas (1988) 'The Tavistock Programme: The Government of Subjectivity and Social Life', in *Sociology*, Vol 22: 171–192.

Miller, Peter and Rose, Nikolas (1994) 'On Therapeutic Authority: Psychoanalytical Expertise Under Advanced Liberalism', in *History of the Social Sciences*, Vol 7, No 3: 29–64.

Miller, Toby and McHoul, Alec (1998a) *Popular Culture and Everyday Life*. London: Sage.

Miller, Toby and McHoul, Alec (1998b) 'Helping the Self', in *Social Text*, 57 (4): 127–155.

Mischler, Elliot G. (1986) *Research Interviewing: Context and Narrative*. Cambridge, Mass: Harvard University Press.

Misztal, Barbara A. (2002) 'Trusting the professional: a managerial discourse for uncertain times', in Mike Dent and Stephen Whitehead (eds) *Managing Professional Identities: Knowledge, Performativity and the 'New' Professional*. London: Routledge.

Moorti, Sujata (1998) 'Cathartic Confessions or Emancipatory Texts: Rape Narratives on the Oprah Winfrey Show', in *Social Text*, 57, Vol 16, No 4, Winter: 83–102.

Morawski, Jill G. (1997) 'Educating the Emotions: Academic Psychology, Textbooks, and the Psychology Industry, 1890–1940', in Joel Pfister and Nancy Schnog (1997) (eds) *Inventing the Psychological: Towards a Cultural History of Emotional Life in America*. New Haven: Yale University Press.

Morris, Colin (1972) *The Discovery of the Individual*. Toronto: University of Toronto.

Morris, Debra (2000) 'Privacy, Privation, Perversity: Toward New Representations of the Personal', in *Signs: Journal of Women in Culture and Society*, Vol 25, No 2: 323–351.

Morrison, K. (1995) *Marx, Durkheim, Weber: Formations of a Modern Social Thought*. London: Sage.

Moskowitz, Eva S. (2001) *In Therapy We Trust: America's Obsession with Self Fulfillment*. Baltimore: The John Hopkins University Press.

Mosley, Rachel (2000) 'Makeover takeover on British Television', in *Screen*, Vol 41, No 3: 299–315.

Mumby, Dennis (ed.) (1993) *Narrative and Social Control: Critical Perspectives*. London: Sage.

Naples, Nancy A. (1997) 'A Feminist Revisiting of the Insider/Outsider Debate: The "Outsider Phenomenon"', in Roseanne Hertz (ed.) *Reflexivity and Voice*. Thousand Oaks: Sage.

Neale, Steve (1986) 'Melodrama and Tears', in *Screen*, Vol 27, No 6: 6–22.

Negus, Keith (2002) 'Identities and Industries: The Cultural Formation of Aesthetic Economies', in P. du Gay and M. Pryke (eds) *Cultural Economy*. London: Sage.

Neill, Alex (1996) 'Empathy and (Film) Fiction', in David Bordwell and Noel Caroll (eds) *Post-Theory: Reconstructing Film Studies*. Madison: University of Wisconsin Press.

Newman, Janet (1991) 'Enterprising Women: Images of Success', in Sarah Franklin, Celia Lury and Jackie Stacey (eds) *Off-Centre: Feminism and Cultural Studies*. London: HarperCollins.

Newton, Tim (1998) 'The Sociogenesis of Emotion: A Historical Sociology', in Gillian Bendelow and Simon J. Williams (eds) *Emotions in Social Life: Critical Themes and Contemporary Issues*. London: Routledge.

Newton, Tim, Handy, Jocelyn and Fineman, Stephen (1995) *Managing Stress: Emotion and Power at Work*. London: Sage.

Nisbet, Robert A. (1969) *Social Change and History: Aspects of the Western Theory of Development*. Oxford: Oxford University Press.

Nixon, Sean and du Gay, Paul (2002) 'Who Needs Cultural Intermediaries?', in *Cultural Studies*, 16 (4): 495–500.

Nolan, James L. (1998) *The Therapeutic State: Justifying Government at the Century's End*. London: New York University Press.

Nolan, James L. (1999) 'Acquiescence or Consensus – Consenting to Therapeutic Pedagogy', in James J. Chriss (ed.) *Counselling and the Therapeutic State*. New York: Aldine de Gruyter.

Nunn, Heather (1999) 'Violence and the Sacred: The Iron Lady, The Princess and the People's PM', in *New Formations*, Vol 36: 92–110.

Nuttall, Anthony D. (1996) *Why does Tragedy Give Pleasure?* Oxford: Clarendon Press.

Oakley, Anne (1981) 'Interviewing Women: A Contradiction in Terms', in Helen Roberts (ed.) *Doing Feminist Research*. London: Routledge.

Offley, N., Brown, H., Larsen, L. and Anderson, B. (2005) *Review of Coaching and Mentoring Research and Evaluation*. NHS Leadership Centre and OPM: London.

Olivero, G., Bane, D. and Kopelman, R. (1997) 'Executive Coaching as a Transfer of Training Tool', *Public Personnel Management*, Winter 1997, 26 (4): 461–469.

Opie, Anne (1992) 'Qualitative Research, Appropriation of the "Other" and Empowerment', in *Feminist Review*, No 40: 52–69.

Palmer, B. (2003) 'Maximizing Value from Executive Coaching', *Strategic HR Review*, Sep/Oct 2003, 2 (6): 26–29.

Parr, Janet (1998) 'Theoretical Voices', in Jane Ribbens and Rosalind Edwards (eds) *Feminist Dilemmas in Qualitative Research: Public Knowledge and Private Lives*. London: Sage.

Parker, Ian (1997) *Psychoanalytic Culture: Psychoanalytic Discourse in Western Society*. London: Sage.

Parker, Ian (1999) *Deconstructing Psychotherapy*. London: Sage.

Parker, Martin (2000) *Organizational Culture and Identity*. London: Sage.

Parker, Martin (1999) *Organizational Culture and Identity: Unity and Division at Work*. London: Sage.

Parkins, Wendy (2001) 'Oprah Winfrey's Change Your Life TV and the Spiritual Everyday', in *Continuum: Journal of Media and Cultural Studies*, Vol 15, No 2: 145–157.

Pearce, Lynne (1995) 'Finding a Place from which to Write: the Methodology of Feminist Textual Practice', in Beverley Skeggs (ed.) *Feminist Cultural Theory: Process and Production*. Manchester: Manchester University Press.

Pearce, Lynne (2004) *The Rhetorics of Feminism: Readings in Contemporary Cultural Theory and the Popular Press*. London: Routledge.

Peck, Janice (1996) 'The Mediated Talking Cure: Therapeutic Framing of Autobiography in Talk Shows', in Sidonie Smith and Julia Watson (eds) *Getting a Life: Everyday Uses of Autobiography*. Minneapolis: University of Minnesota Press.

Peele, Stanton (1995) *Diseasing of America: How We Allowed Recovery Zealots and the Treatment Industry to Convince Us We Are Out of Control*. New York: Lexington.

Pfister, Joel (1995) *Staging Depth: Eugene O'Neill and the Politics of Psychological Discourse*. Chapel Hill: The University of North Carolina Press.

Pfister, Joel (1997a) 'On Conceptualising the Cultural History of Emotional and Psychological Life in America', in Joel Pfister and Nancy Schnog (eds) *Inventing the Psychological: Towards a Cultural History of Emotional Life in America*. New Haven: Yale University Press.

Pfister, Joel (1997b) 'Glamorising the Psychological: The Politics of the Performances of Modern Psychological Identities', in Joel Pfister and Nancy Schnog (1997) (eds) *Inventing the Psychological: Towards a Cultural History of Emotional Life in America*. New Haven: Yale University Press.

Pfister, Joel and Schnog, Nancy (1997) (eds) *Inventing the Psychological: Towards a Cultural History of Emotional Life in America*. New Haven: Yale University Press.

Phoenix, Ann (1994) 'Practising Feminist Research: The Intersection of Gender and "Race" in the Research Process', in Mary Maynard and Jane Purvis (eds) *Researching Women's Lives from a Feminist Perspective*. London: Taylor and Francis.

Pile, Steve and Thrift, Nigel (eds) (1995) *Mapping the Subject*. London: Routledge.

Pilgrim, David (1997) *Psychotherapy and Society*. London: Sage.

Plummer, Ken (1995) *Telling Sexual Stories: Power, Change and Social Worlds*. London: Routledge.

Plummer, Ken (2001) *Documents of Life 2: An Invitation to Critical Humanism*. London: Sage.

Polkinghorne, Donald E. (1988) *Narrative Knowing and the Human Sciences*. New York: State University of New York Press.

Polsky, Andrew J. (1991) *The Rise of the Therapeutic State*. Oxford: Princeton University Press.

Porter, Roy (1994) 'Quacks: An Unconscionable Time Dying', in Susan Budd, and Sharma Ursula (eds) *The Healing Bond: The Patient-Practitioner Relationship and Therapeutic Responsibility*. London: Routledge.

Porter, Roy (ed.) (1997) *Rewriting the Self: Histories from the Renaissance to the Present*. London: Routledge.

Probyn, Elspeth (1993) *Sexing the Self: Gendered Positions in Cultural Studies*. New York: Routledge.

Probyn, Elspeth (2002) *Teaching Affect: An Ethology of the Classroom*, paper given at the seminar series Feminist Pedagogy and Interdisciplinarity, Lancaster University, 18 Oct 2002.

Puttick, Elizabeth (2000) 'Personal Development: The Spiritualisation and Secularisation of the Human Potential Movement', in Steven J. Sutcliffe and Marion Bowman (eds) *Beyond New Age: Exploring Alternative Spirituality*. Edinburgh: Edinburgh University Press.

Rabinach, Anson (1992) *The Human Motor: Energy, Fatigue, and the Origins of Modernity*. Berkeley: University of California Press.

Radner, Hilary (1995) *Shopping Around: Feminine Culture and the Pursuit of Pleasure*. London: Routledge.

Radway, Janice A. (1987) *Reading the Romance*. London: Verso.

Rakos, Richard F. (1991) *Assertive Behaviour: Theory, Research and Training*. London: Routledge.
Ramazanoglu, Caroline and Holland, Janet (1994) 'Power and Interpretation in Researching Young Women's Sexuality', in Mary Maynard and Jane Purvis (eds) *Researching Women's Lives from a Feminist Perspective*. London: Taylor and Francis.
Ramazanoglu, Caroline and Holland, Janet (2002) *Feminist Methodology: Challenges and Choices*. London: Sage.
Rand, Nicholas (2001) 'The Talking Cure: Origins of Psychoanalysis', in Shelley I. Salamensky (ed.) *Talk, Talk, Talk: The Cultural Life of Everyday Conversation*. London: Routledge.
Rapping, Elayne (1996) *The Culture of Recovery: Making Sense of the Self-Help Movement in Women's Lives*. Boston, Mass: Beacon Press.
Reddy, William M. (2001) *The Navigation of Feeling: A Framework for the History of Emotions*. Cambridge: Cambridge University Press.
Ree, Jonathan (1990) 'Funny Voices: Stories, Punctuation, and Personality Identity', in *New Literary History*, Vol 21: 1039–1058.
Reinarman, Craig (1995) 'The Twelve-Step Movement and Advanced Capitalist Culture: The Politics of Self-Control in Postmodernity', in Marcy Darnovsky, Barbara Epstein and Richard Flacks (eds) *Cultural Politics and Social Movements*. Philadelphia: Temple University Press.
Reinharz, Shulamit (1992) *Feminist Methods in Social Research*. New York: Oxford University Press.
Reynolds, Robert (1996) 'Confessing to Change', in *Meanjin*, Vol 55, Issue 1: 138–153.
Ribbens, Jane and Edwards, Rosalind (eds) (1998) *Feminist Dilemmas in Qualitative Research: Public Knowledge and Private Lives*. London: Sage.
Richards, Barry (1989) *Images of Freud*. London: J.M. Dent and Sons.
Richards, Graham (2002) *Putting Psychology in its Place: A Critical Historical Overview*. London: Routledge.
Richardson, Laurel (1990) *Writing Strategies: Reaching Diverse Audiences*. London: Sage.
Ricoeur, Paul (1980) 'Narrative Time', in *Critical Inquiry*, Vol 7, No 1: 169–190.
Rieff, Philip (1966) *The Triumph of the Therapeutic: Uses of Faith after Freud*. New York: Harper Torchbooks.
Rimke, Marie Heidi (2000) 'Governing Citizens through Self-Help Literature', in *Cultural Studies*, Vol 14, No 1: 61–78.
Romero, Lora (1997) *Home Fronts: Domesticity and its Critics in the Antebellum United States*. London: Duke University Press.
Rose, Nikolas (1989) *Governing the Soul: The Shaping of the Private Self*. London: Routledge.
Rose, Nikolas (1996a) *Inventing Our Selves: Psychology, Power and Personhood*. Cambridge: Cambridge University Press.
Rose, Nikolas (1996b) 'Identity, Genealogy, History', in Stuart Hall and Paul du Gay (eds) *Questions of Cultural Identity*. London: Sage.
Rose, Nikolas (2000) *Power in Therapy: Techne and Ethos for Academy for the Study of the Psychoanalytic Arts* accessed http://www.academyanalyticarts.org/rose2/html 13 March 2001.
Rose, Nikolas and Miller, Peter (1992) 'Political Power Beyond the State: Problematics of Government', in *British Journal of Sociology*, Vol 43, No 2: 173–205.

Rosen, Richard D. (1978) *Psychobabble.* London: Wildwood House.
Rosenwald, G.C. and Ochberg, R.L. (1992) *Storied Lives: The Cultural Politics of Self-Understanding.* New Haven: Yale University Press.
Ross, Andrew (1991) *Strange Weather: Culture, Science and Technology in the Age of Limits.* London: Verso.
Ross, Andrew (1992) 'New Age Technoculture', in Lawrence Grossberg, Cary Nelson and Paula Treichler (eds) *Cultural Studies.* London: Routledge.
Rouse, Roger (1995) 'Thinking through Transnationalism: Notes on the Cultural Politics of Class Relations in the Contemporary United States', in *Public Culture,* No 7: 353–402.
Rowan, John (1988) *Ordinary Ecstasy: Humanistic Psychology in Action.* 2nd edition. London: Routledge.
Russell, Janice (1993) *Out of Bounds: Sexual Exploitation in Counselling and Therapy.* London: Sage.
Saks, Mike (1995) *Professions and the Public Interest: Medical Power, Altruism and Alternative Medicine.* London: Routledge.
Salaman, Graeme (2002) 'Understanding Advice: Towards a Sociology of Management Consultancy', in Timothy Clarke and Robin Fincham (eds) *Critical Consulting: New Perspectives on the Management Advice Industry.* Oxford: Blackwell.
Sampson, Edward E. (1977) 'Psychology and the American Ideal', in *Journal of Personality and Social Psychology,* Vol 35, No 11: 767–781.
Schafer, Roy (1976) *A New Language for Psychoanalysis.* New Haven, CT: Yale University Press.
Schafer, Roy (1980) 'Narration in the Psychoanalytic Dialogue', in *Critical Inquiry,* Vol 7: 29–53.
Schafer, Roy (1983) *The Analytic Attitude.* New York: Basic Books.
Schnog, Nancy (1997a) 'On Inventing the Psychological', in Joel Pfister and Nancy Schnog (eds) *Inventing the Psychological: Towards a Cultural History of Emotional Life in America.* New Haven: Yale University Press.
Schnog, Nancy (1997b) 'Changing Emotions: Moods and the Nineteenth-Century American Woman Writer', in Joel Pfister and Nancy Schnog (eds) *Inventing the Psychological: Towards a Cultural History of Emotional Life in America.* New Haven: Yale University Press.
Schrager, Cynthia D. (1993) 'Questioning the Promise of Self-Help: A Reading of Women Who Love Too Much', in *Feminist Studies* Vol 19, No 1: 177–192.
Schur, Edward (1977) *The Awareness Trap: Self Absorption Instead of Social Change.* New York: McGraw-Hill.
Scott, Joan (1992) 'Experience', in Judith Butler and Joan W. Scott (eds) *Feminists Theorize the Political.* New York: Routledge.
Scott, Sara and Payne, Tracey (1984) 'Underneath We're All Loveable', in *Trouble and Strife,* Summer: 21–24.
Sedgwick, Eve Kosofsky (1994) *Tendencies.* London: Routledge.
Sedgwick, Eve Kosofsky (2003) *Touching Feeling: Affect, Pedagogy, Performativity.* Durham: Duke University Press.
Sedgwick, Eve Kosofsky and Frank, Adam (eds) (1995) *Shame and its Sisters: A Silvan Tomkins Reader.* Durham: Duke University Press.
Seitler, Ellen, Borcher, Hans, Kreutzner, Gabriele and Warth, Eva-Maria (eds) (1989) *Remote Control: Television, Audiences and Cultural Power.* London: Routledge.
Seltzer, Mark (1993) *Bodies and Machines.* London: Routledge.

Seltzer, Mark (1998) *Serial Killers: Death and Life in America's Wound Culture*. London: Routledge.
Sennett, Richard (1986) *The Fall of Public Man*. London: Faber.
Shakespeare, Tom (2000) *Help*. Birmingham: Venture Press.
Sharma, Ursula (1995). *Complementary Medicine Today: Practitioners and Patients* (revd). London: Routledge.
Shattuc, Jane M. (1997) *The Talking Cure: TV, Talk Shows and Women*. London: Routledge.
Shepherd, Simon (1994) 'Pauses of Mutual Agitation', in Jacky Bratton, Jim Cook and Christine Gledhill (eds) *Melodrama: Stage, Picture, Screen*. London: BFI.
Shilling, Karen and Fuerher, Ann (1993) 'The Politics of Women's Self-Help Books', in *Feminism and Psychology*, Vol 3, No 3: 418–422.
Shotter, John and Gergen, Kenneth J. (1989) *Texts of Identity*, London: Sage.
Silber, Ilana (1998) 'Modern Philanthropy: Reassessing the Viability of a Maussian Perspective', in Nick Allen and Wendy James (eds) *Marcel Mauss Today*. Oxford: Berghahn.
Silverman, David (1997) *Discourses of Counselling: HIV Counselling as Social Interaction*. London: Sage.
Silverman, David (2000) *Doing Qualitative Research: A Practical Handbook*. London: Sage.
Silverman, David (2001) *Interpreting Qualitative Data: Methods for Analysing Talk, Text and Interaction*. Second Edition. London: Sage.
Simonds, Wendy (1992) *Women and Self Help Culture: Reading between the Lines*. New Brunswick: Rutgers University Press.
Simonds, Wendy (1996) 'All Consuming Selves: Self-Help Literature and Women's Identities', in D. Grodin and T.R. Lindlof (eds) *Constructing the Self in a Mediated World*. London: Sage.
Skeggs, Beverley (1994) 'Situating the Production of Feminist Ethnography', in Mary Maynard and Jane Purvis (eds) *Researching Women's Lives from a Feminist Perspective*. London: Taylor and Francis.
Skeggs, Beverley (ed.) (1995) *Feminist Cultural Theory: Process and Production*. Manchester: Manchester University Press.
Skeggs, Beverley (1997) *Formations of Class and Gender: Becoming Respectable*. London: Sage.
Skeggs, Beverley (2002) 'Techniques for Telling the Reflexive Self', in Tim May (ed.) *Qualitative Research in Action*. London: Sage.
Skeggs, Beverley (2004) *Class, Self, Culture*. London: Routledge.
Smith, Jonathan (1994) 'Reconstructing Selves: An Analysis of Discrepancies Between Women's Contemporaneous and Retrospective Accounts of the Transition to Motherhood', in *British Journal of Psychology*, No 85: 371–392.
Smith, Sidonie and Watson, Julia (eds) (1996) *Getting a Life: Everyday Uses of Autobiography*. Minneapolis: University of Minnesota Press.
Spelman, Elizabeth V. (2002) *Repair: The Impulse to Restore in a Fragile World*. Boston: Beacon Press.
Spence, Donald (1982) *Narrative Truth and Historical Truth: Meaning and Interpretation in Psychoanalysis*. New York: Norton.
Squire, Corinne (2000) 'The Public Life of Emotions', in *International Journal of Psychology*, No 1: 35–52.
Stacey, Jackie (1994) *Star Gazing: Hollywood Cinema and Female Spectatorship*. London: Routledge.

Stacey, Jackie (1995) 'The Lost Audience: Methodology, Cinema History and Feminist Film Criticism', in Beverley Skeggs (ed.) *Feminist Cultural Theory: Process and Production*. Manchester: Manchester University Press.
Stacey, Jackie (1997) *Teratologies: A Cultural Study of Cancer*. London: Routledge.
Stacey, Jackie (2000) 'The Global Within: Consuming Nature, Embodying Health', in Sarah Franklin, Celia Lury and Jackie Stacey *Global Nature, Global Culture*. London: Sage.
Standing, Kay (1998) 'Writing the Voices of the Less Powerful: Research on Lone Mothers', in Ribbens, Jane and Edwards, Rosalind (eds) *Feminist Dilemmas in Qualitative Research: Public Knowledge and Private Lives*. London: Sage.
Stanley, Liz (2000) 'From "Self-Made Women" to "Women Made Selves" – Audit Selves, Simulation and Surveillance in the Rise of Public Woman', in Tess Coslett, Celia Lury and Penny Summerfield (eds) *Feminism and Autobiography: Texts, Theories and Methods*. London and New York: Routledge.
Starker, Steven (1989) *Oracle at the Supermarket: The American Preoccupation with Self-Help Books*. New Brunswick: Transaction Publishers.
Stearns, Peter N. (1989) 'Suppressing Unpleasant Emotions: The Development of a Twentieth-Century American Style', in A. Barnes and P. Stearns (eds) *A Social History in Human Consciousness*. New York: New York University Press.
Stearns, Peter (1995) 'Emotion', in Rom Harre and Peter Stearns (eds) *Discursive Psychology in Practice*. London: Sage.
Stearns, Peter and Stearns, Carole Z. (1987) 'Emotionology: Clarifying the History of Emotions and Emotional Standards', in Geoffrey Cocks and Travis L. Crosby (eds) *Psycho/history: Readings in the Method of Psychology, Psychoanalysis, and History*. London: Yale University Press.
Steedman, Carolyn (1986) *Landscape for a Good Woman: A Story of Two Lives*. New Brunswick, New Jersey: Rutgers University Press.
Steedman, Carolyn (1994) *Strange Dislocations: Childhood and the Idea of Human Interiority 1780–1930*. Cambridge, Mass.: Harvard University Press.
Steedman, Carolyn (2000) 'Enforced Narratives: Stories of Another Self', in Tess Coslett, Celia Lury and Penny Summerfield (eds) *Feminism and Autobiography: Texts, Theories and Methods*. London and New York: Routledge.
Stevens, Richard (1996) *Understanding the Self*. London: Sage.
Stewart, Susan (1993) *On Longing: Narratives of the Miniature, the Gigantic, the Souvenir, the Collection*. Durham: Duke University Press.
Strathern, Marilyn (1990) *The Gender of the Gift*. Berkeley: Los Angeles: University of California Press.
Strathern, Marilyn (1992) *After Nature: English Kinship in the Late Twentieth Century*. Cambridge: Cambridge University Press.
Strathern, Marilyn (1999) *Property Substance and Effect*. London: The Athlone Press.
Sturdy, Andrew (2002) 'Front-line Diffusion: The Production and Negotiation of Knowledge through Training Interaction', in Timothy Clarke and Robin Fincham (eds) *Critical Consulting: New Perspectives on the Management Advice Industry*. Oxford: Blackwell.
Sturdy, Andrew, Handley, Karen, Clark, Timothy and Fincham, Robin (2009) *Management Consultancy, Boundaries and Knowledge in Action*. Oxford: Oxford University Press.
Susman, Warren J. (1985) *Culture as History: The Transformation of American Society*. New York: Pantheon.

Swan, Elaine (2004) *Worked Up Selves*. PhD Lancaster University.

Swan, Elaine (2006) 'Gendered Leadership and Management Development: Therapeutic Cultures at Work', in D. McTavish and K. Miller (eds) *Women in Leadership and Management*. Cheltenham: Edward Elgar.

Swan, Elaine (2008) "You Make Me Feel Like a Woman": Therapeutic Cultures and the Contagion of Femininity', *Gender, Work and Organization*, Vol 15 (1): 88–107.

Swan, Elaine, Stead, Valerie and Elliot, Carole (2009) 'Feminist Challenges and Futures: Women, Diversity & Leadership', *Management Learning*, Vol 40(4): 431–437.

Swan, Elaine and Fox, Stephen (2009) 'Becoming Flexible: Self-flexibility and Its Pedagogies', *British Journal of Management*, Vol 20, Issue 1: 149–159.

Swanson, Gillian (2000a) 'Subjectivity, the Individual and the Gendering of the Modern Self', in Jane Crisp, Kay Ferres and Gillian Swanson (eds) *Deciphering Culture: Ordinary Curiosities and Subjective Narratives*. London: Routledge.

Swanson, Gillian (2000b) 'Memory, Subjectivity and Intimacy: the Historical Formation of the Modern Self', in Susannah Radstone (ed.) *Memory and Methodology*. Oxford: Berg.

Swidler, Ann (2003) *Talk of Love: How Culture Matters*. Chicago: The University of Chicago Press.

Sykes, Charles J. (1992) *A Nation of Victims: The Decay of the American Character*. New York: St. Martin's Press.

Taylor, Charles (1989) *Sources of the Self: The Making of Modern Identity*. Cambridge: Cambridge University Press.

Taylor, Charles (1991) *Ethics of Authenticity*. Cambridge, Mass.: Harvard University Press.

Taylor, Charles (1992) *Sources of the Self: The Making of Modern Identity*. Cambridge: Cambridge University Press.

Taylor, Charles (1994) 'The Politics of Recognition', in Amy Gutman (ed.) *Multiculturalism*. Princeton, New Jersey and Chichester: Princeton University Press.

Testart, Alain (1998) 'Uncertainties of the "Obligation to Reciprocate": A Critique of Mauss', in Nick Allen and Wendy James (eds) *Marcel Mauss Today*. Oxford: Berghahn.

Thedvall, Renita (2004) '"Do it yourself": Making up the Self-employed Individual at a Swedish Public Employment Office', in Garsten, Christina and Kerstin Jacobsson (eds) *Learning to be Employable. New Agendas on Work, Responsibility and Learning in a Globalising World*. Basingstoke: Palgrave.

Thomas, Keith (1993) 'Introduction', in Jan Bremmer and Herman Roodenburg (eds) *A Cultural History of Gesture*. Cambridge: Polity.

Thompson, Paul and Findlay, Patricia (1999) 'Changing the People: Social Engineering in the Contemporary Workplace', in Larry Ray and Andrew Sayer (eds) *Culture and Economy: After the Cultural Turn*. London: Sage.

Thrift, Nigel (1999) 'Capitalism's Cultural Turn', in Larry Ray and Andrew Sayer (eds) *Culture and Economy After the Cultural Turn*. London: Sage.

Tipton, Steven (1983) 'Making the World Work: Ideas of Social Responsibility in the Human Potential Movement', in Eileen Barker (ed.) *Of Gods and Men*. Macon: Mercer University Press.

Titmuss, Richard M. (1971) *The Gift Relationship. From Human Blood to Social Policy*. London: Allen and Unwin.

Tonkiss, Fran (1998) 'Analysing Discourse', in Chris Searle (ed.) *Researching Society and Culture*. London: Sage.
Tosey, Paul and Gregory, Josie (2002) *Dictionary of Personal Development*. London: Whurr Publishers.
Townley, Barbara (1994) *Reframing Human Resource Management: Power, Ethics and the Subject at Work*. London: Sage.
Townley, Barbara (1995) '"Know Thyself": Self-awareness, Self-formation and Managing', in *Organisation*, Vol 2, No 2: 271–289.
Tucker, James (1999) 'Therapy, Organizations, and the State: A Blackian Perspective', in James J. Chriss (ed.) *Counselling and the Therapeutic State*. New York: de Gruyter.
Turnbull, Sharon (1999) 'Emotional Labour in Corporate Change Programmes', *Human Resource Development International*, Vol 2, No 2: 125–146.
Turner, Ralph H. (1976) 'The Real Self: From Institution to Impulse', in *American Journal of Sociology*, Vol 81, No. 5: 989–1015.
Usher, Robin, Bryant, Ian and Johnston, Rennie (1997) *Adult Education and the Postmodern Challenge: Learning Beyond the Limits*. London: Routledge.
Valentine, Gill (1997) 'Tell Me About...: Using Interviews as a Research Methodology', in Robin Flowerdew and David Martin (1997) *Methods in Human Geography: A Guide for Students Doing a Research Project*. Harlow: Addison Wesley Longman.
Van Zoonen, Lisbet (1994) *Feminist Media Studies*. London: Sage.
Vickers, Margaret and Kouzmin, Alexander (2001) 'Employee Assistance Programmes (EAPs): From Crisis Support to Sanctioned Coercion and Panopticist Practices', in *Critical Psychology*, Issue 2: 61–84.
Vincent-Buffault, Anne (1991) *The History of Tears: Sensibility and Sentimentality in France*. Basingstoke: Macmillan.
Vitz, Paul C. (1994) *Psychology as Religion: The Cult of Self-Worship*. 2nd edition. Carlisle: Paternoster Press.
Wainwright, David and Calnan, Michael (2002) *Work Stress: The Making of a Modern Epidemic*. Buckingham: Open University Press.
Walker, Janet (1993) *Couching Resistance*. Minneapolis: University of Minnesota Press.
Wallis, Roy (1989) 'Betwixt Therapy and Salvation: the Changing Form of the Human Potential Movement', in R. Kenneth Jones (ed.) *Sickness and Sectarianism*. Aldershot: Gower.
Walter, Tony (1999) *On Bereavement: The Culture of Grief*. Buckingham: Open University Press.
Warhol, Robyn (2003) *Having a Good Cry: Effeminate Feelings and Pop-Culture Forms*. Columbus: The Ohio State University Press.
Warhol, Robyn and Michie, Helena (1996) '12-Step Teleology – Narratives of Recovery', in Sidonie Smith and Julia Watson (eds) *Getting a Life: Everyday Uses of Autobiography*. Minneapolis: University of Minnesota Press.
Waters, Michael (1996) *The Element Dictionary of Personal Development*. Dorset: Element Books.
Webb, Janette (2004) 'Organizations, Self-identity and the New Economy', *Sociology*, Vol 38 (4): 719–738.
Webb, Janette (2006) *Organizations, Identities and the Self*. Basingstoke: Palgrave Macmillan.

Weber, Max (1978) *Economy and Society: An Outline of Interpretive Sociology*. Berkeley: University of California Press.
Weldon, Fay (1999) 'Mind at the End of its Tether', in Colin Feltman (ed.) *Controversies in Psychotherapy and Counselling*. London: Sage.
Wellenkamp, Jane C. (1988) 'Notions of Grief and Catharsis among the Toraja', in *American Ethnologist*, Vol 15, No 1: 63–83.
Wetherell, Margaret, Taylor, Stephanie and Yates, Simon J. (2001) *Discourse as Data: A Guide for Analysis*. London: Sage.
White, Mimi (1992) *Tele-advising: Therapeutic Discourse in American TV*. Chapel Hill: University of North Carolina Press.
Wiener, Wendy J. and Rosenwald, George C. (1993) 'A Moment's Monument: The Psychology of Keeping a Diary', in Ruthellen Josselson and Amia Lieblich (eds) *The Narrative Study of Lives*. London: Sage.
Williams, S. and Offley, N. (2005) *Research and Reality: Innovations in Coaching*. NHS Modernisation Agency Leadership Centre.
Williams, Simon J. (2000) 'Reason, Emotions and Embodiment: Is "Mental" Health a Contradiction in Terms', in *Sociology of Health and Illness*, Vol 22, No 5: 559–581.
Williams, Simon J. (2001) *Emotion and Social Theory*. London: Sage.
Wilmott, Hugh (1993) 'Strength is Ignorance: Slavery is Freedom: Managing Culture in Modern Organisations', in *Journal of Management Studies*, 30 (4): 515–552.
Wilson, David (1992) *A Strategy for Change: Concepts and Controversies in the Management of Change*. London: Thomson Learning.
Wolcott, Harry F. (1994) *Transforming Qualitative Data: Description, Analysis and Interpretation*. London: Sage.
Wolcott, Harry F. (1999) *Ethnography: A Way of Seeing*. London: AltaMira Press.
Woolfolk, Robert L. and Richardson, Frank C. (1984) 'Behaviour Therapy and the Ideology of Modernity', in *American Psychologist*, Vol 39, No 7: 777–786.
Wouters, Cas (1986) 'Formalization and Informalization: Changing Tension Balances in Civilizing Processes', in *Theory Culture and Society*, Vol 3, No 2: 1–35.
Wouters, Cas (1987) 'Developments in the Behaviour Codes between the Sexes: The Formalization of Informalization in the Netherlands 1930–85', in *Theory, Culture and Society*, Vol 4: 405–427.
Wouters, Cas (1989) 'The Sociology of Emotions and Flight Attendants: Hochschild's Managed Heart', in *Theory, Culture and Society*, Vol 6: 95–123.
Wouters, Cas (2002) 'The Quest for New Rituals in Dying and Mourning: Changes in the We-I Balance', in *Body and Society*, Vol 8, No 1: 1–27.
Zaretsky, Eli (1976) *Capitalism, the Family and Personal Life*. London: Pluto Press.
Zaretsky, Eli (2000) 'Charisma or Rationalisation – Domesticity and Pyscho-analysis in the U.S. in the 1950s', in Lauren Berlant (ed.) *Intimacy*. Chicago: Chicago University Press.

Index